MW01640077

STATISTICAL PATTERN RECOGNITION

STATISTICAL PATTERN RECOGNITION

Chi-hau Chen

Southeastern Massachusetts University

HAYDEN BOOK COMPANY, INC.
Rochelle Park, New Jersey

ISBN 0-87671-177-8
Library of Congress Catalog Card Number 72-75714

Printed in the United States of America

Spartan Books are distributed throughout the world by Hayden Book Company, Inc., 50 Essex Street, Rochelle Park, N.J. 07662, and its agents.

1 2 3 4 5 6 7 8 9 PRINTING

73 74 75 76 77 78 YEAR

Dedicated to WANDA

Preface

During the past 15 years, there have been vigorous efforts in applying statistical methods to various problems of pattern recognition. It is this author's belief that the enormous amount of results, particularly those which have appeared in the last six years, will have widespread application not only in designing better recognition machines but also in such areas as statistical data processing, communication and control systems, and the computer-related fields. This book is an attempt to organize some of those results into a coherent, logical framework useful to students and researchers alike. Every effort is made to provide the readers with broad and balanced views in reasonable depth on various approaches in statistical pattern recognition.

It is not the author's intent to compile and present all results. This would require a volume several times larger. Readers are introduced to the primary developments in selected topics and presented with some important results. Having gained an understanding of a topic, serious readers may always pursue further studies from the references cited and the bibliographies following each chapter. Topics such as the use of stochastic automata and the linguistic approaches are not treated in this book.

The selection of features for recognition is one of the most important problems in pattern recognition. This is related to the fundamental problem, the design of experiments, in mathematical statistics. Limited success in solving this problem can be considerably balanced by efforts in other directions such as the use of nonlinear decision boundaries, proper representation of the pattern, contextual analysis, feedback, etc., each of which provides improved performance which we would expect from a better feature set.

Chapter 1 introduces basic concepts in statistical pattern recognition. As the primary objective of most recognition systems is the maximum number of correct recognitions, optimum decision boundaries must first be established; this is the subject of chapter 2. Chapter 3 describes some best ways to represent patterns. This problem is no less important than, but often misrecognized as, the feature selection discussed in chapter 4. Information statistics provide a fairly general criterion to select feature sets indirectly for almost all kinds of patterns. Learning (or estimation) with and without supervision, as presented in chapters 5 and 6, with recursive or nonrecursive algorithms, may be considered as an area with much success in statistical pattern recognition. Such algorithms are useful particularly in control system parameter estimation. The stochastic approximation and related techniques in chapter 6 need not use parameter statistics completely. Real solution to the statistical pattern recognition problem, however, needs the nonparametric (distribution-free) statistical methods discussed in chapter 7 because the assumption of parameter statistics is often unjustified.

Another important development in pattern recognition is the analysis of data structure to seek for best clusters and modes, as presented in chapter 8. The objectives are to define the pattern class and reduce the amount of data, in addition to minimizing errors. While a fixed number of features is processed in most recognition techniques, not all of the features are really required. Sequential decision theory (chapter 9) makes it possible to select, on the average, a smaller number of features for a specified performance. The real advantage of the sequential approach lies in processing properly ordered features. Features may be ordered in a predetermined manner or through information feedback. The problem of recognition systems with the finite memory constraint, as described in chapter 10, is a fundamental one and deserves more attention. In almost all recognition applications, there is dependence among successive patterns. Chapter 11 includes contextual analysis for designing an optimum recognition system. Finally, in chapter 12, we present the application of learning algorithms to adaptive signal detection and communication receivers.

With the exception of chapters 8, 10, and 11 an early version of the manuscript constituted my lecture notes for a graduate course at Northeastern University, Boston, in the fall of 1968. Written as a graduate level text, this book may also be used for seminars or short courses or even self-study purposes. Both reference sources and a bibliography are provided at the end of each chapter. Problems are also given, partly to supplement the discussions in the text and partly for computer recognition experiments. Lengthy derivations are minimized and replaced by intuitive interpretations. A number of computer recognition results are included, and they are highly dependent on the data sets available. Readers are encouraged to have their own data sets generated and to test some of the techniques described. Fortunately, during the past few years several researchers have made their character recognition data sets available to the pattern recognition community, such as Dr. W. H. Highleyman of Data Trends, Inc.; Dr. A. L. Knoll of Honeywell, Inc.; and Dr. J. Munson of Stanford Research Institute. With a common data set, it is possible to compare the performance of different recognition techniques.

Statistical pattern recognition has been interfaced with almost every fundamental problem in mathematical statistics. No doubt its progress has benefited considerably from recent developments in statistical decision theory. The reverse is also true. The field progresses much faster theoretically than practically. Both the theoretical and practical aspects of statistical pattern recognition will remain a challenging field in the years to come.

C. H. Chen

Acknowledgments

The author would like to express his gratitude to Dr. K. S. Fu, Dr. S. H. Chang, and Lt. Col. Russell B. Ives for their encouragement in this project. Thanks are due to Dr. W. H. Highleyman for his helpful comments and criticisms on various versions of the manuscript, and to Dr. A. L. Knoll for carefully reading the first two chapters and providing detailed comments and suggestions. Partial support of the Air Force Office of Scientific Research is gratefully acknowledged.

The author was fortunate in having had the opportunity to study under Professor K. S. Fu at Purdue University. Discussion with him has always been fruitful and stimulating. Thanks also go to Mrs. Beverly Zexter for her capable typing of the final manuscript.

Finally, to my wife, I owe a special debt. Her encouragement and understanding were essential to the completion of the manuscript.

Contents

STATISTICAL PATTERN RECOGNITION

CHAPTER I
Introduction

1. Description of Patterns

A pattern is a model, guide, or plan used in making things, according to one of the dictionary definitions. It can be concrete or abstract. Almost anything which is within the reach of our five senses can be chosen as a pattern—a character, a photograph, a biological waveform, speech pattern, odors, tastes, etc.

A pattern class is a group of patterns with certain properties. For instance, in recognizing electrocardiograms there are two pattern classes, namely, the heart is normal and abnormal. In speech patterns, the pattern classes may be various spoken words or various speakers. The problem of pattern recognition is that of classifying a pattern into one of the pattern classes on the ground of certain measurements or observations. These certain measurements or observations are made subjectively, since different types of classification may use different measurements.

Figure 1.1 shows a typical set of patterns which are character samples and time series patterns. Depending on the points of view, the variations of the members of a pattern class can be deterministic (nonrandom) or random in nature. For example, in character recognition where the characters are from a known font, variations in the digital pattern for an "A" will be due to ink variations in the typewriter ribbon, noise entering the digitization process, etc., which can be deterministic or statistical in nature. If we use the statistical pattern recognition approach, the variations of the pattern from the stored reference, which is the ideal or average pattern, are considered as random. It is necessary then, to describe such variations with a probabilistic quantity. Either school of thought has provided us many fruitful results during the development of pattern recognition in the last two decades. This book deals mainly with the statistical and statistically-related approaches to the field of pattern recognition.

2. Probabilistic Formulation of Pattern Recognition

Having been given the measurement of a pattern, a pattern classifier or a recognition, the machine classifies the pattern into one of several classes. The recog-

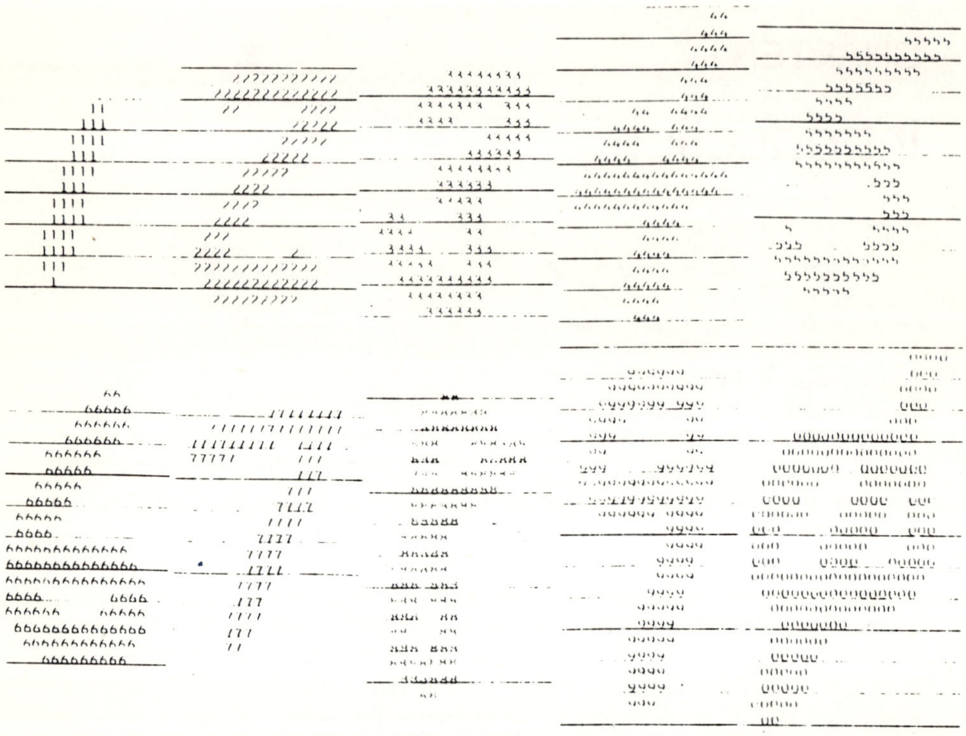

Fig. 1.1(a) Computer Printout of Numerals Written for Fortran Program (Samples provided by Dr. J. Munson of Stanford Research Institute)

nition machine can be described by the block diagram in figure 1.2. The receptor is concerned with the preprocessing of patterns to select or extract the features which characterize the pattern. The categorizer decides to which class the pattern belongs, i.e., it is concerned with the classification problem. Up to now, much effort has been made to improve the percentage of correct recognitions by using a better classification scheme; comparatively much less work has been done on the problem of selecting features.

Suppose that the pattern is random, we shall sort out its characteristics with certain statistics. Each measurement we make is denoted as x. We can also consider x as a point in the N-dimensional measurement (sample) space. Each pattern class corresponding to a certain state of nature is denoted as ω_i, with a priori probability $P_i = P(\omega_i)$, $i = 1,2, \ldots, m$, where m is the total number of classes. If the recognition machine makes a wrong decision on the jth class according to the measurement x while the ith class actually is the true one, there is a loss. Let $L(\omega_i, d_j)$ be the loss associated with the decision, $P = \{P(\omega_i)\}$ be the set of

Fig. 1.1(b) Typical Samples of Hand-Printed Numerals (Supplied by Dr. A. Knoll of Honeywell)

a priori probabilities, and $p(x/\omega_i)$ be the probability density function of the ith class. Then the average risk function is

$$R(P; d_j) = \int_{\Omega_x} \sum_{i=1}^{m} L(\omega_i, d_j) P_i \, p(x/\omega_i) dx \tag{1.1}$$

where the integration is over the space of x, denoted as Ω_x. The recognition machine then chooses the pattern class so that the average risk given by equation (1.1) is the smallest. The categorization problem is exactly the same as that of statistical decision theory.

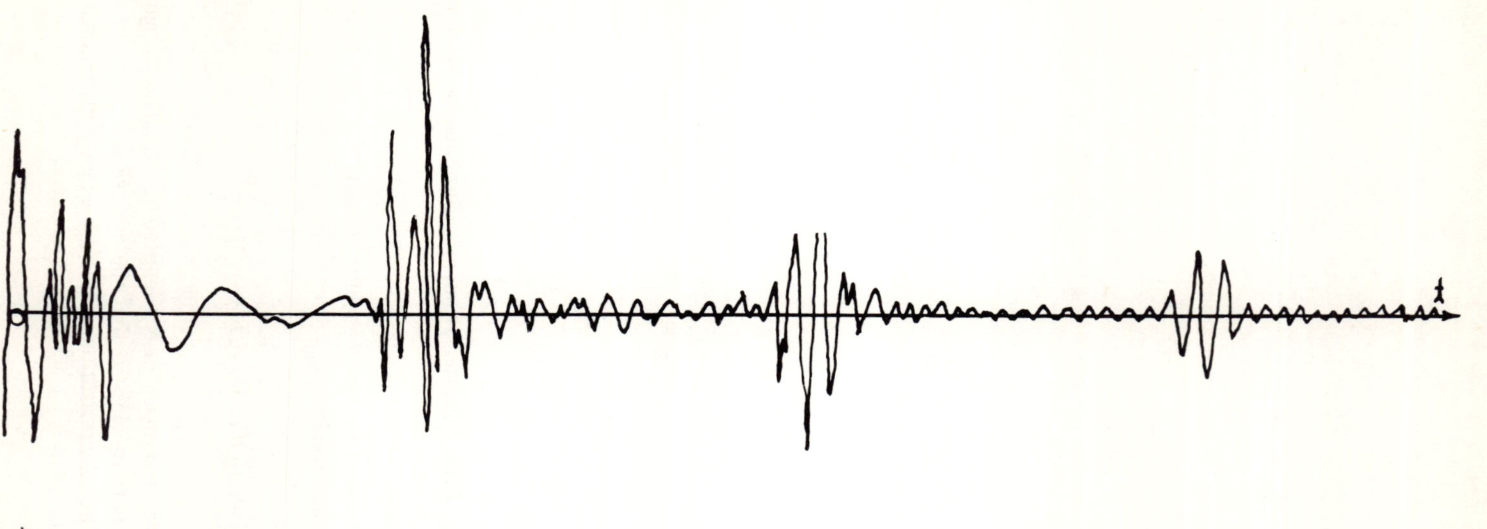

Fig. 1.1(c) A Typical Set of Marine Seismic Data (Supplied by K. Prada of Woods Hole Oceanographic Institution) See also, C. H. Chen, *On the Application of Pattern Recognition Techniques to Oceanographic Signal Processing*, 1970 IEEE International Conference on Engineering in the Ocean Environment, Panama City, Fla.

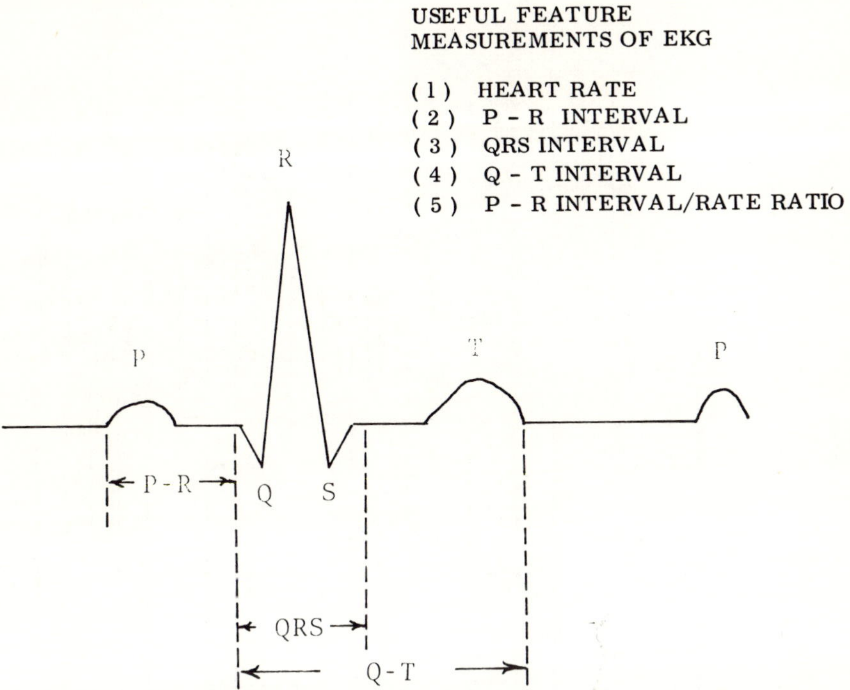

Fig. 1.1(d) A Typical Segment of Electrocardiogram

Thus many useful results from mathematical statistics can be applied to pattern classification. As to the receptor, the equivalence is not so obvious. However, we may extremize the information measure, a probabilistic quantity, to obtain a feature set with the largest discrimination power among all classes. There are some instances† in which statistical approaches are neither desirable nor feasible. But each problem can be formulated probabilistically so that the statistical solution is available at least theoretically. In addition to statistical decision theory, other statistical criteria will also be discussed.

3. Geometrical Interpretations

Geometrical interpretations are usually explicit and convenient ways to explain some basic concepts in pattern recognition. Let us assume that there is a set of two-dimensional measurements of two pattern classes A and B, as shown

†For example, in optical character recognition the dimension of a pattern may be so large that the statistical method of reducing the dimension is not useful.

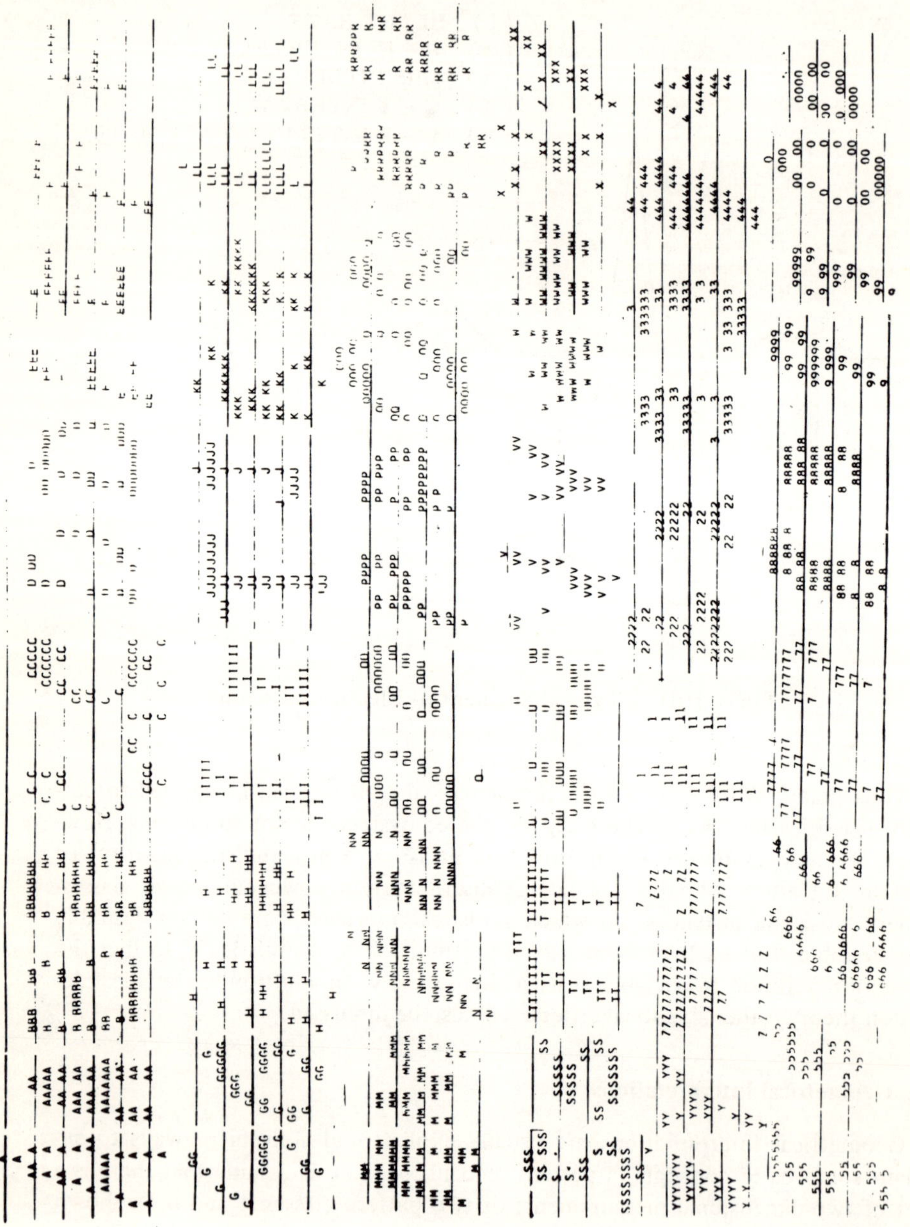

Fig. 1.1(e) Typical Samples of Highleyman's Data Set

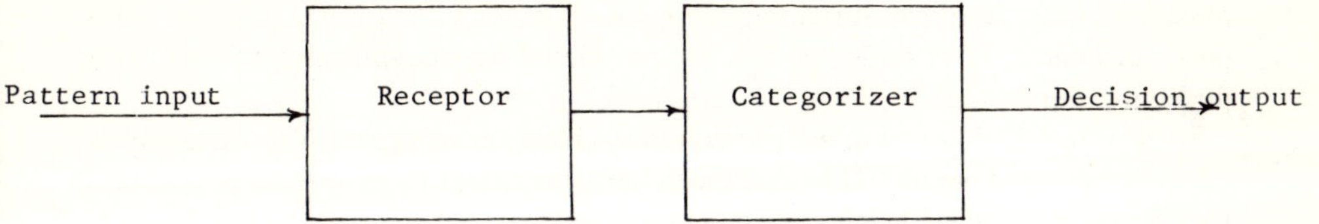

Fig. 1.2 Recognition Machine

in figure 1.3. In figure 1.3a, a nonlinear decision boundary can be constructed to partition the sample space into class *A* and class *B* without an error. The two classes which are disjoint in the sample space are said to be separable. If the decision boundary is linear, as shown by the dashed line, the two classes are linearly separable. However, the two classes are often not separable by a single decision surface, as shown in figure 1.3b. The sample space can be partitioned with a minimum error if statistical decision theory is applied. We should also notice that the probabilistic formulation of pattern classification is more convenient and feasible in the typical sample space, as shown in figure 1.3b. The number of pattern classes may or may not be fixed. In figure 1.3c we still have classes *A* and *B*. But class *A* is divided into two disjoint subclasses, A_1 and A_2. The optimum decision boundaries between subclass A_1 and class *B* and between subclass A_2 and class *B* can be constructed. If A_1 and A_2 are not disjoint, they may also be partitioned by an optimum decision boundary.

4. Applications of Statistical Pattern Recognition

In order to mechanize the enormous number of recognition tasks in information processing, which heretofore have been performed primarily by humans, we

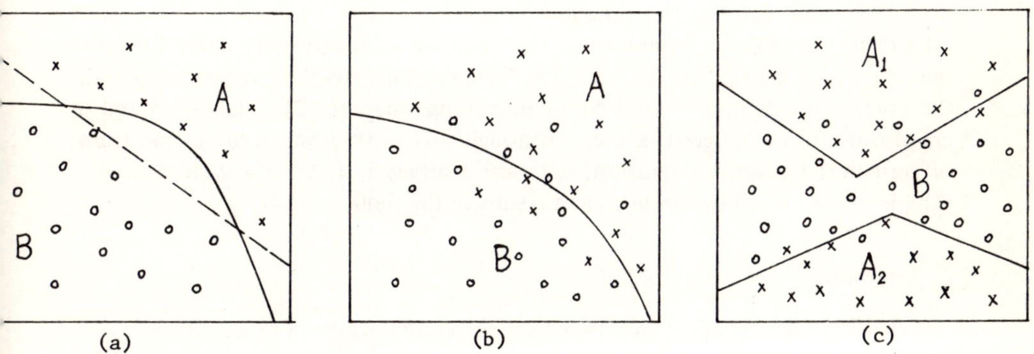

Fig. 1.3 Typical Two-Class Two-Dimensional Sample Spaces

must construct hardware-oriented recognition devices or general purpose computer programs, both of which can be considered as recognition machines with different applications.

To distinguish these two, we can compare character recognition to the analysis of an electrocardiogram. Thousands of characters must be processed per minute for recognition in a business environment; thus special recognition hardware is required. However, the analysis of an electrocardiogram can be done at a much more leisurely pace (i.e., several minutes) by a general purpose computer and still be more efficient than manual analysis, provided the computer can detect the important features the physician sees.

Statistical pattern recognition is one of the mathematical theories underlying the design and analysis of recognition machines. By properly incorporating an input device (such as a scanner) to the digital, analog, or hybrid computer system, a statistical recognition machine is formed. In addition to the characters (numerals and alphabets) and biomedical waveforms, statistical recognition methods have been successfully applied to patterns in weather prediction, photointerpretation, multispectral crop classification, and many other areas. What is equally important is that the computational schemes developed in statistical recognition techniques are very useful in many other disciplines such as statistical data processing, communication and control theories, computer-related fields and in the general systems area, not to mention the interaction of statistical pattern recognition with many nonengineering disciplines, such as mathematical statistics and psychology.

5. Scope of Statistical Pattern Recognition

In spite of the fast development in pattern recognition in recent years, statistical pattern recognition is still in its infancy. To a newcomer, this area appears highly diversified with a number of scattered results. Many of the results are quite uncorrelated. This work attempts to provide a unified treatment of the field. We shall develop the fundamental concepts and background of statistical pattern recognition (chapters 1,2,4). Then we shall introduce several important methodologies (chapters 3,5,6,7,9,10,11) and discuss their relationship with the computer (chapter 8) and communications (chapter 12). Chapters 5 and 6 are also useful in the control area. Although this work covers a broad spectrum of statistical pattern recognition, it is not a survey but rather a systematic development of a few key methods and results in the field.

6. Literature

Following each chapter are two lists of related works: (1) the References, which list those works referred to in the text and (2) a Bibliography of works pertinent to the subject matter of the chapter.

The following is a list of publications which introduce or survey the area of statistical pattern recognition.

Books

1. Bongard, M. *Pattern Recognition.* Translated from Russian by T. Cheron. Edited by J. K. Hawkins. Spartan Books, New York, 1970.
2. Fu, K. S. *Sequential Methods in Pattern Recognition and Machine Learning.* Academic Press, New York, 1968.
3. Kanal, L. N., ed. "Pattern Recognition." In *Proc. of the IEEE Workshop on Pattern Recognition*, held at Dorado, Puerto Rico, Thompson, Washington, D.C., 1968. Particularly Part III.
4. Mendel, J. M. and K. S. Fu, eds. *Adaptive Learning and Pattern Recognition Systems: Theory and Applications.* Academic Press, New York, 1970. Particularly Part I.
5. Nilsson, N. J. *Learning Machines.* McGraw-Hill, New York, 1965.
6. Sebestyen, G. S. *Decision Making Processes in Pattern Recognition.* Macmillan, New York, 1962.
7. Watanabe, S., ed. *Methodologies of Pattern Recognition.* Academic Press, New York, 1969.
8. Fu, K. S., ed. "Pattern Recognition and Machine Learning." *Proceedings of the Japan-U.S. Seminar on the Learning Process in Control Systems.* Nagoya, Japan (August 1970). Plenum Press, New York. Particularly Part I.

Articles and Reports

1. Abramson, N., D. Braverman, and G. S. Sebestyen. "Pattern Recognition and Machine Learning." *IEEE Trans. on Information Theory*, IT-9 (October 1963), 257–261.
2. Braverman, D. "Theories of Pattern Recognition." In *Advances in Communications Systems*, vol. 1, edited by A. V. Balakrishnan. Academic Press, New York, 1964.
3. Ho, Y. C. and A. K. Agrawala. "On Pattern Classification Algorithms: Introduction and Survey." *Proc. of IEEE* (October 1968).
4. Kanal, L., et al. "Adaptive Modelling of Likelihood Classification-1." RADC-TR-66-190 (AD 636519), June 1966.
5. Kanal, L., B. Chandrasekaran, and T. J. Harley, Jr. "On Methodologies of Pattern Recognition," Philco Technical Report, March 1969.
6. Kovalevsky, V. A. "The Problem of Character Recognition from the Point of View of Mathematical Statistics." In *Character Readers and Pattern Recognition*, edited by V. A. Kovalevsky. Spartan Books, New York, 1968.
7. Nagy, G. "State of the Art in Pattern Recognition." *Proc. of IEEE*, 56 (May 1968), 836-863.
8. Tsypkin, Y. Z. "Pattern Recognition," chapter 4 in *Adaptation and Learning in Automatic Systems.* Translated by Z. J. Nikolic. Academic Press, New York, 1971.

CHAPTER II

Linear and Nonlinear Classification Theories

1. Introduction

When we talk about the linear and nonlinear classification theories, we mean the partitioning of the sample space by the linear and nonlinear decision boundaries, respectively. The function defining the decision boundary is known as the decision function or the discriminant function.† Optimum decision boundaries usually are nonlinear and no doubt are more complex to implement. The piecewise linear boundaries are easier to implement and can be constructed to approximate the optimum nonlinear decision boundaries. Once the decision boundaries are established, we can assign an unknown pattern to the class which is determined by the decision boundaries. Therefore, the construction of decision boundaries is a fundamental task of pattern recognition.

Optimum decision boundaries become linear in some cases. For instance, when two pattern classes are normally distributed with equal covariance matrices but different mean vectors, then the optimum decision boundary is a linear one. Generally speaking, the sample space is multiply-connected and multimodal. So the linear boundaries may not be adequate to provide us with a reasonably accurate classification.

In this chapter, we shall first introduce the elementary Bayes decision theory which is fundamental to the development of the discriminant function. Later, we shall discuss the linear and nonlinear discriminant functions in detail.

2. Elementary Bayes Decision Theory

Consider two classes ω_1 and ω_2 with a priori probabilities of occurrence P_1 and P_2 ($P_1 + P_2 = 1$). Let the observation (measurement) x be an N-dimensional vector which is uniquely classified into one of the two classes by the decision criterion, i.e., the decision criterion partitions the sample space of all ob-

†The discriminant function $U(x)$ is defined such that if $U(x) \geqslant C$, class 1 is true and if $U(x) < C$, class 2 is true, where C is a constant.

servations R into R_1 (class ω_1) and R_2 (class ω_2). Let $p(x/\omega_1)$ and $p(x/\omega_2)$ represent the conditional probability densities associated with measurement x, given that the unknown pattern came from class ω_1 or class ω_2 respectively. For all regions of the space R in which both probability densities are greater than zero, a finite probability of misclassification exists. The overall probability of correctly classifying patterns from class ω_1 is then given by

$$P(d_1/\omega_1) = \int_{R_1} p(x/\omega_1)dx$$

where $d_j, j = 1,2$, denotes the decision that the jth class is true and $dx = dx_1 \cdot dx_2, \cdots, dx_N$ while the probability of misclassifying patterns from class ω_1 is given by

$$P(d_2/\omega_1) = \int_{R_2} p(x/\omega_1)dx$$

Similarly, the probabilities of correctly and incorrectly classifying patterns from class 2 are

$$P(d_2/\omega_2) = \int_{R_2} p(x/\omega_2)dx \quad \text{and} \quad P(d_1/\omega_2) = \int_{R_1} p(x/\omega_2)dx$$

respectively. Let $L(\omega_i, d_j)$, $i, j = 1,2$, be the loss incurred with the decision d_j when the ith class is true. With the exception of chapter 9, we assume the cost of taking an observation to be zero. Thus $L(\omega_1, d_1) = L(\omega_2, d_2) = 0$. Also $L(\omega_1, d_2) > 0$ and $L(\omega_2, d_1) > 0$. Then the average (expected) loss from misclassification is

$$P_1 L(\omega_1, d_2)P(d_2/\omega_1) + P_2 L(\omega_2, d_1)P(d_1/\omega_2) \tag{2.1}$$

It is this average loss that we would like to minimize. That is, we want to divide the sample space into regions R_1 and R_2 such that the average loss is as small as possible. The procedure that minimizes equation (2.1) is called a Bayes procedure.

When the a priori probabilities are *unknown*, the conditional expected loss if the observation is from class 1 is

$$r(\omega_1, R) = L(\omega_1, d_2)P(\omega_2/\omega_1)$$

and the expected loss if the observation is from class 2 is

$$r(\omega_2, R) = L(\omega_2, d_1)P(\omega_1/\omega_2)$$

A procedure is minimax if the maximum expected loss $r(\omega_1, R)$ is a minimum.

When the a priori probabilities are *known*, the decision rule is to minimize the average loss given by equation (2.1). The rule is to choose R_1 and R_2 according to

$$\begin{aligned} R_1&: P_1 p(x/\omega_1) L(\omega_1, d_2) \geqslant P_2 p(x/\omega_2) L(\omega_2, d_1) \\ R_2&: P_1 p(x/\omega_1) L(\omega_1, d_2) < P_2 p(x/\omega_2) L(\omega_2, d_1) \end{aligned} \tag{2.2}$$

When the equality holds, the observation can be classified as either from class 1 or class 2. We have arbitrarily put it into R_1. Let

$$K = \frac{P_2 L(\omega_2, d_1)}{P_1 L(\omega_1, d_2)} \tag{2.3}$$

Another way of writing equation (2.2) is

$$\begin{aligned} R_1&: \frac{p(x/\omega_1)}{p(x/\omega_2)} \geqslant K \\ R_2&: \frac{p(x/\omega_1)}{p(x/\omega_2)} < K \end{aligned} \tag{2.4}$$

Consider two multivariate normal distributions with the means M_1 and M_2 and equal covariance matrix V.

$$p(x/\omega_i) = \frac{1}{(2\pi)^{N/2} \mid V \mid^{1/2}} \exp\left[-\frac{1}{2}(x - M_i)' V^{-1} (x - M_i)\right], i = 1, 2$$

The logarithm of the ratio of densities is

$$\begin{aligned} U = \log \frac{p(x/\omega_1)}{p(x/\omega_2)} &= -\frac{1}{2}[(x - M_1)' V^{-1} (x - M_1) \\ &\quad - (x - M_2)' V^{-1} (x - M_2)] \\ &= x' V^{-1} (M_1 - M_2) \\ &\quad - \frac{1}{2}(M_1 + M_2)' V^{-1} (M_1 - M_2) \end{aligned} \tag{2.5}$$

The first term is the well known (Fisher's) linear discriminant function. It is a linear function of the observation vector x. U, the test statistic, can be compared with the threshold $\log K$, where K is given by equation (2.3). In the particular case when $P_1 = P_2$ and $L(\omega_2, d_1) = L(\omega_1, d_2)$, $\log K = 0$.

Now let the square of the distance between the two normal distributions be

$$\alpha = (M_1 - M_2)' V^{-1} (M_1 - M_2) \tag{2.6}$$

which is the square of the Euclidean distance between M_1 and M_2 when $V = I$, the identity matrix. The test statistic U has a normal distribution with the mean and the variance when class 1 is true given by

$$E_1 U = \int p(x/\omega_1) \log \frac{p(x/\omega_1)}{p(x/\omega_2)} dx = \frac{1}{2} (M_1 - M_2)' V^{-1} \cdot (M_1 - M_2) = \frac{1}{2} \alpha$$

$$\sigma_1^2(U) = (M_1 - M_2)' V^{-1} (M_1 - M_2) = \alpha$$

Similarly, the mean and the variance of U when class 2 is true are given by

$$E_2 U = \int p(x/\omega_2) \log \frac{p(x/\omega_1)}{p(x/\omega_2)} dx = -\frac{1}{2} \alpha$$

and

$$\sigma_2^2(U) = \alpha$$

As a remark, $E_i U$, $i = 1,2$ are called the directed divergences, and the divergence between the two distributions is[1]

$$J = E_1 U - E_2 U = \alpha \tag{2.7}$$

The probability of misclassification if the observation is from class 1 is

$$P(d_2/\omega_1) = \int_{-\infty}^{c} \frac{1}{\sqrt{2\pi\alpha}} e^{-(z-\alpha/2)^2/2\alpha} dz = \int_{-\infty}^{(c-\alpha/2)/\sqrt{\alpha}} \cdot \frac{1}{\sqrt{2\pi}} e^{-y^2/2} dy \tag{2.8}$$

where $C = \log K$ and the probability of misclassification if the observation is from class 2 is

$$P(d_1/\omega_2) = \int_{c}^{\infty} \frac{1}{\sqrt{2\pi\alpha}} e^{-(z+\alpha/2)^2/2\alpha} dz = \int_{(c+\alpha/2)/\sqrt{\alpha}}^{\infty} \cdot \frac{1}{\sqrt{2\pi}} e^{-y^2/2} dy \tag{2.9}$$

The random variable z is equal to the test statistic U given that class 1 (equation 2.8) or class 2 (equation 2.9) be true. Figure 2.1 shows the two probabilities of misclassification as the shaded portions in the tails.

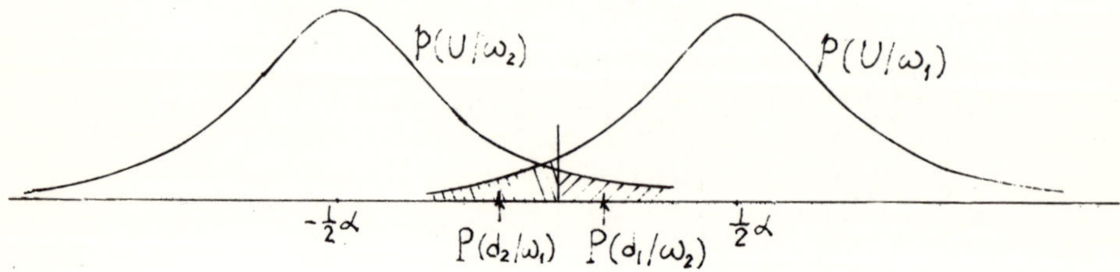

Fig. 2.1 Probabilities of Misclassification

If the a priori probabilities are not available, we may select the threshold $C = \log K$ on the basis of making the expected losses equal due to the misclassifications. This is called the minimax solution. We choose C so that

$$L(\omega_2, d_1)P(d_1/\omega_2) = L(\omega_1, d_2)P(d_2/\omega_1)$$

In practice, the mean and the covariance of each class are estimated from samples. Let K_1 and K_2 be the number of samples (observations) belonging to class 1 and class 2 respectively. The sample mean and covariance matrices are

$$\hat{M}_i = \frac{1}{K_i} \sum_{j=1}^{K_i} x_{ji}$$

$$\hat{V}_i = \frac{1}{K_i - 1} \sum_{j=1}^{K_i} (x_{ji} - \hat{M}_i)(x_{ji} - \hat{M}_i)' \tag{2.10}$$

where x_{ji} is the jth sample of the ith class, $i = 1,2$. This procedure is asymptotically optimal (convergent in probability) since

$$\lim_{K_i \to \infty} \hat{M}_i \overset{p}{=} M_i$$

and

$$\lim_{K_i \to \infty} \hat{V}_i \overset{p}{=} V_i$$

The common covariance matrix of the two classes may also be estimated from the samples as

$$(K_1 + K_2 - 2)\hat{V} = \sum_{j=1}^{K_1} (x_{ji} - \hat{M}_1)(x_{ji} - \hat{M}_1)' + \sum_{j=1}^{K_2} (x_{j2} - \hat{M}_2)(x_{j2} - \hat{M}_2)' \tag{2.11}$$

and $\hat{V}$ will converge in probability to the common population covariance matrix V.

The distribution of V or $A = (k - 1)V$, often called the Wishart distribution, is fundamental to multivariate statistical analysis. When $V = I$, the distribution is in a sense a generalization of the chi-squared distribution.

The Bayes discriminant function $f_{12}(x)$ defining the decision boundary between classes 1 and 2 can be obtained from equation (2.2) which is normalized by

$$p(x) = \sum_{i=1}^{2} P_i p(x/\omega_1)$$

The result is

$$f_{12}(x) = \frac{1}{p(x)} [P_1 L(\omega_1, d_2) p(x/\omega_1) - P_2 L(\omega_2, d_1) p(x/\omega_2)] \tag{2.12}$$

For the multiple pattern classes, the Bayes discriminant function between the ith and the jth classes is given by

$$f_{ij}(x) = \frac{1}{p(x)} \sum_{\ell=1}^{m} P_\ell r_\ell(i,j) p(x/\omega_\ell) \quad 1 \leqslant i,j \leqslant m \tag{2.13}$$

where

$$f_{ij}(x) = -f_{ji}(x)$$

and

$$r_\ell(i,j) = \begin{cases} L(\omega_\ell, d_j) - L(\omega_\ell, d_i); & \ell \neq i,j \\ L(\omega_i, d_j) - L(\omega_i, d_i); & \ell = i \\ -L(\omega_j, d_i) + L(\omega_j, d_j); & \ell = j \end{cases}$$

Using the function given by equation (2.13), the expected risk due to misclassification is minimized by deciding that x belongs to the ith class if

$$f_{ij}(x) \geqslant 0, \quad j = 1,2,\cdots,m, \quad j \neq i \tag{2.14a}$$

or the jth class if

$$f_{ij}(x) < 0, \quad j = 1,2,\cdots,m, \quad j \neq i \tag{2.14b}$$

In the case of normal distributions with a common covariance matrix, each pattern class is bounded by, at most, $m - 1$ hyperplanes (linear Bayes discriminant functions). In general, to determine the probability of misclassification, the joint probability distribution of $m - 1$ discriminant functions must be known. It is usually more convenient to determine the probability of correct decision, $P(d_i/\omega_i)$, $i = 1,2,\cdots,m$ satisfying $\sum_{i=1}^{m} P(d_i/\omega_i) = 1$. For the decision rule given by equation (2.14), the probability of correct decision when the ith class is true is given by

$$\begin{aligned} P(d_i/\omega_i) = P\,[&f_{i1}(x) \geqslant 0, f_{i2}(x) \geqslant 0, \cdots, f_{ii-1}(x) \geqslant 0, \\ &f_{ii+1}(x) \geqslant 0, \cdots, f_{im}(x) \geqslant 0] \end{aligned} \tag{2.15}$$

For zero-one loss functions, viz., $L(\omega_i, d_i) = 0$ for all i and $L(\omega_i, d_j) = 1$ for all i, j such that $i \neq j$, then

$$\begin{aligned} P(d_i/\omega_i) = P\,[&U_{i1} \geqslant C_{i1}, U_{i2} \geqslant C_{i2}, \cdots, U_{ii-1} \geqslant C_{ii-1}, \\ &U_{ii+1} \geqslant C_{ii+1}, \cdots, U_{im}(x) \geqslant C_{im}] \end{aligned} \tag{2.16}$$

which is usually easier to evaluate than equation (2.15). (Consider, for example, the multiple classes with normal distributions and a common covariance matrix.) Here $U_{ij} = \log\,[P(x/\omega_i)/p(x/\omega_j)]$ and $C_{ij} = \log P_j/P_i$, $i \neq j$. The average probability of error (misclassification) is

$$P_e = 1 - \sum_{i=1}^{m} P_i P(d_i/\omega_i) \tag{2.17}$$

It is remarked that the computation of the exact probability of error is often difficult for $m > 2$ except for special types of distributions. Thus many researchers attempt to find the bounds of the probability of error.

3. Statistical Criteria and Discriminant Functions

The Bayes decision rule discussed in the preceding section is optimum in the sense that it minimizes the expected risk with respect to the a priori probabilities and loss functions. There are other criteria of optimality.[2] Each criterion will determine a discriminant function wherein the linear discriminant function is a special case. In this section we shall present Fisher's and the least mean square criteria and the discriminant functions.

The Fisher's criterion[3] regards the value of the discriminant function $U(x)$ as a random variable and postulates the measure of effectiveness of U to be the quantity

$$L = \frac{(\overline{U}_1 - \overline{U}_2)^2}{\sigma_1^2(U) + \sigma_2^2(U)} \tag{2.18}$$

where $\overline{U}_i = E_i U$ and $\sigma_i^2(U)$, $i = 1,2$ are the mean and the variance respectively. To maximize L, the distance between the means, i.e., the interclass distance, must be large and the samples of each class must be clustered with respect to its mean, i.e., the intraclass distance must be small.

It should be noted that the Fisher criterion does not require a decision rule to be stated before an optimal function $U(x)$ can be found. The optimal U in the Fisher sense is chosen only on the basis of the measure L; any use made of the function for decision purposes is left to the discretion of the experimenter. One obvious and intuitively appealing way to use an optimal U is to choose class 1 if $|U - \overline{U}_1| < |U - \overline{U}_2|$ and class 2 otherwise. The optimal U denoted as U_0 as derived in appendix A is

$$U_0(x) = [p(x/\omega_1) - p(x/\omega_2)] \frac{1}{p(x/\omega_1) + p(x/\omega_2)} \tag{2.19}$$

where $\beta = \dfrac{P_2}{P_1 C}$ and C is some constant. Choose class 1 if $U_0(x) \geqslant 0$ and class 2 otherwise. Here we notice that this is essentially a likelihood ratio test which chooses class 1 if $\dfrac{P_1 p(x/\omega_1)}{P_2 p(x/\omega_2)} \geqslant \dfrac{1}{C}$ and class 2 otherwise. Whether equation (2.19) is a linear function of x will depend on the distributions considered.

The least mean square (lms) measure of the effectiveness of a discriminant function $U(x)$ is taken to be

$$\begin{aligned} \overline{e^2} &= \int (U - \delta_1)^2 \, p(x/\omega_1)dx + \beta \int (U - \delta_2)^2 \, p(x/\omega_2)dx \\ &= E_1[(U - \delta_1)^2] + E_2[(U - \delta_2)^2] \end{aligned} \tag{2.20}$$

where δ_i is the desired value of U if ω_i is true, $i = 1, 2$. And $\overline{e^2}$, defined by the equation, is a measure of the mean square distance between U and δ_i, $i = 1,2$. The closer $\overline{e^2}$ is to zero, the better U is in the lms sense. Similar to the Fisher criterion, the lms measure requires no specific decision rule until an optimal U (also in the lms sense) has been found.

The optimal form of U denoted as $U_0(x)$ that minimizes $\overline{e^2}$ can be obtained by the calculus of variations as

$$U_0(x) = \frac{1}{[p(x/\omega_1) + \beta p(x/\omega_2)]} \{\delta_1 p(x/\omega_1) + \beta \delta_2 p(x/\omega_2)\} \tag{2.21}$$

4. Linear Decision Functions

How do we obtain the linear decision function†? Each criterion discussed in the preceding two sections may result in a linear decision function for certain distributions. We may also treat the problem by approximating the true distribution with a particular form of probability distribution, e.g., Gaussian. This particular form will provide us with a linear boundary. Hence our problem becomes the estimation of the parameters of the approximating distribution. Since the true distribution of a pattern is generally unknown, it is better not to make assumptions about the distribution but to restrain the form of the decision boundary to be linear. This last approach is essentially an approximation to a nonparametric estimator (the hyperplane).[4]

For every pair of pattern classes, one hyperplane can be constructed to separate them. For m pattern classes, there are $\frac{1}{2}\, m(m - 1)$ possible linear boundaries, which is the maximum number. Figure 2.2 illustrates the linear decision function for three pattern classes in a two-dimensional space. Figure 2.2a shows the optimum linear decision function in dashed lines and the optimum nonlinear decision functions in solid curves. In general, there is no guarantee that the linear decision boundaries will meet at a point as shown in figure 2.2b. Classification of a sample point is performed on a class pair basis. The sample point A is classified as belonging to classes 2, 3, 2 respectively by using the boundaries B_{12}, B_{13}, B_{23}. These boundaries classify point B as belonging to classes 2, 1, 3 respectively. Thus sample B is rejected as it does not belong to any class. This occurs only when we restrain to the linear boundaries in the multiple pattern class case.

In the remainder of this section, we shall consider two pattern classes only. The linear discriminant function is given by $f(x) = w \cdot x + w_0$, where $w \cdot x$ is the dot product of the measurement vector x and the weighting vector w. The hyperplane is then

$$f(x) = w \cdot x + w_0 = \sum_{i=1}^{N} w_i x_i + w_0 = 0 \tag{2.22}$$

where w_i, $i = 1,2, \cdots, N$ are the coefficients (weights) of the hyperplane and w_0 is some constant corresponding to the threshold. An unknown pattern x is

†This term is the same as the linear discriminant function. It is also called the hyperplane. For an N-dimensional measurement space, the hyperplane has a dimension of $N - 1$.

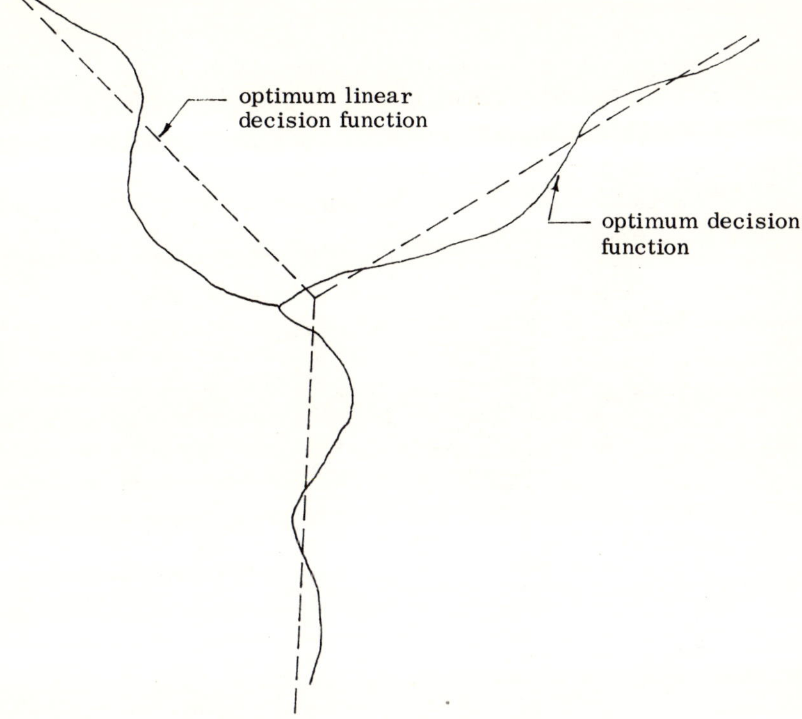

Fig. 2.2(a) Linear Decision Functions

assigned to class 1 if $f(x) \geqslant 0$, i.e., $\sum_{i=1}^{N} w_i x_i \geqslant -w_0$, and class 2 if $f(x) < 0$. Here the equality sign is arbitrarily assigned to class 1. It is noted that equation (2.5) is the same as equation (2.22) with $w' = V^{-1}(M_1 - M_2)$ and $w_0 = -\frac{1}{2}(M_1 + M_2)' V^{-1}(M_1 - M_2)$.

Equation (2.22) can be easily synthesized by a resistive network. The weights and the threshold can be adjusted iteratively by changing the network parameters to reach optimum. This is done by using the sequence of training samples whose correct classifications are known. Figure 2.3 shows an ADALINE (an abbreviation of the adaptive linear network or adaptive logic element[5,6]) which implements the hyperplane, equation (2.22). The output of the summing element is $f(x)$. The output of the threshold element indicates +1 (class 1) or −1 (class 2). Define the error when the kth pattern vector is received as $\epsilon(k) = d(k) - w_0 - w(k) \cdot x(k)$ where $d(k)$ is the desired output. Then ADALINE minimizes the mean square error averaged over k, denoted as ϵ^2, by properly

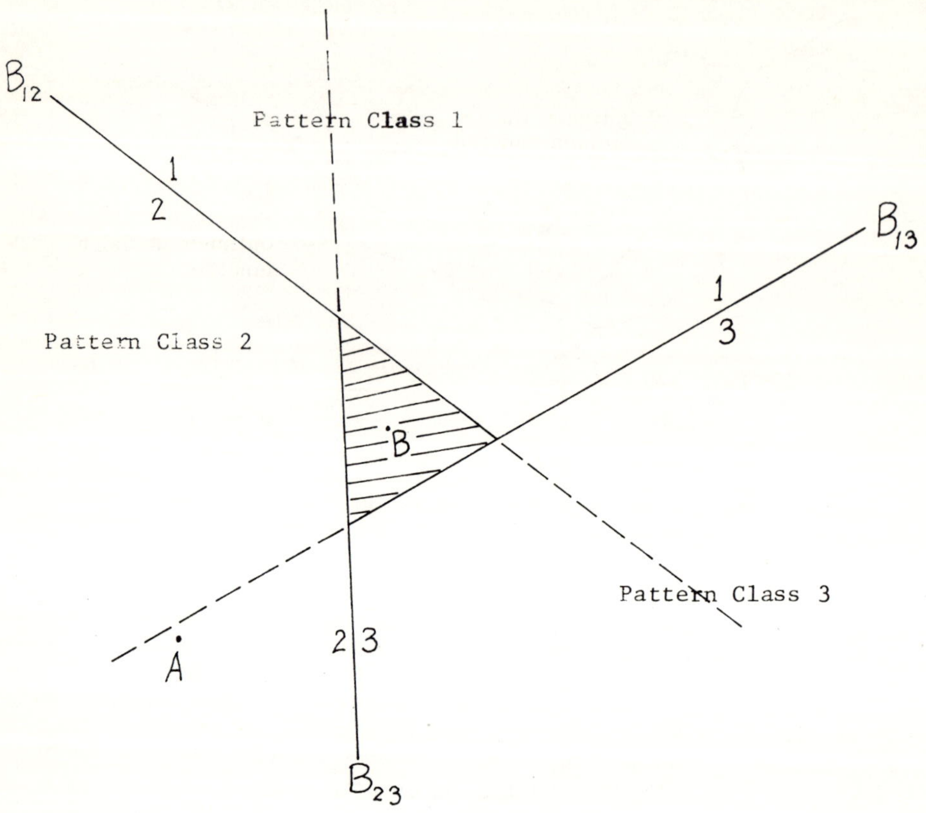

Fig. 2.2(b) Linear Decision Functions

selecting the weight vector w. The weight vector is usually determined iteratively,

$$w(k+1) = w(k) + C(k), \quad k = 1,2, \cdots \tag{2.23}$$

where $C(k)$ is the correction vector which is related to the pattern vector $x(k)$ by a training rule or error-correction procedure. For example, if $x(k)$ is from class 1 but $f(x(k)) < 0$, then let $C(k) = \alpha x(k)$, where $\alpha > 0$ is the correction increment. On the other hand, if $x(k)$ is from class 2 but $f(x(k)) > 0$, then let $C(k) = -\alpha x(k)$. Let $C(k) = 0$ if the classification is correct. In general, it is necessary that the training rule be convergent, i.e., $C(k) \to 0$ as $k \to \infty$. If the training samples are linearly separable, i.e., if there exists a linear decision boundary that can classify them all correctly, then the convergence is guaranteed after a finite number of corrections.

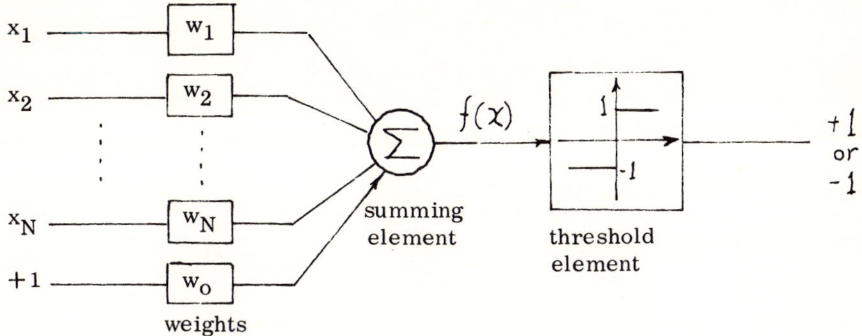

Fig. 2.3 Adaptive Linear Network (ADALINE)

The linear decision function is of prime importance to the pattern classification because it not only is simple to implement but also often leads to the optimum or near-optimum solution.

5. Piecewise Linear Decision Functions

When one or both pattern classes are multimodal or multiply-connected, it requires segments of hyperplanes to separate the two classes linearly. The assemblage of these segments of hyperplanes forms a boundary or a set of boundaries, which is called the piecewise linear decision function. This function has been geometrically explained in figure 1.2 where class A has two disjoint regions A_1 and A_2. The piecewise linear boundaries may also be considered as the approximation of the nonlinear boundaries. Each hyperplane has the equation of the form given by equation (2.14). If we implement and assemble the hyperplanes, we shall have a complete piecewise linear machine.

6. Minimum Distance Classifier

Let each pattern class be assigned a reference point P_i, $i = 1,2,\cdots,m$, which may be, for example, the sample mean of a number of samples from the ith class. The Euclidean distance, $d(x, P_i)$, from an arbitrary point x to the point P_i is defined as

$$d(x,P_i) = |x - P_i| = \sqrt{(x - P_i) \cdot (x - P_i)}$$

or

$$d^2(x,P_i) \sim -2x \cdot P_i + P_i^2 \tag{2.24}$$

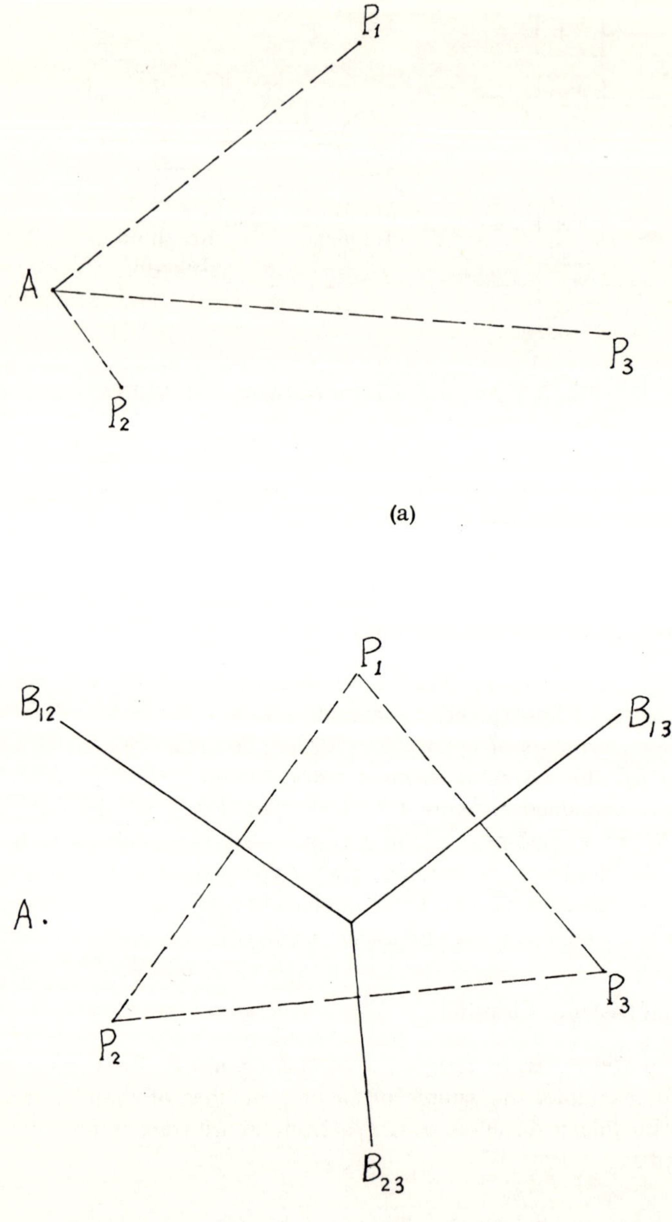

Fig. 2.4 The Relation of a Minimum Distance Classifier to a Linear Decision Function: (a) Minimum Distance Classifier, (b) Linear Decision Function Equivalent

The minimum distance classifier compares $d(x, P_i)$, $i = 1,2, \cdots, m$ and selects the smallest one. Point x is assigned to the class which has the smallest $|x - P_i|^2$. Figure 2.4a is an example of the minimum distance classifier with three classes. A sample point A is identified with the class represented by that reference point to which it is closest in a Euclidean sense. Equation (2.24) indicates that the minimum distance classifier is a linear machine. Consider reference points P_1 and P_2 and the hyperplane B_{12} (figure 2.4b) which is a perpendicular bisector of the line joining P_1 and P_2. The statement that A is closer to P_2 than to P_1 is equivalent to the statement that the point lies on the 2 side of B_{12}. By constructing such a hyperplane for every pair of reference points, a linear decision function equivalent to the minimum distance decision function is obtained. Thus the minimum distance classifier is a subclass of linear decision functions. In general, for every minimum Euclidean distance classifier, there exists a classifier based on a linear decision function which is at least as good.[4] It is well known that maximizing an appropriately normalized crosscorrelation function, or matched filtering, is equivalent to minimizing a Euclidean distance. Sebestyen[7] considered the non-Euclidean minimum distance decision function and the problem of setting threshold or bias in correlation operation or matched filtering.

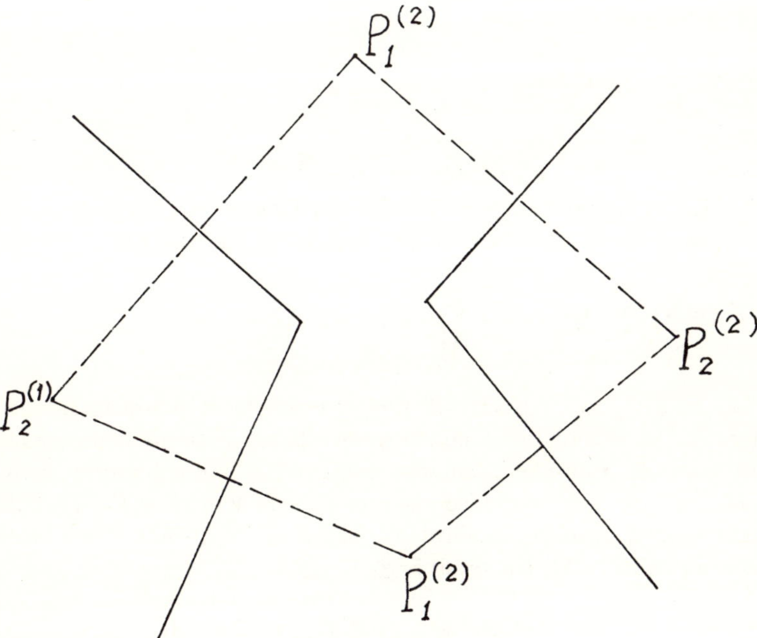

Fig. 2.5 Piecewise Linear Decision Function and Minimum Distance Classifier

When the reference is a point set, which may have more than one point, then the distance between x and the point set P_i is defined as

$$d(x,P_i) = \min |x - P_i^{(j)}| \quad j = 1,2, \cdots, n_i \tag{2.25}$$

where n_i denotes the number of points of P_i. The linear separation of two classes requires the piecewise linear decision boundaries. Equation (2.25) may be considered as the defining equation of piecewise linear decision function. Figure 2.5 is an example of such a minimum distance classifier. Again it can be shown that the performance of using the piecewise linear decision boundaries is at least as good as the minimum distance classifier. It is also noted that all samples of known classification may be used as reference points. In this case n_i is the total number of samples from all classes. Equation (2.25) then defines the nearest-neighbor decision rule to be discussed in chapter 7.

7. Nonlinear Classification Theory

The nonlinear classification theory provides us with the most general method of partitioning the sample space. Since the sample space is usually very complicated, it often requires nonlinear decision boundaries to partition it into a finite number of classes. The nonlinear discriminant function can be written in the general form as

$$f(x) = \sum_{i=1}^{r} w_i f_i(x) + w_0 \tag{2.26}$$

where $f_i(x), i = 1,2, \cdots, r$ are functions of x.

For the linear discriminant function discussed earlier, $r = N, f_i(x) = x_i$. An important class of the decision boundaries takes the quadratic form

$$f(x) = \sum_{k=1}^{N} \sum_{j=1}^{N} w_{kj} x_k x_j + \sum_{i=1}^{N} w_i x_i + w_0 \tag{2.27}$$

where w_{kj} and w_i are constants. A typical example of the quadratic decision boundary is the boundary of normally distributed patterns with unequal covariance matrices. Consider again two multivariate normal distributions with means M_1 and M_2 and covariance matrices V_1 and V_2, $V_1 \neq V_2$. Then the discriminant function can be obtained by taking the logarithm of the likelihood ratio as in equation (2.5). The result is

$$x'(V_1^{-1} - V_2^{-1})x - 2x'(V_1^{-1} M_1 - V_2^{-1} M_2) + M_1' V_1^{-1} M_1 - M_2' V_2^{-1} M_2 + \log |V_1| - \log |V_2| = 0 \tag{2.28}$$

Without assuming a distribution function†, we can constrain the decision boundary to be nonlinear with the polynomial form given by equation (2.26) with

$$f_i(x) = \underbrace{x_k^m \; x_j^n \cdots x_p^1}_{\text{Product of } N-1 \text{ terms}} \qquad \begin{aligned} &k, j, \cdots, p = 1,2, \cdots, N \\ &m + n + \cdots + 1 \leqslant N - 1 \\ &m, n, \cdots, 1 = 0,1, \cdots, N - 1 \end{aligned}$$

The coefficients of the polynomial function, also known as the generalized discriminant function,[7,8] can be theoretically estimated from the sequence of training samples. Frequently, some approximation of the generalized discriminant function by using a simple form is desirable. There is then some irreducible probability of misrecognition or expected risk as compared with the performance of the system using the generalized discriminant function.

8. Discussion of Multiple Pattern Classification

The number of pattern classes is usually more than two. To classify an unknown pattern as belonging to one of several pattern classes, the following are two commonly used methods:

a. Parallel processing. Compute the probability density of the likelihood function of each class and select the class with the largest probability density or likelihood function. This requires knowledge of the distribution of each class. If such knowledge is not available, then the minimum distance categorizer can be used.
b. Sequential processing. Determine, one class at a time, whether or not the class contains the unknown pattern. If it does, the final decision is made. If it doesn't, reject such class from consideration and proceed to the remaining classes. When only one class is left, it is accepted as the recognized class. In determining whether a class should be rejected, the likelihood function (or probability density) of the class can be normalized[9] by, say, the product of the likelihood functions of all classes and then compared with a threshold. If the normalized quantity falls below the threshold, then the class is rejected.

The second method is obviously more efficient with less error because we are dealing with fewer classes most of the time; the number of classes decreases with each rejection. The drawback is that any rejection of the correct class leads to an incorrect decision.

An alternate procedure for the second method is to group all the pattern

†In this nonparametric case, the assumption can be made that the samples are locally Gaussian, i.e., normally distributed at the immediate vicinity of each sample.

classes into two groups and proceed with the group which most likely contains the pattern. The procedure continues until the pattern is recognized.†

If we constrain the decision boundary to be, say, linear, then the parallel processing mentioned above is not applicable. In addition to the sequential processing method, the following are two possibilities:[10]

a. For each class, one decision is made—whether the pattern belongs to the class or not. If each decision has a probability of correct decision p, the net probability of correct decision for the combined decision if all binary decisions are independent is p^m, which is quite low.
b. The pattern is classified from the discriminant function between every pair of classes. The majority voting rule can be applied to the results to determine the final classification. This method requires an excessive number of pairwise decisions when the number of classes is large. The majority rule does not perform well when most of the pairwise decisions differ from one another.

Therefore, sequential processing appears to be the best choice for multiple pattern classification.[9,10]

9. Remarks

For the beginner in decision theory we recommend the book by Chernoff and Moses.[11] This book is concerned with one-dimensional measurements. For vector measurements, chapter 6 of Anderson[12] contains the most comprehensive discussion of elementary decision theory.

Other statistical criteria of the discriminant functions are the Kullback criteria[1] and the uncertainty criterion,[2] based on some ideas from information theory. Digital computer methods can be used to seek for a linear discriminant function which is optimal with respect to some given discriminant function criteria.[2] Highleyman[4,13] also described computational algorithms to search for a hyperplane that minimizes the expected loss.

As for the deterministic approaches to pattern recognition, notably the ADALINE and perception types of machines, Nilsson[14] provides a very clear treatment of discriminant functions. For two pattern classes, the single discriminant function which Nilsson considered is consistent with ours. Much statistical literature is concerned with the linear and quadratic discriminant functions with emphasis on their asymptotic optimal properties. In engineering literature the emphasis is more on the iterative methods of error correction for determining the optimum discriminant function (e.g., Duda and Fossum[15]).

We indicated earlier that the multivariate Gaussian distributions lead to the optimum linear and quadratic discriminant functions. It can be shown[16] that any family of probability density functions for which the quadratic discrimina-

†This procedure is similar to the cluster and mode-seeking technique to be discussed in chapter 8.

tion is optimum is representable in the form

$$p(x/\omega_i) = K(m_i, V_i)\, \phi\,(x) \exp\left\{-\frac{1}{2}(x - M_i)' V_i^{-1} (x - M_i)\right\} \tag{2.29}$$

where $K(M_i, V_i)$ is a normalizing constant, M_i and V_i are the mean vector and the covariance matrix of the ith class, and $\phi(x)$ is an arbitrary scalar function of x. The family of probability density functions for which linear discrimination is optimum can be obtained by setting $V_i = V$ for all i in equation (2.29), where V is a positive definite symmetric matrix.

The class of nonlinear transformations that result in nonlinear discriminant functions is too general to yield a practical solution. Sebestyen[7] obtained the polynomial function by minimization of the Euclidean distance measured after a continuous nonlinear transformation of the sample space. The nonlinear methods in pattern classification remain important topics for further study.

PROBLEMS

1. Prove that the average risk associated with the loss function

$$L(w_i, d_j) = \begin{cases} 0, & i = j \\ 1, & i \neq j \end{cases}$$

is also the probability of misrecognition.

2. Consider three pattern classes denoted as $\omega_1, \omega_2, \omega_3$. Let a pattern be received by a recognition machine through a random environment. Define $P(d_j/\omega_i)$ as the probability that the *a* pattern is assigned to the jth class while ω_i is the true class. The table of the probabilities and the loss are as follows:

$P(d_j/\omega_i)$	d_1	d_2	d_3
w_1	0.5	0.2	0.3
w_2	0.6	0.2	0.2
w_3	0.7	0.1	0.2

$L(\omega_1, d_j)$	d_1	d_2	d_3
w_1	0	L_1	L_1
w_2	L_2	0	L_2
w_3	L_3	L_3	0

Determine the Bayes decision rule for making d_1, d_2, d_3. Assume the three pattern classes are equally probable.

3. A recognition machine compares the one-dimensional measurement x with a threshold and decides that the pattern class ω_1 is true or the pattern class ω_2 is true. The measurement x has a normal distribution $N(m_1, \sigma_1^2)$ in ω_1 and $N(m_2, \sigma_2^2)$ in ω_2. The a priori probabilities are P_1 and P_2. The loss functions are $L(w_1, d_1) = L(w_2, d_2) = 0$, $L(w_1, d_2) = L_1$, and $L(w_2, d_1) = L_2$.
   a. Obtain an expression for the threshold which would minimize the expected loss.
   b. What decision rule should be followed with respect to this threshold?

4. Find the Bayes decision rule to choose between two classes ω_1 and ω_2, whose prior probabilities are $\frac{5}{8}$ and $\frac{3}{8}$ respectively. The conditional probability densities are

$$p(x/\omega_1) = \sqrt{\frac{2}{\pi}}\, e^{-x^2/2}$$

and

$$p(x/\omega_2) = e^{-x}$$

x being always positive. Let the losses of the two kinds be equal, i.e., $L(\omega_1, d_2) = L(\omega_2, d_1) = L$. Find the minimum average probability of error.

5. Consider a pattern x, a scalar random variable, which belongs to one of two pattern classes ω_1 and ω_2 and that x has a normal distribution $N(m_1, \sigma_1^2)$ in ω_1 and $N(m_2, \sigma_2^2)$ in ω_2. The likelihood ratio criterion results in a quadratic discriminant function if $\sigma_1 \neq \sigma_2$. Show that if the quadratic discriminant function may be factored into two linear discriminant functions, then the probabilities of misclassifications are the same for both linear discriminant functions and that both of them should be used for classification (reference 17).

6. Determine the quadratic discriminant function by using equation (2.28) for a bivariate normal distributed pattern with the following means and covariance matrices:

$$M_1 = \begin{bmatrix} 1 \\ 1 \end{bmatrix}, \quad V_1 = \begin{bmatrix} 1 & 0 \\ 0 & 0.25 \end{bmatrix}, \quad M_2 = \begin{bmatrix} 2 \\ 0 \end{bmatrix}, \quad V_2 = \begin{bmatrix} 0.01 & 0 \\ 0 & 4 \end{bmatrix}$$

7. Determine and discuss the average probability of error for discriminating between two multivariate normal distributions with different means but the same covariance matrix.

REFERENCES

1. Kullback, S. *Information Theory and Statistics.* Wiley, New York, 1958.
2. Peterson, D. W. "Discriminant Functions: Properties, Classes, and Computational Techniques." Stanford Electronics Laboratories. Technical Report 6761-2, April 1965.
3. Fisher, R. A. *Statistical Methods for Research Workers.* 13th ed., rev. Hafner, New York, 1963.
4. Highleyman, W. H. "Linear Decision Functions with Applications to Pattern Recognition." *Proc. of IRE*, 50 (June 1962), 1501–1514.
5. Widrow, B. and M. E. Hoff. "Adaptive Switching Circuits." Stanford Electronics Laboratories. Technical Report 1553-1, June 1960.

6. Widrow, B. "Generalization and Information Storage in Networks of ADALINE 'NEURONS'." In *Self-Organizing Systems*, edited by M. C. Yovits, G. T. Jacobi, and G. D. Goldstein, pp. 435–461. Spartan Books, Washington, D.C. 1962.
7. Sebestyen, G. *Decision-Making Processes in Pattern Recognition.* Macmillan, New York, 1962.
8. Specht, D. F. "Generation of Polynomial Discriminant Functions for Pattern Recognition." *IEEE Trans. on Electronic Computers*, EC=16 (June 1967), 308–319.
9. Reed, F. C. "A Sequential Multi-decision Procedure." In *Proc. Symposium on Decision Theory and Applications to Electronic Equipment Development.* USAF Development Center, Rome, N.Y., 1960.
10. Chaplin, W. G. and V. S. Lavadi. "A Generalization of the Linear Threshold Decision Algorithm to Multiple Classes." In *Computer and Information Sciences*, edited by J. Tou and R. Wilcox. Academic Press, New York, 1966.
11. Chernoff, H. and E. Moses. *Elementary Decision Theory.* Wiley, New York, 1959.
12. Anderson, T. W. *Introduction to Multivariate Statistical Analysis.* Wiley, New York, 1958.
13. Highleyman, W. H. "Linear Decision Functions, with Applications to Pattern Recognition." Ph.D. dissertation, Electrical Engineering Dept., Polytechnic Inst., Brooklyn, June 1961.
14. Nilsson, N. J. *Learning Machines.* McGraw-Hill, New York, 1965.
15. Duda, R. O. and H. Fossum. "Pattern Classification by Iteratively Determined Linear and Piecewise Linear Discriminant Functions." *IEEE Trans. on Electronic Computers*, EC-15 (April 1966), 220–232.
16. Day, N. E. "Linear and Quadratic Discrimination in Pattern Recognition." *IEEE Trans. on Information Theory*, IT-15 (May 1969), 419–420.
17. Rao, P. S. R. S. "On the Linear and Quadratic Discriminators for Pattern Recognition." Technical Report 12, Information Research Associates, Inc., Lexington, Mass., July 1967.

Bibliography

1. Amari, S. "A Theory of Adaptive Pattern Classifiers." *IEEE Trans. on Electronic Computers*, EC-16 (June 1967).
2. Anderson, T. W. and R. Bahadur. "Classification into Two Multivariate Normal Distributions with Different Covariance Matrices." *Ann. Math. Stat.*, 33 (1962), 422–431.
3. Cooper, P. W. "Hyperplanes, Hyperspheres and Hyperquadrics as Decision Boundaries." In *Computer and Information Sciences*, edited by J. Tou and R. Wilcox. Spartan Books, Washington, D.C., 1964.
4. Cooper, P. W. "Quadratic Discriminant Functions in Pattern Recognition." *IEEE Trans. on Information Theory*, IT-11 (April 1965), 313–315.
5. Das, S. K. and D. F. Stanat. "A Modified Training Procedure for Linear Threshold Devices." *IEEE Transactions on Computers.* Correspondence (April 1972), 396–397.
6. Fukunaga, K. and D. R. Olsen. "Piecewise Linear Discriminant Functions

and Classification Errors for Multiclass Problems." In *IEEE Transactions on Information Theory* (correspondence), vol. IT-16, No. 1 (January 1970), 99, 100.

7. Greenberg, H. J. and A. G. Konheim. "Linear and Nonlinear Methods in Pattern Classification." *IBM Jour. of Res. and Dev.*, (July 1964), 299–307. This reference is concerned with the nonstatistical approach.
8. Hoffman, R. L. and M. L. Moe. "A Sequential Algorithm for Piecewise Linear Classification Functions." In Seventh Symposium on Discrete Adaptive Processes. Los Angeles, December 1968.
9. Koford, J. S. and G. F. Groner. "The Use of an Adaptive Threshold Element to Design a Linear Optimal Pattern Classifier." *IEEE Trans. on Information Theory*, 12 (January 1966), 42–50.
10. Patterson, J. D. and B. F. Womack. "An Adaptive Pattern Classification System." *IEEE Trans. on Systems Science and Cybernetics*, SSC-2 (August 1966), 62–67.
11. Peterson, D. W. and R. L. Mattson. "A Method of Finding Linear Discriminant Functions for a Class of Performance Criteria." In *IEEE Transactions on Information Theory*, vol. IT-12 (July 1966), 380–387.
12. Pitt, J. M. and B. F. Womack. "A Sequentialization of the Pattern Classifier." *Proc. of IEEE* (letter), December, 1966), 1987.
13. Pitt, J. M. and B. F. Womack. "Additional Features of an Adaptive, Multicategory Pattern Classification System." *IEEE Transactions on Systems Science and Cybernetics*, SSC-5, 3 (July 1969), 183–191.
14. Roy, R. J. "Two Viewpoints of K-Tuple Pattern Recognition." *IEEE Transactions on Systems Science and Cybernetics*, SSC-3, 2 (November 1967), 117–120.
15. Smith, F. W. "Small-Sample Optimality of Design Techniques for Linear Classifiers of Gaussian Patterns." *IEEE Transactions on Information Theory*, IT-18, 1 (January 1972), 118–126.
16. Wee, W. G. and K. S. Fu. "An Adaptive Procedure for Multi-Class Pattern Classification." *IEEE Trans. on Computers* (February 1968), 178–182.
17. Yau, S. S. and P. C. Chung. "Feasibility of Using Linear Pattern Classifiers for Probabilistic Pattern Classes." *Proc. of IEEE* (letter), (December 1966), 1957–1959.

CHAPTER III

Representation of Patterns

1. Introduction

Once the measured variables or attributes $x_1, x_2, \ldots, x_N$ characterizing the patterns are determined, then an important problem we face is how to represent the patterns. The problem is that of abstracting the information in the samples into a compact functional form $f(x_1, x_2, \ldots, x_N)$ from which the decision regarding the classification of an unknown pattern can be made. The desirable properties of such functional forms are that they must be easy to evaluate or implement and that they fully represent the genuine variations of the patterns belonging to the same class. In the statistical sense, such functionals may be in the forms of probability distributions or probability density functions. Generally speaking, they assume forms without the properties of the probability distribution or the probability density function. The methods in solving pattern representation problems are closely related to the nature of patterns† and the particular set of attributes selected.

In this chapter we shall introduce various series expansion methods in the binary measurements (sections 2 and 3) and the numerical measurements (sections 4 and 5). These methods have the advantage of being rather independent of the true probability distributions of the patterns. However, one realizes that in practice only a finite number of terms in the series expansion is implemented, which may be considered an approximation to the unknown probability density (distribution) function, the random function, or the stochastic process characterizing the pattern class. Discussion of methods involving stochastic approximation procedures is postponed until chapter 6.

†In some recognition problems, the pattern is not a "deterministic signal" plus "noise" in nature. Rather the signal may have been significantly contaminated by nonadditive noise (such as multiplicative noise, random time base compression, or random phase shift). Averaging to reduce the effect of noise in many classification problems (such as communication systems, optical character recognition, etc.) may not work because the signal may be eliminated by the averaging operation. One example of such a pattern is the spontaneous electroencephalogram.

2. Representation of Binary Random Patterns: Orthogonal Series Expansion Procedures

In many pattern recognition problems, e.g., classification of photographic data, we usually use optical devices to preprocess the patterns. Using optical means results in a two-dimensional array of binary random variables.

To apply the statistical classification procedures to the joint distributions of binary random variables, we often invoke the assumption that the variables are statistically independent or their joint distributions are multivariate normal. The first assumption, while leading to a simple result, is obviously very limiting. The multivariate normal approach is also limited and requires special development when the sample covariance matrices are singular. For the analysis and application of the latter see reference 1.

Since the vector measurements are almost always correlated, the dependency, i.e., nonlinear relations among features, has great effects on the recognition results and must be taken into consideration. The orthogonal series expansion procedures are obviously possible solutions. For the n binary variables, $x = (x_1, x_2, \ldots, x_n)$, each x_i taking on values 1 and 0 with probabilities P_i and $1 - P_i$ respectively, a set of 2^n polynomials on x can be defined as

$$\phi_0(x) = 1, \quad \phi_1(x) = 2x_1 - 1, \quad \phi_2(x) = 2x_2 - 1, \ldots, \quad \phi_n(x) = 2x_n - 1$$

$$\phi_{n+1}(x) = (2x_1 - 1)(2x_2 - 1), \ldots, \quad \phi_{2^n-1}(x) = \prod_{i=1}^{n} (2x_i - 1)$$

where $\phi_j(x)$, for $j > n$, is a finite product of $\phi_1, \phi_2, \ldots, \phi_n$. This set is an orthonormal basis in the vector space of real value functions on x. Letting $P(x)$ denote a probability distribution, if $P(x)$ is nonzero for all values of x, we can write

$$P(x) = \sum_{i=0}^{2^n-1} a_i \phi_i(x) \tag{3.1}$$

where

$$a_i = \frac{1}{2^n} \sum_{\text{all } x} \phi_i(x) P(x) \tag{3.2}$$

An obvious procedure for approximating the expansion is simply to omit the higher-order terms. For instance, the first- and second-order approximations would retain the first $1 + n$ and $1 + n + \binom{n}{2}$ terms respectively in the series expansion. The coefficients in the series expansion are

$$a_0 = \left(\frac{1}{2}\right)^n, \quad a_i = \left(\frac{1}{2}\right)^n [P(x_i = 1) - P(x_i = 0)] = \frac{1}{2^n} (2P_i - 1) \text{ for } 1 \leqslant i \leqslant n$$

and a typical term for $n < i \leqslant \binom{n}{2}$ is, from equation (3.2),

$$a_{n+1} = \frac{1}{2^n} \sum_{\text{all } x} \phi_{n+1}(x)\, P(x)$$

$$= \frac{1}{2^n} [P(x_1 = 1, x_2 = 1) + P(x_1 = 0, x_2 = 0) - P(x_1 = 0, x_2 = 1) - P(x_1 = 1, x_2 = 0)]$$

Generally, the coefficient of the jth-order term is an algebraic sum of the joint probabilities of the corresponding jth order, which is determined by the modulo two sum of the variables x_i's. For example, the coefficient of the first-order term, say a_1, is evaluated from the marginal probability $P(x_1)$ and the second-order coefficients, say a_{n+1}, is evaluated from the second-order probability $P(x_1, x_2)$. No higher-order probability is required for evaluating any lower-order coefficients. There is, however, a serious difficulty in this procedure. The approximation obtained by omitting the higher order terms in equation (3.1) may not be a probability distribution at all. The approximation may fail to be nonnegative for some x. Normalization of the truncated series expansion to get a unit sum will lead to a probability distribution. To avoid the difficulty of nonnegativeness, additional terms in the series expansion may be taken or the logarithm of the probability function can be made. The former increases the complexity, the latter requires higher-order probabilities in computing any order of coefficients. We conclude that a better series expansion method remains to be investigated for the binary measurement.

3. Representation of Binary Random Patterns: Markov Dependence Considerations

In the preceding section, the dependence among variables assumes their most general form. It appears that the complexity of the system is unavoidable. A special assumption that is of common interest is the Markov dependence among neighboring variables.

By definition the joint probability distribution $P(x_1, x_2, \ldots, x_n)$ can be written as a product of the conditional probabilities:

$$P(x_1, x_2, \ldots, x_n) = P(x_1)\, P(x_2/x_1)\, P(x_3/x_2, x_1) \ldots P(x_n/x_{n-1}, \ldots, x_2, x_1) \tag{3.3}$$

For a first-order Markov chain dependence, the following relationship holds:

$$P(x_i/x_{i-1}, x_{i-2}, \ldots, x_2, x_1) = P(x_i/x_{i-1})$$

and equation (3.3) becomes

$$P(x) = \prod_{i=1}^{n} P(x_i/x_{i-1})$$

Define the transition probabilities

$$\alpha_0(i) = P(x_i = 1/x_{i-1} = 0)$$

$$\alpha_1(i) = P(x_i = 1/x_{i-1} = 1)$$

and

$$\beta_m(i) = 1 - \alpha_m(i), \; m = 0, 1$$

Then

$$\begin{aligned} P(x_i/x_{i-1}) &= [\beta_0(i)]^{1-x_i} [\alpha_0(i)]^{x_i} \quad \text{if } x_{i-1} = 0 \\ &= [\beta_1(i)]^{1-x_i} [\alpha_1(i)]^{x_i} \quad \text{if } x_{i-1} = 1 \end{aligned}$$

or simply

$$P(x_i/x_{i-1}) = \left\{\beta_0(i) \left[\frac{\alpha_0(i)}{\beta_0(i)}\right]^{x_i}\right\}^{1-x_{i-1}} \left\{\beta_1(i) \left[\frac{\alpha_1(i)}{\beta_1(i)}\right]^{x_i}\right\}^{x_{i-1}}$$

with the convention that x_0 is always 0.

The logarithm of the first-order chain approximation to $P(x)$ becomes

$$\log P(x) = \log \prod_{i=1}^{n} P(x_i/x_{i-1}) = w_0 + \sum_{i=1}^{n} w_1(i)\, x_i + \sum_{i=2}^{n} w_2(i)\, x_i x_{i-1} \tag{3.4}$$

where w_0, $w_1(i)$, $w_2(i)$ are weights depending on the transition probabilities. Because of the dependence among x_i's, log $P(x)$ is no longer linear in x's but quadratic in x's. However, due to the chain dependence, only $n - 1$ quadratic terms are required.

For the first-order Markov chain it can be shown† that for $k < n$,

†$P(x_k/x_1, x_2, \ldots, x_{k-1}, x_{k+1}, \ldots, x_n) = \dfrac{P(x_1, x_2, \ldots, x_n)}{P(x_1, \ldots, x_{k-1}, x_{k+1}, \ldots, x_n)}$

$= \dfrac{P(x_k/x_{k-1})\,P(x_{k+1}/x_k)}{P(x_{k+1}/x_{k-1})} = \dfrac{P(x_{k-1})\,P(x_k/x_{k-1})\,P(x_{k+1}/x_k)}{P(x_{k-1})\,P(x_{k+1}/x_{k-1})}$

$= \dfrac{P(x_{k-1}, x_k, x_{k+1})}{P(x_{k-1}, x_{k+1})} = P(x_k/x_{k-1}, x_{k+1})$

$$P(x_k/x_1, x_2, \ldots, x_{k-1}, x_{k+1}, \ldots, x_n) = P(x_k/x_{k-1}, x_{k+1})$$

so that any point is only dependent on its two nearest neighbors, one on either side. The first-order chain can be easily extended to the second-order and higher. For the rth-order Markov chain, the following relationship holds:

$$P(x_k/x_1, x_2, \ldots, x_{k-1}) = P(x_k/x_{k-r}, \ldots, x_{k-1})$$

Then we have

$$P(x_k/x_1, x_2, \ldots, x_{k-1}, x_{k+1}, \ldots, x_n) = P(x_k/x_{k-r}, \ldots, x_{k-1}, x_{k+1}, \ldots, x_{k+r}) \tag{3.5}$$

The converse is not true, in general. The assumption of dependence on the r nearest neighbors on each side does not imply an rth-order Markov chain dependence. A Markov chain is a special case of dependence on the $2r$ nearest neighbors.

The Markov chain assumption of the nearest neighbor dependence given by equation (3.5) implies a one-dimensional process of sequence. For the classification of two-dimensional patterns, one must scan the patterns and apply the chain assumption to the scanned output. This is still a one-dimensional process. A better process for two-dimensional patterns is called Markov mesh,[2] which is considered as a two-dimensional Markov chain. This use of neighbor dependence approximation for the two-dimensional patterns was first studied by Chow.[3] Basically, this two-dimensional Markov chain is characterized by a transition probability matrix $P_{m,n}$ defined as

$$P_{m,n} = \begin{bmatrix} p_{1,1} & p_{1,2} & \cdots & p_{1,b-1} & p_{1,b} & \cdots & p_{1,n} \\ p_{2,1} & p_{2,2} & \cdots & p_{2,b-1} & p_{2,b} & \cdots & p_{2,n} \\ \vdots & \vdots & & \vdots & \vdots & & \vdots \\ p_{a-1,1} & p_{a-1,2} & \cdots & p_{a-1,b-1} & p_{a-1,b} & \cdots & p_{a-1,n} \\ \vdots & \vdots & & \vdots & \vdots & & \vdots \\ p_{m,1} & p_{m,2} & \cdots & p_{m,b-1} & p_{m,b} & \cdots & p_{m,n} \end{bmatrix} \tag{3.6}$$

where $p_{ij} = P(x_j/x_i)$ is the transition probability.

A similar relationship like equation (35) can be obtained for the two-dimensional case (see reference 2 and problem 3).

Recently Chow[4] introduced the tree dependence which includes the neighbor dependence described above as a special case. The basic assumption is that each variable x_i may be conditioned upon any one, not necessarily the immediate, of the preceding variables, namely,

$$P(x_i/x_{i-1}, x_{i-2}, \ldots, x_2, x_1) = P(x_i/x_{j(i)}, 0 \leqslant j(i) < i)$$

The indexed set $\{j(i)/0 \leqslant j(i) < i\}$ defines a tree of dependence. That is, $j(i) = 0$ indicates that x_i is not conditioned. Under the assumption of tree dependence, the expansion similar to equation (3.4) is given by

$$\log P(x) = w_0 + \sum_{i=1}^{n} w_1'(i) x_i + \sum_{i=2}^{n} w_1''(i) x_{j(i)} + \sum_{i=2}^{n} w_2(i) x_i x_{j(i)} \tag{3.7}$$

where the weights w_0, $w_1'(i)$, $w_1''(i)$, and $w_2(i)$ depend on the transition probabilities. The tree dependence requires the knowledge $j(i)$. The number of parameters representing the complexity is n, $2n$, $4n, \ldots, 2^r n$ respectively for the first- (i.e., independent), the second- (i.e., first-order dependent), the third- and the rth-order approximations. The corresponding numbers in the orthogonal expansion are $n, n + \binom{n}{2}, n + \binom{n}{2} + \binom{n}{3}$, and $\sum_{i=1}^{r} \binom{n}{i}$.

4. Karhunen-Loeve Expansion for Patterns, and Its Properties

For the binary measurements discussed in the preceding section, if we want to get a complete description of the pattern, we almost invariably need to consider the nonlinear relationship among the variables. The linear system, i.e., the independence assumption, usually fails to provide a good description of the pattern. For numerical measurements, the Karhunen-Loeve (K-L) expansion has been commonly used.[5,6,7] The K-L expansion attempts to characterize the pattern by a set of coordinate systems whose components are independent. The dependency consideration is removed but the number of independent coordinates may have to be considerably increased as compared with the finite coordinate systems.

Let $\{\phi_i(x)\}$, $i = 1, 2, \ldots$ be a complete set of orthonormal functions defined in the domain $[a, b]$.

$$\int_a^b \phi_i^*(x)\, \phi_j(x)\, dx = \delta_{ij} \tag{3.8}$$

where * denotes the complex conjugate and δ_{ij} is the Dirac delta function, equal to one if $i = j$ and zero otherwise. Then, any function $f(x)$ which is deterministic can be expressed as

$$f(x) = \sum_{i=1}^{\infty} C_i \phi_i(x) \tag{3.9}$$

with

$$C_i = \int_a^b \phi_i^*(x) f(x)\, dx \tag{3.10}$$

and

$$\sum_{i=1}^{\infty} |C_i|^2 = 1 \tag{3.11}$$

Substituting equation (3.10) in equation (3.9) results in

$$f(x) = \int_a^b f(y) \sum_{i=1}^{\infty} \phi_i^*(y)\, \phi_i(x)\, dy$$

which shows the inverse orthogonality of equation (3.8):

$$\sum_{i=1}^{\infty} \phi_i^*(y)\, \phi_i(x) = \delta(x - y)$$

where $\delta(\cdot)$ is the unit impulse function, with area equal to one when $x = y$ and zero otherwise.

If $f(x)$ is a random function with a known probability density function $p(x)$, then $f(x)$ can still be expressed as equation (3.9) where the coefficients C_i's are random variables. The covariance function, $K(x, y)$, for the random function $f(x)$ is

$$K(x, y) = E[f(x) f^*(y)] \tag{3.12}$$

Substituting equation (3.9) in equation (3.12), we have

$$K(x, y) = \sum_i \sum_j \phi_i(x)\, \phi_j^*(y)\, E(C_i C_j^*)$$

Let the random coefficients C_i's satisfy the conditions

$$E(C_i C_j^*) = \sigma_i^2 \delta_{ij} \tag{3.13}$$

Then the covariance function $K(x, y)$ becomes

$$K(x, y) = \sum_{i=1}^{\infty} \sigma_i^2 \phi_i(x) \phi_i^*(y) \tag{3.14}$$

That is, if the general expansion in equation (3.9) exists for the random function $f(x)$ and the random coefficients satisfy equation (3.13), then the covariance function $K(x,y)$ must have the representation given by equation (3.14). Furthermore, multiplying equation (3.14) by $\phi_j(y)$ and integrating over all the value of y, we have

$$\begin{aligned} \int_a^b K(x, y) \phi_j(y) \, dy &= \int_a^b \sum_{j=1}^{\infty} \sigma_j^2 \phi_j(x) \phi_i^*(y) \phi_j(y) \, dy \\ &= \sum_{j=1}^{\infty} \sigma_j^2 \phi_j(x) \int_a^b \phi_i^*(y) \phi_j(y) \, dy \\ &= \sigma_i^2 \phi_i(x) \end{aligned} \tag{3.15}$$

if the summation and integration may be interchanged. Thus we have an integral equation defined in equation (3.15) to be satisfied by $\{\sigma_i^2\}$ and $\{\phi_i(x)\}$. Equation (3.9) with the orthonormal functions $\{\phi_i(x)\}$ satisfying equation (3.15) is called the Karhunen-Loeve expansion.[8] In the language of integral equations, $\{\phi_i(x)\}$ are characteristic functions or eigenfunctions and $\{\sigma_i^2\}$ are the characteristic values or eigenvalues of the kernel $K(x, y)$.

The function $f(x)$ can be a probability density function or it may represent a continuous waveform [then $f(x)$ must be replaced by $f(t)$], such as in speech recognition. The following are two important properties of the K-L expansion:[5]

a. The K-L method minimizes the entropy function defined as

$$-\sum_i \rho_i \log \rho_i \tag{3.16}$$

where ρ_i is the eigenvalue of the integral equation (3.15), i.e.,

$$\rho_i = \sigma_i^2 \tag{3.17}$$

For a given ensemble of measurements, the values of ρ_i vary depending on the choice of the orthogonal coordinate system. In order to work on a small number of features or attributes, it is desirable that the ρ's are concentrated on a few components instead of being widely spread over many components. This objective is accomplished by minimizing the entropy function, equation (3.16).

b. The K-L method minimizes the mean-squared error resulting from using only a finite number, say k, of terms in the series expansion. The mean-squared error for a given k in the ensemble of measurements is

$$\int_a^b \left| f(x) - \sum_{i=1}^{k} C_i \phi_i(x) \right|^2 dx = \sum_{i=k+1}^{\infty} \left| C_i \right|^2 = 1 - \sum_{i=1}^{k} \rho_i \tag{3.18}$$

There may be a number of orthogonal coordinate systems representing the pattern classes. Only the K-L coordinate system can minimize both the entropy function and the mean-squared error given by equations (3.16) and (3.18) respectively by taking the first k terms, in the series expansion, which have the largest eigenvalues.

Although the Karhunen-Loeve theory has been developed in the context of integral equations and continuous time signals, the method can be digitally implemented by replacing the continuous signal with a time-sampled representation.

$$f = \begin{bmatrix} f_1 \\ f_2 \\ \cdot \\ \cdot \\ \cdot \\ f_M \end{bmatrix}, \quad f_k = \sum_{i=1}^{\infty} C_{ik}\, \phi_{ik}, \quad k = 1, \ldots, \tag{3.19}$$

The C_{ik}'s are random coefficients and ϕ_{ik} is the kth component of the ith coordinate vector $\{\phi_i\}$ which is a set of orthonormal coordinate vectors. The discrete analog given by equation (3.18) can be obtained with no loss of information if the signal $f(t)$, $0 \leqslant t \leqslant T$ is described by M numbers, according to Shannon's Sampling Theorem, where $M = 2WT$, W = bandwidth of $f(t)$, and where the N numbers are the sampled values of the signal at the time interval $\frac{1}{2W}$. Therefore, for practical purposes the Karhunen-Loeve method can be considered equivalent to its discrete analogy, which is well known in multivariate statistical theory as the principal component analysis.[9]

5. Other Orthogonal Expansion Procedures

In the preceding section we have treated the pattern class as a random function or a stochastic process and obtained the Karhunen-Loeve expansion, which is a linear process. However, in many pattern recognition problems, the random process we encounter (such as conditional probability density, decision functions, etc.) are highly nonlinear. To synthesize the nonlinear functionals, there are some other orthogonal expansion procedures, e.g., the Wiener's Hermite-Laguerre expansion.[10,11] In this section we shall describe the Gram-Charlie and Edgeworth series as a general representation of probability density functions, examine the Wiener's canonical forms (Hermite-Laguerre expansion procedures) and the implementation problems, and then discuss the use of Walsh functions.

Gram-Charlie and Edgeworth Series

Suppose that we are given an arbitrary density function $f(x)$ representing a pattern class and wish to express it by the series

$$f(x) = \sum_{n=0}^{\infty} a_n \, \alpha(x) \, H_n(x), \qquad -\infty < x < \infty \tag{3.20}$$

where $\alpha(x) = \frac{1}{\sqrt{2\pi}} e^{-(x^2/2)}$, $-\infty < x < \infty$ is the normal density, $H_n(x)$ is called a Hermite polynomial,

$$H_n(x) = x^n - \frac{n(n-1)}{2 \cdot 1!} x^{n-2} + \frac{n(n-1)(n-2)(n-3)}{2^2 \cdot 2!} x^{n-4} + \frac{n(n-1)(n-2) \cdots (n-5)}{2^3 \cdot 3!} x^{n-6} + \cdots \tag{3.21}$$

which has a number of interesting properties.[12] The $H_n(x)$ are orthogonals over the interval $(-\infty, \infty)$ with respect to the weighting function $\alpha(x)$; that is,

$$\int_{-\infty}^{\infty} \alpha(x) \, H_m(x) \, H_n(x) \, dx = n! \, \delta_{mn} \tag{3.22}$$

where δ_{mn} is the Dirac delta function, equal to one when $m = n$ and zero otherwise. After multiplying both sides of equation (3.22) by $H_m(x)$ and integrating from $-\infty$ to ∞, we obtain

$$a_n = \frac{1}{n!} \int_{-\infty}^{\infty} f(x) \, H_n(x) \, dx \tag{3.23}$$

using the orthogonality relationship of equation (3.22). This formal expansion of $f(x)$ as given by equation (3.20) is called the Gram-Charlie series. If we substitute $H_n(x)$ as given by equation (3.21) in equation (3.23), we have

$$a_n = \frac{1}{n!} \left[u'_n - \frac{n(n-1)}{2 \cdot 1} u'_{n-2} + \frac{n(n-1)(n-2)(n-3)}{2^2 \cdot 2!} u'_{n-4} + \cdots \right] \tag{3.24}$$

where u'_n is the nth moment of $f(x)$, about the origin,

$$u'_n = \int_{-\infty}^{\infty} x^n f(x)\,dx \tag{3.25}$$

In using equation (3.20) it is necessary to know that the series converges and does represent the pattern class. The series may be used to determine the approximate form of a density by using the first few terms of the series together with the estimates of the first few moments $u'_3, u'_4, \ldots, u'_n$. In this case, the rate of convergence must be examined also to determine whether a very few terms would give a good approximation to $f(x)$. Unfortunately, the series given by equation (3.20) may not converge even for the well-behaved functions. So we shall regroup the terms in equation (3.20) to form another series which converges. A commonly used regrouping is called the Edgeworth series,[13] defined in terms of the normalized variable $y = \dfrac{x - m}{\sigma}$, where m and σ are the mean and the standard deviation, respectively, of $f(x)$. The series is

$$\begin{aligned} f(y) = \alpha(y) &- \frac{1}{3!}\frac{u_3}{\sigma^3}\,\alpha^{(3)}(y) + \frac{1}{4!}\left(\frac{u_4}{\sigma^4} - 3\right)\alpha^{(4)}(y) + \frac{10}{6!}\left(\frac{u_3}{\sigma^3}\right)^2 \alpha^{(6)}(y) \\ &- \frac{1}{5!}\left(\frac{u_5}{\sigma^5} - 10\,\frac{u_3}{\sigma^3}\right)\alpha^{(5)}(y) - \frac{35}{7!}\left(\frac{u_4}{\sigma^4} - 3\right)\alpha^{(7)}(y) \\ &- \frac{280}{9!}\left(\frac{u_3}{\sigma^3}\right)^3 \alpha^{(9)}(y) + \cdots \end{aligned} \tag{3.26}$$

where

$$\alpha(y) = \frac{1}{\sqrt{2\pi}}\, e^{-(y^2/2)}, \quad \alpha^{(n)}(y) = \frac{d^n \alpha(y)}{dy^n}$$

and the nth moment of $f(y)$ is

$$\frac{u_n}{\sigma^n} = \int_{-\infty}^{\infty} y^n f(y)\,dy$$

Wiener's Canonical Form

Brick and Zames[11] showed that the Wiener-like functionals could be applied to decision theory to obtain canonical mathematical forms which could, in turn, be synthesized in terms of electronic circuit structures for the desired Bayes optimum system, when the underlying phenomena were members of a broad class of stochastic processes. The important advantage of their scheme is that it can be easily adapted to different processes simply by adjusting amplifier gains or, mathematically, the constant coefficients while the functional dependence remains invariant. These adjustments can be made automatically for ergodic or quasi-ergodic processes from a set of training samples.

It is shown[11] that the ratio, W_R, of the probability density function describing the statistical behavior of each member of a stochastic process, $V(t)$, to the probability density function characterizing an identical member, path, or time history of a Wiener (or Brownian) process, $x(t)$, can be expanded canonically at $t = 0$ as

$$W_R(\beta) \sim \lim_{p\to\infty} \sum_{k_1=0}^{\infty} \cdots \sum_{k_p=0}^{\infty} b_{k_1,\ldots,k_p} \prod_{r-1}^{p} H_{k_r}[V_r(\beta)] \tag{3.27}$$

Likewise, the ratio of the probability density function of $V(t)$ conditioned on a parameter S to that of $x(t)$ can be expanded at $t = 0$ as

$$W_R(\beta/S) \sim \lim_{p\to\infty} \sum_{k_1=0}^{\infty} \cdots \sum_{k_p=0}^{\infty} \overset{(S)}{b}_{k_1,\ldots,k_p} \prod_{r=1}^{p} H_{k_r}[V_r(\beta)] \tag{3.28}$$

where β is an indexing variable, $0 \leqslant \beta \leqslant 1$, which labels each member or path of the process, $V(t)$, except for a set of probability measure zero. Both $V(t)$ and $x(t)$ are assumed to run from $t = -\infty$ to $t = 0$. Since time is always taken as the present time, no explicit time dependence is shown in equations (3.27) and (3.28). H_{kr} is a Hermite polynomial of the order k_r and $V_r(\beta)$ is the coefficient of the rth term in a Laguerre function expansion of the path of $V(t)$, i.e.,

$$V_r(\beta) = \int_0^{\infty} \phi_r(t)\, dV(-t, \beta) \tag{3.29}$$

where $V(t, \beta)$ denotes a member of a stochastic (random) time process for $t = -\infty$ to 0, and

$$\phi_r(t) = L_i(t) = \frac{e^{t/2}}{1!} \frac{d^i}{dt^i} (t^i e^{-t}) \tag{3.30}$$

which forms an orthonormal set over $0 \leqslant t \leqslant \infty$. The Hermite polynomial is given by equation (3.21). $\{H_{k_r}[V_r(\beta)]\}$ can be interpreted circuitwise as the Hermite polynomial nonlinear operations performed on the outputs of Laguerre filters.[10] The coefficients $b_{k_1\ldots k_p}$ which are determined from

$$\left.\begin{matrix} b_{k_1\ldots k_p} \\ \text{or} \\ \overset{(s)}{b}_{k_1\ldots k_p} \end{matrix}\right\} = \int_0^1 \left\{\begin{matrix} W_R(\beta) \\ \text{or} \\ W_R(\beta/S) \end{matrix}\right\} \prod_{r=1}^{p} H_{k_r}[V_r(\beta)]\, d\beta \tag{3.31a, 3.31b}$$

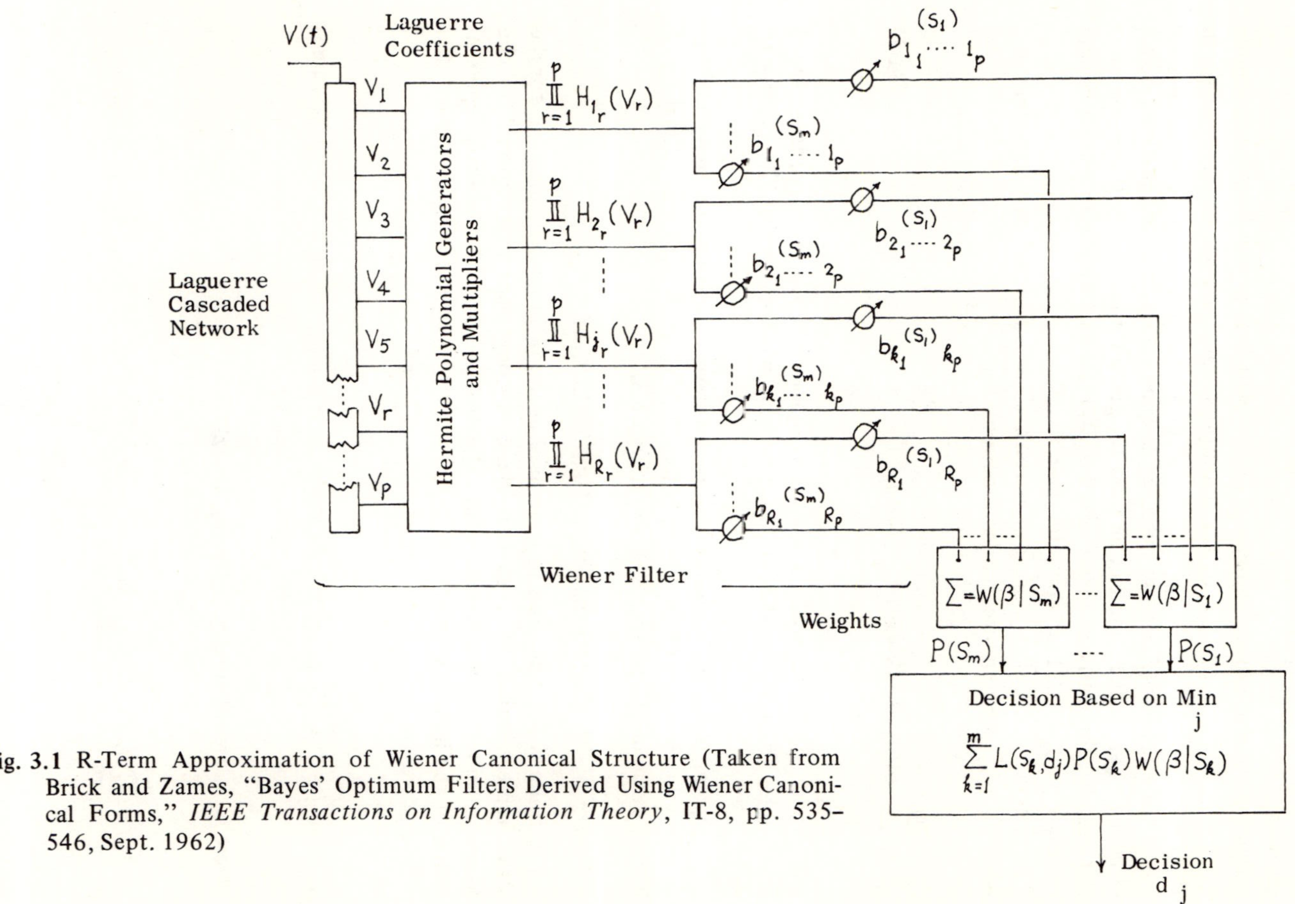

Fig. 3.1 R-Term Approximation of Wiener Canonical Structure (Taken from Brick and Zames, "Bayes' Optimum Filters Derived Using Wiener Canonical Forms," *IEEE Transactions on Information Theory*, IT-8, pp. 535–546, Sept. 1962)

can be instrumented as the amplifier gains on the respective nonlinear circuit outputs.

For an ergodic process, equation (3.31), which is in the form of ensemble averages, can be converted to the appropriate time average of $H_{kr}[V_r(\beta)]$. In this case, a sufficiently long sample of the process either characterized by parameter S for equation (3.31b) or averaged over all values of S for equation (3.31a) obtained at an earlier time can be used for preadjusting the b's. If the process is not ergodic, the statistics of the process $V(t)$ must be known or estimated and used in equation (3.31) to compute the b's.

In making a decision among m pattern classes, denoted as parameters ω_1, $\omega_2, \ldots, \omega_m$, we compute the risk function,

$$\sum_{k=1}^{m} L(\omega_k, d_j) P(\omega_k) p(\{v\}/\omega_k) \tag{3.32}$$

and choose the jth class which minimizes equation (3.32). Here $\{v\}$ is the set of observables from $V(t)$ and $p(\{v\}/\omega_k)$ is the conditional probability density of $\{v\}$.

In implementing the canonical form, we have to restrict the finite number of terms in equation (3.28) or equation (3.27). An R-term approximation of Wiener's canonical structure is shown in figure 3.1.

Finite Walsh Functions and a Generalization

The finite Walsh functions may be used as the orthonormal functions for the series representation of a pattern class. A convenient description[14] of the N-length finite Walsh functions wal(k, j), exists in terms of the binary representation of the indices k and j, $k = 0, 1, 2, \cdots, N - 1, j = 0, 1, 2, \cdots, N - 1$. Let N be a power of 2, i.e., $N = 2^n$, then

$$\text{wal}(k,j) = \prod_{r=0}^{n-1} (-1)^{(k_{n-r} + k_{n-r-1})\, j_r} \tag{3.33}$$

where j_r, k_r are the binary digits of j, k; viz.,

$$j = \sum_{r=0}^{n-1} j_r 2^r, \quad k = \sum_{r=0}^{n-1} k_r 2^r.$$

Note that $j_n = k_n = 0$. We may illustrate this definition by the 8-length finite Walsh functions, which we can express as an 8×8 matrix,

$$\text{wal}(k,j) = \begin{array}{c} j = \;0\;\;1\;\;2\;\;3\;\;4\;\;5\;\;6\;\;7 \\ \left[\begin{array}{cccccccc} 1 & 1 & 1 & 1 & 1 & 1 & 1 & 1 \\ 1 & 1 & 1 & 1 & - & - & - & - \\ 1 & 1 & - & - & - & - & 1 & 1 \\ 1 & 1 & - & - & 1 & 1 & - & - \\ 1 & - & - & 1 & 1 & - & - & 1 \\ 1 & - & - & 1 & - & 1 & 1 & - \\ 1 & - & 1 & - & - & 1 & - & 1 \\ 1 & - & 1 & - & 1 & - & 1 & - \end{array}\right] \end{array} \begin{array}{c} k = \\ 0 \\ 1 \\ 2 \\ 3 \\ 4 \\ 5 \\ 6 \\ 7 \end{array} \tag{3.34}$$

where "–" denotes the value -1. It is noted that the index k or j denotes the number of zero crossings of a binary waveform over a unit time interval as shown in figure 3.2. The orthogonality condition holds as

$$\begin{aligned} \sum_{j=0}^{N-1} \text{wal}(k,j)\,\text{wal}(\ell,j) &= N, \quad k = \ell \\ &= 0, \quad k \neq \ell \end{aligned} \tag{3.35}$$

The pattern $x(t)$ can be represented at discrete sampling instants as

$$x(j) = \sum_{k=0}^{N-1} A(k)\,\text{wal}(k,j), \qquad j = 0, 1, 2, \cdots, N-1 \tag{3.36}$$

where

$$A(k) = \frac{1}{N} \sum_{j=0}^{N-1} x(j)\,\text{wal}(k,j), \quad k = 0, 1, 2, \cdots, N-1 \tag{3.37}$$

Equations (3.36) and (3.37) are known as a Walsh transform pair. To generalize equation (3.33) to nonbinary, say m-ary, case, $N = m^n$, we start with rewriting equation (3.33) as

$$\phi(x;j) = x_0^{j_0} \cdots x_{n-1}^{j_{n-1}} = \prod_{r=0}^{n-1} x_r^{j_r} \tag{3.38}$$

where $x_r = (-1)^{(k_{n-r} + k_{n-r-1})}$ is either $+1$ or -1 and $x = (x_0, x_1, \cdots, x_{n-1})$ is a vector with binary attributes. For m-ary case, a generalized finite Walsh function is defined as[15]

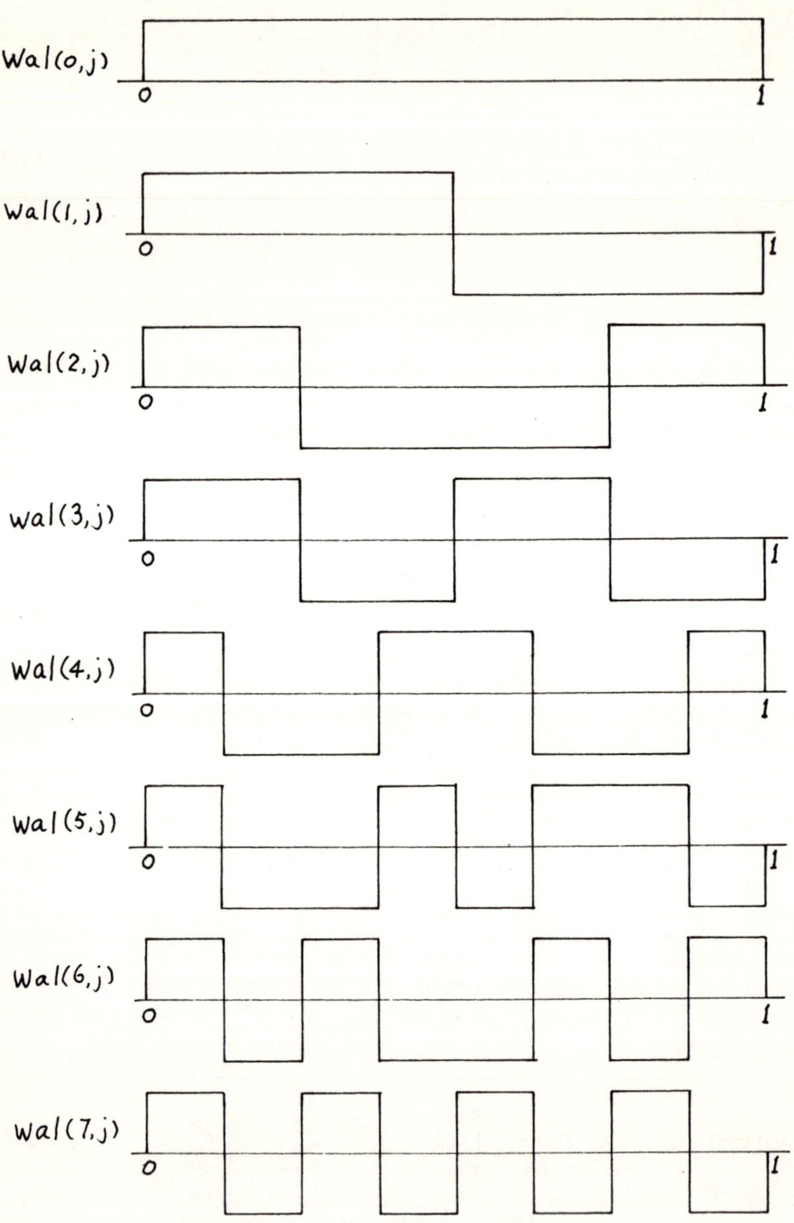

Fig. 3.2 Binary Square Waves for Walsh Functions

$$\left.\begin{aligned} \Phi(x;j) &= m^{-(n/2)}\,\phi(x;j) \\ \phi(x;j) &= x_0^{j_0}\cdots x_{n-1}^{j_{n-1}} \end{aligned}\right\} \qquad \begin{aligned} j &= 0, 1, \cdots, m^n - 1 \\ j &= \sum_{r=0}^{n-1} j_r m^r \end{aligned} \tag{3.39}$$

Here x_i's are the roots of the equation $\alpha^m - 1 = 0$. Consider, for example $n = 2$ and $m = 3$, all the elements of $x = \{x_0, x_1\}$ are

$$x = \{(1,1), (\omega,1)\,(\omega^2,1), (1,\omega), (\omega,\omega), (\omega^2,\omega), (1,\omega^2), (\omega,\omega^2), (\omega^2,\omega^2)\}$$

where $\omega = \exp(2\pi\sqrt{-1}/m)$ and all of the Φ functions are

$$\begin{aligned} &\Phi(x;0) = \tfrac{1}{3}, && \Phi(x;1) = \tfrac{1}{3}x_1, && \Phi(x;2) = \tfrac{1}{3}x_1^2, \\ &\Phi(x;3) = \tfrac{1}{3}x_2, && \Phi(x;4) = \tfrac{1}{3}x_1x_2, && \Phi(x;5) = \tfrac{1}{3}x_1^2x_2, \\ &\Phi(x;6) = \tfrac{1}{3}x_2^2, && \Phi(x;7) = \tfrac{1}{3}x_1x_2^2, && \Phi(x;8) = \tfrac{1}{3}x_1^2x_2^2 \end{aligned}$$

where each x_i takes the value $1, \omega$, or ω^2.

The Φ functions are clearly orthogonal and a representation of the pattern class, $f(x)$, can be approximated by

$$f_M(x) = \sum_{j=0}^{M-1} C(j)\,\Phi(x;j), \qquad M = 1, 2, \cdots, m^n \tag{3.40}$$

where

$$C(j) = \sum_{\text{all } x} f(x)\,\Phi^*(x;j) \tag{3.41}$$

In the binary representation of Walsh functions—equations (3.33), (3.36), and (3.38)—no multiplication is involved, thus reducing the amount of computation and storage. Even in the multivalued representation in equations (3.39) and (3.40), the complex multiplication involves only roots of one. Thus the finite Walsh functions will become increasingly important in pattern recognition because of the advantages in computation and implementation.

6. Remarks

As the true probability density function of patterns is often unavailable, we have been concerned with the orthogonal series representation of a pattern class in this chapter. When such representation is established, the decision criterion for classifying the patterns is usually the maximum likelihood decision rule or the Bayes decision rule. Explicit expressions for the probability of misrecognition have not been obtained. The orthogonal series expansion may also be used to describe the decision boundaries. Implementation should be the primary factor in determining which series expansion should be used for a particular recognition problem. For Wiener's nonlinear expansion procedure described in section 5, Bose[16] and Winkler[17] have considered the instrumentation by using gate functions.

The problem of probability distribution approximation for binary patterns has also been studied by Lewis[18,19] and Brown,[20] who considered the possibility of storing several of the lower-order component distributions and using these to approximate the higher-order distributions with the criterion of maximum entropy. They considered, for example, the product of functions of the variables x_j and x_k for all pairs x_j and x_k $(j \neq k)$. Their product form leads to procedures similar to those given by the orthogonal series expansion (section 2), so far as the functional structure and the number of parameters are concerned. That is, for the second-order approximation, the pairwise dependence contains all $\binom{n}{2}$ quadratic terms.

PROBLEMS

1. Suppose we wish to classify patterns each consisting of N independent binary components (each $x_i = 1$ or 0). Let us assume that there are two classes, i.e., $m = 2$ and zero-one loss function is used. Define the notations:

$$P(x_i = 1/\omega_1) = p_i$$
$$P(x_i = 0/\omega_1) = 1 - p_i$$
$$P(x_i = 1/\omega_2) = q_i$$
$$P(x_i = 0/\omega_2) = 1 - q_i \qquad i = 1, 2, \cdots, N$$

Let the a priori probabilities of the two classes be P_1 and P_2.
   a. Write the expression of the optimum decision boundary.
   b. Draw a block diagram using the results of part a. See references 21, 22, 23.
2. In problem 1, if the binary components are correlated, show that the probability distribution function of the patterns can be written as a series expansion.

$$P(x/\omega_1) = P_0(x/\omega_1)\left[1 + \sum_{i<j} r_{ij} Z_i Z_j + \sum_{i<j<k} r_{ijk} Z_i Z_j Z_k + \cdots \right.$$
$$\left. + r_{1,2,\ldots,M}\, Z_1 Z_2 \ldots Z_n\right]$$

where

$$Z_i = \frac{x_i - p_i}{\sqrt{p_i(1 - p_i)}}$$

$$r_{ij} = \overline{Z_i \cdot Z_j}, \qquad i<j$$

$$r_{ijk} = \overline{Z_i \cdot Z_j \cdot Z_k}, \qquad i<j<k$$

$$r_{1,2,\ldots,N} = \overline{Z_1 \, Z_2 \cdots Z_N}$$

and $P_0(x/\omega_1)$ is the probability distribution function when all N components are independent. See reference 24.

3. The probability matrix $P_{m,n}$ is defined by equation (3.6). Let $P_{m,n}^{a,b}$ be such matrix with elements $p_{i,j}$, $a < i \leqslant m, b < j \leqslant n$, deleted $(a < m, b < m)$. Show that

a. $P(P_{a,b}/P_{m,n}^{a,b}) = p(P_{a,b}/P_{a-1,b}, P_{a-1,b-1}, P_{a,b-1})$

b. $$P(P_{a,b}/P_{m,n}) = p\left[p_{a,b} \middle| \begin{matrix} p_{a-1,b-1} & p_{a-1,b} & p_{a-1,b+1} \\ p_{a,b-1} & & p_{a,b+1} \\ p_{a+1,b-1} & p_{a+1,b} & p_{a+1,b+1} \end{matrix}\right]$$

Note: Part a implies b but b does not imply a. See reference 2.

4. Draw a block diagram for the tree dependence scheme described in section 3.
5. In section 4, the random function $f(x)$ is generated by a single stochastic process and the K-L expansion is given by equations (3.9) and (3.10). In general, the random function may be generated from several, say m, stochastic processes,

$$f_i(x) = \sum_{k=1}^{\infty} C_{ik}\phi_k(x), \quad i = 1, 2, \cdots, m$$

Equations (3.12) and (3.13) must be written as

$$K(x, y) = \sum_{i=1}^{m} P_i E\,[f_i(x) f_i^*(y)]$$

and

$$\sum_{i=1}^{m} P_i E(C_{ik} C_{ij}^*) = \sigma_k^2 \, \delta_{kj}$$

respectively, where P_i is the a priori probability of the ith class. Show that the optimum properties of the K-L expansion still hold in this multiple-stochastic process case. See reference 25.

REFERENCES

1. Kanal, L. N. and N. C. Randall. "Recognition System Design by Statistical Analysis. In *Proc. Nineteenth National Meeting ACM,* Paper No. D2.5. August 1964.
2. Abend, K., T. J. Harley, and L. N. Kanal. "Classification of Binary Random Patterns," *IEEE Trans. on Information Theory,* IT-11 (October 1965), 538–544.
3. Chow, C. K. "A Recognition Method Using Neighbor Dependence." *IRE Trans. on Electronic Computers,* EC-11 (October 1962), 683–690.
4. Chow, C. K. "A Class of Nonlinear Recognition Procedures." *IEEE Trans. on Systems Science and Cybernetics,* 1 (December 1966).
5. Watanabe, S. "Karhunen-Loeve Expansion and Factor Analysis: Theoretical Remarks and Applications." In *Proc. Fourth Prague Conference on Information Theory, Statistical Decision Functions, Random Processes.* September 1965.
6. Davenport, W. B. and W. L. Root. *An Introduction to the Theory of Random Signals and Noise.* McGraw-Hill, New York, 1958.
7. Selin, I. *Detection Theory.* Princeton University Press, Princeton, N.J., 1965. Chapter 7.
8. Loeve, M. *Probability Theory.* 3rd ed. Van Nostrand, Princeton, N.J., 1963.
9. Wilks, S. S. *Mathematical Statistics.* Wiley, New York, 1960. Chapter 18.
10. Wiener, N. *Nonlinear Problems in Random Theory.* Wiley, New York, and M.I.T. Press, Cambridge, Mass., 1958.
11. Brick, D. B. and G. Zames, "Bayes' Optimum Filters Derived Using Wiener Canonical Forms." *IRE Trans. on Information Theory,* IT-8 (September 1962), 535–546.
12. Kendall, M. G. and A. Stuart. *The Advanced Theory of Statistics,* vol. I. 2nd ed. Hafner, New York, 1963.
13. Cramer, H. *Mathematical Methods of Statistics.* Princeton University Press, Princeton, N.J., 1948. P. 228.
14. Pratt, W. K., J. Kane, and H. C. Andrews. "Hadamard Transform Image Coding." *Proc. of IEEE,* 57 (January 1969), 58–68.
15. Uesaka, Y. "Construction of a Complex-Valued Nonlinear Discriminant Function for Pattern Recognition." *IEEE Trans. on Systems, Man, and Cybernetics,* XMC-1 (July 1971), 194–215.
16. Bose, A. G. "A Theory of Nonlinear Systems." M.I.T. Research Laboratory of Electronics, Cambridge, Mass., Technical Report 309, May 1956.
17. Winkler, G. "Bayes' Optimum Filters Derived Using Bose Forms." *Archiv der Elektrischen Ubertragung.* (March 1965), 321–325. Also presented at the International Conference on Microwaves, Circuit Theory and Information Theory; Tokyo, Japan; 1964.
18. Lewis, P. M. "Approximating Probability Distributions to Reduce Storage Requirements." *Information and Control,* 2 (1959), 214–225.

19. Lewis, P. M. "A Note on the Realization of Decision Networks using Summation Elements." *Information and Control,* 4 (September 1961), 282–290.
20. Brown, D. T. "A Note on Approximations to Discrete Probability Distribution." *Information and Control,* 2 (1959), 386–392.
21. Nilsson, N. J. *Learning Machines.* McGraw-Hill, New York, 1965.
22. Minsky, M. "Steps Toward Artificial Intelligence." *Proc. of IRE,* 49 (January 1961), 14.
23. Minsky, M. and O. G. Selfridge. "Learning in Random Nets." In *Proc. Fourth London Symposium on Information Theory,* edited by C. Cherry. Academic Press, New York, 1961.
24. Bahadur, R. R. "A Representation of the Joint Distribution of Response to n Dichotomous Items." In *Studies in Item Analysis and Prediction,* edited by H. Solomon, pp. 158–176. Stanford University Press, Stanford, Calif., 1961.
25. Chien, Y. T. and K. S. Fu. "On the Generalized Karhunen-Loeve Expansion." *IEEE Trans. on Information Theory,* IT-13 (July 1967), 518–520.

Bibliography

1. Brick, D. B. "Pattern Recognition and Self-Organization Using Wiener's Canonical Forms." In *Cybernetics of The Nervous System.* Progress in Brain Research, vol. 17. Edited by N. Wiener and J. P. Schade. Elsevier, New York, 1965.
2. Brick, D. B. "Wiener's Nonlinear Expansion Procedure Applied to Cybernetic Problems." *IEEE Trans. on Systems Science and Cybernetics,* SSC-1 (November 1965), 67–74.
3. Brick, D. B. "On the Applicability of Wiener's Canonical Expansions." *IEEE Trans. on Systems Science and Cybernetics,* SSC-4 (February 1968).
4. Chow, C. K. and C. N. Liu. "An Approach to Structure Adaptation in Pattern Recognition." *IEEE Trans. on Systems Science and Cybernetics,* SSC-2 (December 1966), 73–80.
5. Chow, C. K. "The Maximum Likelihood Estimate of A Dependence Tree." In *Pattern Recognition,* edited by L. Kanal, pp. 323–328. Thompson, Washington, D.C., 1968.
6. Chow, C. K. and C. N. Liu. "Approximating Discrete Probability Distributions with Dependence Trees." *IEEE Trans. on Information Theory,* IT-14 (May 1968), 462–467.
7. Glaser, E. "Signal Detection by Adaptive Filters." *IRE Trans. on Information Theory,* IT-7 (April 1961), 87–98.
8. Gose, E. E. "An Adaptive Network for Producing Real Functions of Binary Inputs." *Information and Control,* 8 (1965), 111–123.
9. Jordan, K. L. "Discrete Representation of Random Signals." M.I.T. Research Laboratory of Electronics, Cambridge, Mass., Technical Report 378, 1961.
10. Kennett, B. L. M. "A Note on the Finite Walsh Transform." *IEEE Trans. on Information Theory,* IT-16 (July 1970), 489–491.
11. Raviv, J. and D. N. Streeter. "Linear Methods for Biological Data Processing." IBM Research Center Report RC-1577, December 1965.
12. Roy, R. J. and J. Sherman. "Two Viewpoints of k-tuple Pattern Recogni-

tion." *IEEE Trans. on Systems Science and Cybernetics,* SSC-3 (November 1967), 117–120.

13. Sears, R. "Adaptive Representation for Pattern Recognition." *IEEE Trans. on Systems Science and Cybernetics,* SSC-1 (November 1965), 59–66.
14. Whelchel, J. E. and D. F. Guinn. "The Fast Fourier-Hadamard Transform and its Use in Signal Representation and Classification," EASCON '68 Convention Record, published by the *IEEE Trans. on Aerospace and Electronic Systems,* pp. 561–573, 1968.
15. Young, T. Y. and W. H. Huggins. "On the Representation of Electrocardiograms." *IEEE Trans. on Bio-medical Electronics* (July 1963), 86–95.

CHAPTER IV

Feature Selection and Extraction

1. Introduction

To determine what variables (attributes) are to be measured is the first and most important step toward designing an efficient recognition machine. The task of determining the variables is called feature selection or extraction. Similar and related terms are property filtering and characteristic selection. Feature selection is usually preceded by preprocessing of patterns, which refers to the processes of sorting, normalization, centralization, filtering, etc. of the input patterns. The desirable requirements of the features selected are: (1) they properly describe the pattern, (2) they are easy to process, and (3) they are invariant to translation and rotation of the pattern. However, to select features which satisfy all three requirements at the same time is almost impossible. The designer usually decides on what to measure from the nature and physics of the pattern. The number of features chosen can be very large. The features must be evaluated and the most effective ones chosen. In mathematical terms, this is known as dimensionality reduction if each pattern is expressed as a vector measurement. By reducing the dimension of the measurement, the amount of computation by digital computer or analog device or other methods can be greatly reduced. The invariant property will be less a problem if the preprocessing task is performed.

The importance of feature selection and extraction has received much attention, although comparatively less effort and success have been reported than for categorization and parameter estimation problems in pattern recognition. This is mainly due to the fact that each pattern has its own particular characteristics. So a unified formulation of the problem is difficult if not impossible. Much of the effort has been experimental, which appears to be quite effective in many cases. All experimental results have shown that the recognition performance will always be improved with the properly selected features.

In this chapter, we will discuss feature selection criteria using information statistics (information theory and mathematical statistics). The features selected will minimize indirectly the probability of misrecognition or the average risk, both of which are, in general, difficult to evaluate exactly and directly. We then compare theoretically the relative merit of each criterion, especially its performance bounds. Finally we examine the fundamental problem of the relationship between dimensionality and sample size in connection with statistical recognizer design.

2. Information Measure of Feature Effectiveness

Intuitively, one hopes to obtain effective features so that the accuracy of recognition may be enhanced, or the number of features required to achieve a given accuracy may be reduced. The effectiveness of a feature may be interpreted from an information-theoretic point of view. The measure of feature effectiveness can be chosen as a measure of information provided by the feature. One such measure proposed by Lindley[1] is similar in form to an entropy function.† This information measure, denoted as $I(x)$, is given by

$$I(x) = \sum_{i=1}^{m} \int P(\omega_i)\, p(x/\omega_i) \log \frac{P(\omega_i/x)}{P(\omega_i)}\, dx \tag{4.1}$$

If x is a discrete random variable, then

$$I(x) = \sum_{\text{all } x} \sum_{i=1}^{m} P(\omega_i, x) \log_2 \frac{P(\omega_i/x)}{P(\omega_i)} \tag{4.2}$$

$$= \sum_{\text{all } x} p(x) \sum_{i=1}^{m} P(\omega_i/x) \log_2 P(\omega_i/x) - \sum_{i=1}^{m} P(\omega_i) \log_2 P(\omega_i) \tag{4.3}$$

Here x may be a vector measurement or simply a one-dimensional measurement. It can be shown that the larger $I(x)$ is, the smaller the probability of misrecognition tends to be. For any measurement x, the probability of misrecognition obtained by maximizing the probability of correct recognition, $P(\omega_i/x)$, is zero if we have

$$I = -\sum_{i=1}^{m} P(\omega_i) \log_2 P(\omega_i)$$

†Entropy may be viewed as a function associated with a random variable x. If x is a discrete random variable which assumes values $x_1, x_2, \cdots, x_n$ with probabilities $P(x_1)$, $P(x_2), \cdots, P(x_n)$, the entropy function is

$$H(x) = \sum_{i=1}^{n} P(x_i) \log \frac{1}{P(x_i)}$$

If x is a continuous random variable with the probability density function $p(x)$, then

$$H(x) = \int p(x) \log \frac{1}{p(x)}\, dx$$

For binary measurements such as obtained in optical character recognition, the information measure I of each binary variable can be evaluated to provide a list of variables of high information. Combinations of these high information variables are used to derive feature sets. The feature set with the highest information is chosen, which has the minimal dimension and satisfies the specified accuracy level, i.e., the probability of correct recognition.[2,3,4] A typical plot of $I(x)$ versus the number of features for handprinted numeric symbols is shown in figure 4.1. Here the features are the high probability points among the two-dimensional array of binary measurements.

For independent numerical measurements which are quantized, Lewis[5] has examined a notion of statistic given by

$$G_j = \sum_{i=1}^{m} \sum_{k=1}^{v_j} P[\omega_i, f_j(k)] \log \varphi \{P[\omega_i, f_j(k)]\} \tag{4.4}$$

for the jth feature, $j = 1, 2, \cdots, N$. Each feature f_j can take v_j values. Here φ is a measure of correlation between f_j and ω_i and is a single-valued function of its argument. It is desirable that the statistic G_j has the following properties:

(i) If $G_j > G_1$, then the probability of correct recognition of using f_j only must be greater than the probability of correct recognition of using f_1 only.

(ii) If $G_j > G_1$, then, for any set of features, F, the probability of correct recognition of using features f_j and F must be greater than the probability of correct recognition of using f_1 and F.

(iii) The probability of correct recognition of using F is a linear function of the sum of statistics evaluated for the features in F.

Although no single-number statistic satisfies both (ii) and (iii) in general, equation (4.4) at least satisfies (ii) and (iii) over a fairly wide range of situations. If we compare equations (4.1) and (4.4), then a possible choice for φ is

$$\varphi \{P[\omega_i, f_j(k)]\} = \frac{P[\omega_i, f_j(k)]}{P(\omega_i)\, P[f_j(k)]} = \frac{P[\omega_i \mid f_i(k)]}{P(\omega_i)} \tag{4.5}$$

Thus

$$G_j = \sum_{i=1}^{m} \sum_{k=1}^{v_j} P[\omega_i, f_j(k)] \log \frac{P[\omega_i \mid f_j(k)]}{P(\omega_i)} \tag{4.6}$$

$$\simeq \sum_{i=1}^{m} \sum_{k=1}^{v_j} P[\omega_i, f_j(k)] \left[\frac{P[\omega_i \mid f_j(k)]}{P(\omega_i)} - 1\right] \tag{4.7}$$

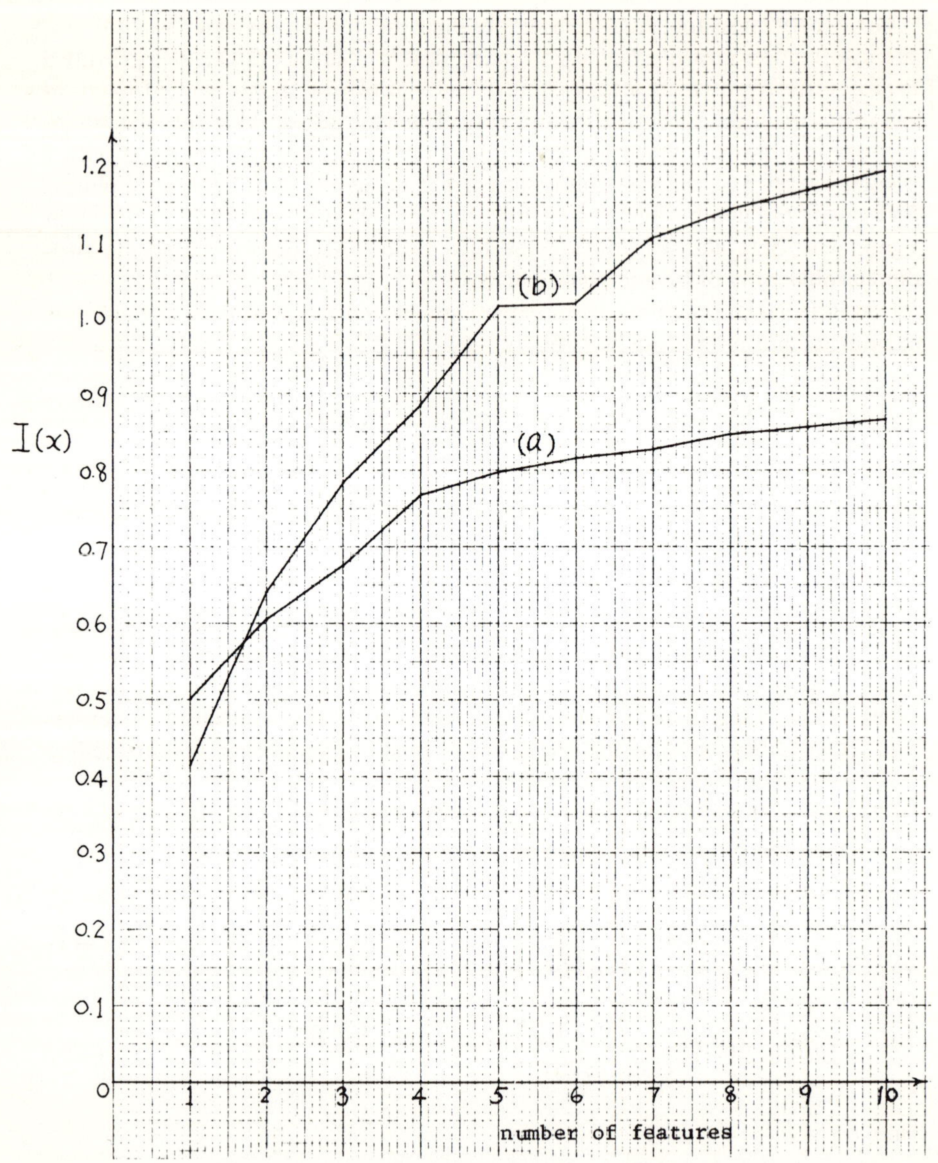

Fig. 4.1 A Typical Plot of Mutual Information Versus the Number of Features for Hand Printed Numeric Symbols—(a) "5" and "6," (b) "3," "5," and "8" (Samples supplied by Dr. A. Knoll of Honeywell)

Both equations (4.2) and (4.6) may be considered as the mutual information between the features f_j and the pattern classes $\omega_1, \omega_2, \cdots, \omega_m$. Although no explicit relationship exists between the probability of correct recognition and equations (4.2) or (4.6), the feasibility of using such information measure has been experimentally proved.[3,5]

3. Distance Measure and Performance Bounds

If we consider the categorization problem as a statistical hypothesis testing, then the selection of variables is similar to the comparison of experiments in mathematical statistics. The "distance" between the two hypotheses or pattern classes has been defined in several ways in the statistical literature. All distance measures, however, are qualitatively related to the probability of misrecognition in the same manner: the larger the distance between the two pattern classes as provided by the variables selected, the smaller the probability of misrecognition. This relationship may be justified by using the comparison of experiments.[6,7]

Consider now two pattern classes. Many distance measures currently being used can be written in the form[8]

$$f\{E[\phi(L)/\omega_1]\} \tag{4.8}$$

where $L = p(x/\omega_1)/p(x/\omega_2)$, $\phi(\cdot)$ is a continuous convex function, $f(\cdot)$ is an increasing real-valued function of a real variable. Typical examples of distance measures are:

a. Kullback-Leibler numbers, also called directed divergence[9]

$$I(1,2) = \int p(x/\omega_1) \log \frac{p(x/\omega_1)}{p(x/\omega_2)}\, dx = E\,[\log L/\omega_1] \tag{4.9}$$

$$I(2,1) = \int p(x/\omega_2) \log \frac{p(x/\omega_1)}{p(x/\omega_2)}\, dx = E\,[L^{-1} \log L/\omega_1] \tag{4.10}$$

If we use the notations of chapter 2, then $I(1,2) = E_1 U$ and $I(2,1) = -E_2 U$

b. Divergence (J-distance)[10]

$$J = I(1,2) + I(2,1) = E\,[(1 - L^{-1}) \log L/\omega_1] \tag{4.11}$$

c. Bhattacharyya distance (B-distance)

$$B = -\log \rho \tag{4.12}$$

$$\text{where } \rho = \int \sqrt{p(x/\omega_1)\, p(x/\omega_2)}\, dx = E\,[L^{-1/2}/\omega_1] \tag{4.13}$$

is called the Bhattacharyya coefficient[11] or Hellinger integral.[12]

d. Matusita's measure of distance[13]

$$d = \left[\int (\sqrt{p(x/\omega_1)} - \sqrt{p(x/\omega_2)})^2 \, dx\right]^{1/2} \tag{4.14}$$
$$\{E\,[(L^{-1/2} - 1)^2/\omega_1]\}^{1/2}$$

Note that $d^2 = 2(1 - \rho)$ (4.15)

and thus Matusita's distance measure is uniquely related to the Bhattacharyya coefficient.

e. Kolmogorov variational distance[14]

$$K = \frac{1}{2}\int |\, P_1\, p(x/\omega_1) - P_2\, p(x/\omega_2) \,|\, dx$$
$$= \frac{1}{2} P_1 E\,[\,|\, P_2 L^{-1}/P_1 - 1 \,|\, /\omega_1] \tag{4.16}$$

In equation (4.16) the integration is over the measurement space R_1 or R_2, where $R_i = \{x/\omega_i$ is chosen when x is measured$\}$.

f. Mahalanobis D^2-statistic

It is the divergence between two Gaussian densities with unequal mean vectors but equal covariance matrices.

To establish the relationships among the distance measures and the probability of misrecognition (or the Bayes risk), we start with the Kolmogorov variational distance,

$$K = \frac{1}{2}\int_{R_1} |\, P_1 p(x/\omega_1) - P_2\, p(x/\omega_2) \,|\, dx = \frac{1}{2} - P_E \tag{4.17}$$

where P_E is the probability of misrecognition,

$$P_E = P_1 \int_{R_2} p(x/\omega_1) dx + P_2 \int_{R_1} p(x/\omega_2) dx$$

over the set of a priori probabilities $P = \{P_1, P_2\}$. Thus the Kolmogorov variational distance is uniquely related to the probability of misrecognition.

An upper bound of K is obtained from the Schwarz inequality as follows:

$$\left[\int |\, P_1\, p(x/\omega_1) - P_2\, p(x/\omega_2) \,|\, dx\right]^2 \leqslant \int |\, \sqrt{P_1\, p(x/\omega_1)} - \sqrt{P_2\, p(x/\omega_2)} \,|^2 \, dx$$

$$x \int | \sqrt{P_1\, p(x/\omega_i)} + \sqrt{P_2\, p(x/\omega_2)}\, |^2\, dx = [1 - 2\sqrt{P_1 P_2}\, \rho]$$

$$\cdot\, [1 + 2\sqrt{P_1 P_2}\, \rho] = 1 - 4P_1 P_2 \rho^2$$

The lower bound is

$$\int | P_1\, p(x/\omega_1) - P_2\, p(x/\omega_2) |\, dx \geqslant \int | \sqrt{P_1\, p(x/\omega_1)}$$

$$- \sqrt{P_2\, p(x/\omega_2)}\, |^2\, dx = 1 - 2\sqrt{P_1 P_2}\, \rho$$

Thus

$$\tfrac{1}{2}\, [1 - 2\sqrt{P_1 P_2}\, \rho] \leqslant K \leqslant \tfrac{1}{2}\sqrt{1 - 4P_1 P_2 \rho^2} \tag{4.18}$$

or, from equation (4.17),

$$\tfrac{1}{4}\, \rho^2 \leqslant P_1 P_2 \rho^2 \leqslant \tfrac{1}{2}\, (1 - \sqrt{1 - 4P_1 P_2 \rho^2}) \leqslant P_E \leqslant \sqrt{P_1 P_2}\, \rho \leqslant \tfrac{1}{2}\, \rho \tag{4.19}$$

for any $\{P_1, P_2\}$. It follows that the minimization of ρ is a reasonable criterion of optimality. Minimization of ρ is equivalent to maximization of the B-distance defined by equation (4.12). The upper and lower bounds given by equation (4.19) are plotted in figure 4.2.

The upper bound on P_E in terms of ρ is quite useful. No similar bound in terms of the divergence J appears to be generally true. However, a lower bound can be written as

$$P_E \geqslant P_1 P_2 \rho^2 > P_1 P_2 \exp(-J/2) \geqslant \tfrac{1}{4} \exp(-J/2) \tag{4.20}$$

which follows via Jensen's inequality,

$$\begin{aligned} -\tfrac{1}{2}\, I(1,2) &= E\, [\log L^{-1/2} \mid \omega_1] \leqslant \log [E(L^{-1/2}/\omega_1)] = \log \rho \\ \text{or } \rho^2 &\geqslant \exp - J/2 \end{aligned} \tag{4.21}$$

For Gaussian patterns, the upper bound of P_E is available[15] and we have

$$P_E \leqslant \sqrt{P_1 P_2}\, \rho < \sqrt{P_1 P_2} \left(\frac{J}{4}\right)^{-1/4} \tag{4.22}$$

The B-distance is much simpler for the Gaussian process with unequal covariances but equal or almost equal means. On the other hand, if two Gaussian

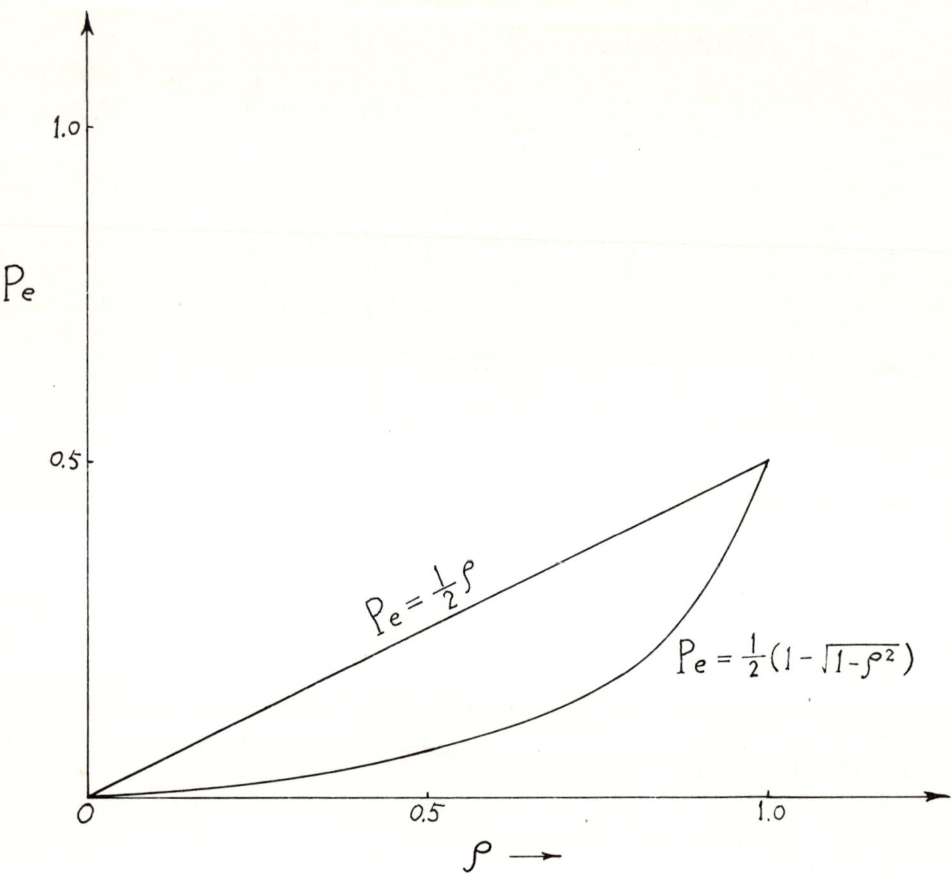

Fig. 4.2 Error Bounds of B-Distance Criterion With $m = 2$

processes are of distinct mean and equal covariance, the divergence (D^2-statistic) is superior. In cases where the average with respect to unknown parameters is required, the B-distance is better.[16] The divergence also has the drawback that a discontinuity occurs when one of the probability densities becomes equal to zero. This problem does not arise in the B-distance or the entropy-type functions. In addition to the feature selection in pattern recognition, the distance measures are useful in estimation, detection, and signal design problems.

4. Multiclass Distance Measures

For multiclass or multihypothesis problems, the average divergence or the expected divergence[17] can be defined as

$$\bar{J} = \sum_{i=1}^{m} \sum_{j=1}^{m} P_i P_j \; J(H_i, H_j) \tag{4.23}$$

where $J(H_i, H_j)$ is the pairwise divergence between the ith and the jth classes. For Gaussian patterns with the same covariance matrix V among all classes, the average divergence is

$$\bar{J} = \sum_{i=1}^{m} \sum_{j=1}^{m} P_i P_j \,(\mu_i - \mu_j)' \, V^{-1} \,(\mu_i - \mu_j) \geqslant d^2 \left(1 - \sum_{i=1}^{m} P_i^2\right) \tag{4.24}$$

where μ_i is the mean vector of the ith class and

$$d^2 = \min_{i \neq j} J(H_i, H_j) \tag{4.25}$$

is the square of the minimum distance among all pattern classes. A feature subset selected to maximize equation (4.25) has been shown experimentally[18] to have a percentage correct recognition close to that using the complete feature set. This maximin method may be very conservative, however. The average divergence may be maximized directly. Even for Gaussian patterns, the case of unequal covariance matrices should be considered. A separability measure[19] has been proposed, which is related to but somewhat more general than the divergence.

A lower bound of the average divergence can be determined as follows.

Let $I(i, j)$ be the Kullback-Leibler number between the ith and the jth classes, then equation (4.23) can be written as

$$\bar{J} = 2 \sum_{i=1}^{m} \sum_{j=1}^{m} P_i P_j^{I}(i, j) \tag{4.26}$$

Vajda[20] has shown that

$$I(i, j) \geqslant \log \left(\frac{2 + K_{ij}}{2 - K_{ij}}\right) - \left(\frac{2K_{ij}}{2 + K_{ij}}\right) \tag{4.27}$$

where K_{ij} is the Kolmogorov variational distance between the ith and the jth classes. From equations (4.26) and (4.27) we have

$$\bar{J} \geqslant 2 \sum_{i=1}^{m} \sum_{j=1}^{m} P_i P_j \left[\log \left(\frac{2 + K_{ij}}{2 - K_{ij}}\right) - \left(\frac{2K_{ij}}{2 + K_{ij}}\right)\right]$$

For multiclass B-distance measure, let ρ_{ij} be the pairwise B-coefficient between the ith and the jth classes. The average B-distance may be defined as

$$\overline{B} = \sum_{\substack{i=1 \\ i<j}}^{m} \sum_{j=1}^{m} \rho_{ij} \tag{4.28}$$

Performance bounds of equation (4.28) have been derived by Lainiotis.[21]

5. Comparison of Feature Selection Criteria

The recognition system designer often has to decide on which feature selection criterion to choose. He may perform the recognition experiment to determine the best feature set and the appropriate feature selection criterion. While experimental results are important in evaluating the feature effectiveness,[19] one drawback with experimental comparison is that incorrect assumptions on the underlying distribution or the limited number of available samples of the pattern may lead to inconsistent or incorrect conclusions. Theoretical comparison, however, should provide us with unique results.

In the preceding section, the relative advantages of the B-distance over the divergence were discussed. It is also noted from equations (4.20) and (4.22) that tighter upper and lower error bounds are available with the B-distance. In this section we compare the performance of the B-distance criterion which minimizes the B-coefficient with that of the entropy criterion which minimizes the equivocation† or the missing information, H. Assume that all classes are equally likely. For the entropy criterion, the Fano bound provides a lower bound of P_E,

$$H \leqslant - P_E \log P_E - (1 - P_E) \log_2 (1 - P_E) + P_E \log_2 (m - 1) \tag{4.29}$$

When the equality of equation (4.29) holds, we have $H = H_{\max}$. P_E is plotted in figure 4.3 as a function of $H_{\max}$ for $m = 2, 4, 8, 10$. It is noted that P_E is a monotonic increasing function of $H_{\max}$ for $P_E \leqslant 1 - (1/m)$. The Fano bound becomes loose as m becomes large. If we take the differential on both sides of equation (4.29), we have

$$\frac{dP_E}{dH} \geqslant [\log_2 (m - 1) + \log_2 (1 - P_E)/P_E]^{-1} \geqslant 0 \tag{4.30}$$

†Using the notations of equation (4.3), we can write the equivocation for binary measurements as

$$H = - \sum_{\text{all } x} p(x) \sum_{i=1}^{m} P(\omega_i/x) \log_2 P(\omega_i/x)$$

For continuous measurements, summation with respect to x must be replaced by integration.

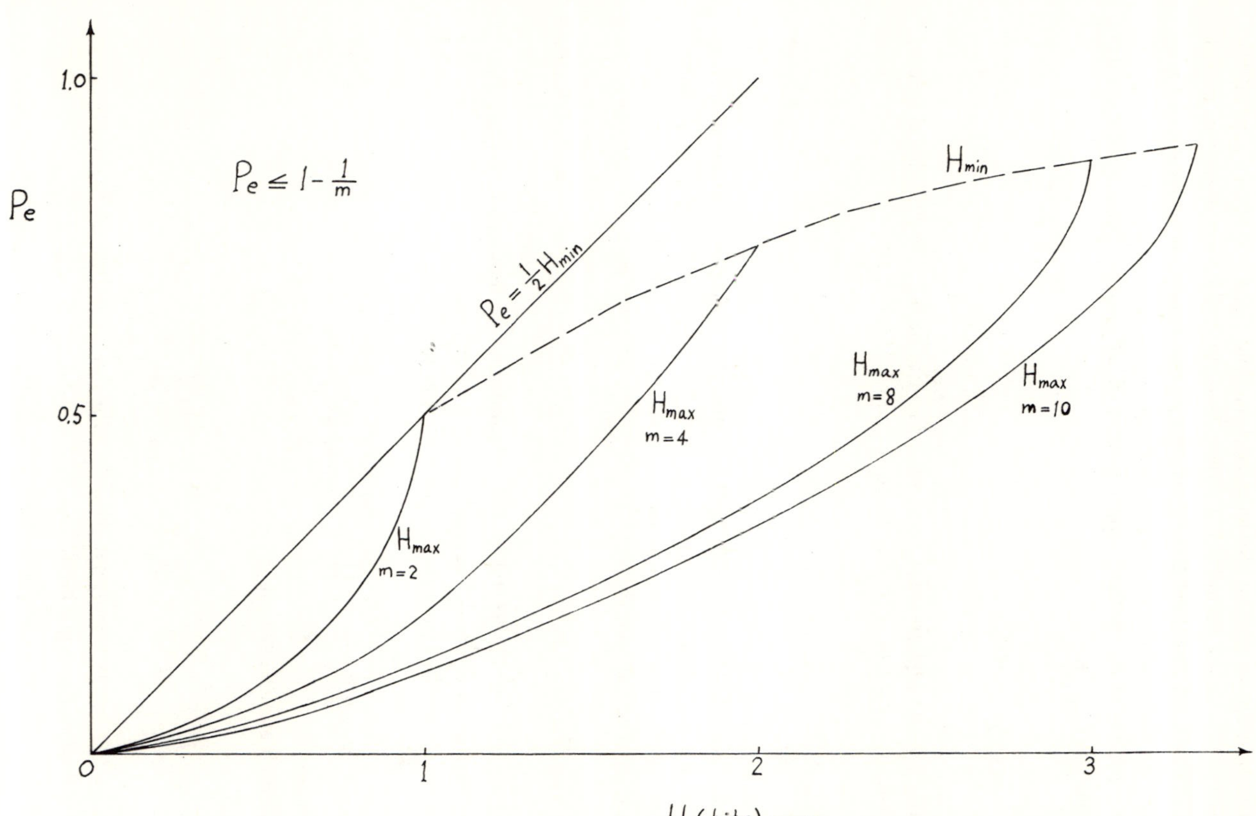

Fig. 4.3 Error Bounds of Entropy Criterion with $m \geqslant 2$

For $m > 2$, the lower bound of P_E with the B-distance criterion is not available, but it cannot be smaller than the lower bound at $m = 2$. Comparison of the lower error bounds would be difficult because the tight bounds in general are not available. The lower bounds of the first derivative of P_E are, however, useful measures. The larger the first derivative of P_E, the faster the decrease of P_E if the feature set dimension is increased; thus the better the performance would be. For $m = 2$ and small P_E, a tight lower bound of $dP_E/d\rho$ is obtained from equations (4.20) and (4.22),

$$\frac{dP_E}{d\rho} \geqslant \sqrt{P_E} - O(P_E) \tag{4.31}$$

where $O(P_E)$ is the higher-order term with P_E. For $m = 2$, the right-hand side of equation (4.30) is greater than that of equation (4.31). Hence

$$\frac{dP_E}{dH} \geqslant \frac{dP_E}{d\rho}; \quad m = 2 \tag{4.32}$$

Here the equality holds when $P_E \simeq 0.1$. Thus the entropy criterion performs better than the B-distance criterion for $m = 2$ according to the lower bounds.

Now the upper bounds of the two criteria are compared. For the entropy criterion, it has been shown that[22,23]

$$P_E \leqslant \tfrac{1}{2} H; \quad m \geqslant 2 \tag{4.33}$$

When the equality holds, H takes the minimum value denoted as $H_{\min}$. $P_E = \frac{1}{2} H_{\min}$ is plotted in figure 4.3 as a solid line. Another expression of the minimum entropy also shown in figure 4.3 is given by the piecewise linear relationship[24]

$$H_{\min} = \log_2 n + n(n+1)\left(\log_2 \frac{n+1}{n}\right)\left(P_E - \frac{n-1}{n}\right); \quad m \geqslant 2 \tag{4.34}$$

where n is such an integer that

$$\frac{n-1}{n} < P_E < \frac{n}{n+1}$$

Equation (4.34) is a better upper bound of P_E than equation (4.33). For $m > 2$, an upper bound of P_E is given by[21]

$$P_E \leqslant \frac{1}{m} \sum_{i<j} \rho_{ij}; \quad m \geqslant 2 \tag{4.35}$$

Now let $\rho' = \max_{i,j} \rho_{ij}$
then H is related to ρ' by[23]

$$H \leqslant K\rho'; \quad m \geqslant 2 \tag{4.36}$$

where K is a constant. For $m = 2$, clearly

$$P_E \leqslant \tfrac{1}{2} H \leqslant \tfrac{1}{2} K\rho \tag{4.37}$$

and the entropy criterion appears superior, which is consistent with our conclusion based on the lower error bounds. Furthermore, from equations (4.32) and (4.37) we have $K < 1$. Hence† for $m > 2$, the upper bound given by equation (4.33) is always smaller than the upper bound given by equation (4.35). Therefore, we conclude that for a finite number of classes, the entropy criterion appears superior to the B-distance criterion when $m \geqslant 2$.

6. Evaluation of Feature Subsets

If the performance of a feature set can be related with that of its feature subset through a tight inequality, then we can not only estimate or evaluate the performance of a feature subset but also determine the required number of features for a specified recognition accuracy in recognizer design. One such inequality is given by Perez[25] as

$$P_E^* \leqslant P_E + \sqrt{2P_E^* (1 - P_E^*) [I - I^*]} \leqslant P_E + \sqrt{\frac{I - I^*}{2}} \tag{4.38}$$

where we have let "*" denote a quantity associated with a feature subset. For example, I and I^* are mutual informations with the feature set and its feature subset respectively. No similar result is available with the B-distance criterion. We may, however, take the Taylor series expansion of the probability of misrecognition and write as a first-order approximation,

$$P_E^* \simeq P_E + \frac{dP_E}{dH} (H^* - H) \leqslant P_E + \frac{1}{2} (H^* - H); \quad m \geqslant 2 \tag{4.39}$$

for the entropy criterion and

$$P_E^* \simeq P_E + \frac{dP_E}{d\rho} (\rho^* - \rho) \leqslant P_E + \frac{1}{2} (\rho^* - \rho); \quad m = 2 \tag{4.40}$$

†The inequality given by equation (4.36) is the tightest when ρ' is the smallest, which occurs when all ρ_{ij}'s in equation (4.35) are equal and denoted as ρ. Then equation (4.35) becomes $P_E \leqslant \frac{1}{2} (m - 1) \rho$ and for $m > 2$, $P_E \leqslant \frac{1}{2} H \leqslant \frac{1}{2} K\rho \leqslant \frac{1}{2} (m - 1)\rho$.

for the B-distance criterion. Equation (4.39) is tighter than equation (4.38) if we consider, for example, the case that all classes are equally probable so that $I = -H, I^* = -H^*$ and thus

$$\sqrt{\frac{(I - I^*)}{2}} = \sqrt{\frac{(H^* - H)}{2}} > \frac{1}{2}\,(H^* - H) \text{ since } H^* - H < 1$$

Equation (4.39) is also tighter than equation (4.40).

7. Algorithm of Dimensionality Reduction

In previous sections, features were selected on the basis of information and distance measures to minimize the probability of misrecognition. Each pattern class must be taken into account in selecting the features. In dimensionality reduction, however, emphasis is on a particular pattern class and a smaller dimension, say d, is selected from N features of the pattern. Effective algorithms are much needed to select a subset of variables from a larger set. The exhaustive search method is obviously not feasible. Here we examine a mean-squared error criterion for Gaussian patterns.[26] Consider the measurement vector x of dimension N to be multivariate Gaussian with mean vector μ and covariance matrix V. Then a set of linearly independent orthonormal feature vectors, $\{a_i,\ i = 1, 2, \cdots, N\}$ can be chosen such that $z = x - \mu$ can be expressed as

$$z = \sum_{i=1}^{N} f_i\,(x)\, w_i\, a_i \tag{4.41}$$

where $f_i(x)$ is a function (a scalar) of x, and w_i is the weighting coefficient. It is desired to reduce N to a smaller dimension d such that the expected square error with respect to x,

$$\epsilon_d\,(a) = E_x\left\{\left|z - \sum_{i=1}^{d} f_i(x)\, w_i a_i\right|^2\right\} \tag{4.42}$$

is minimized. The orthogonality condition states that

$$a_i'\, a_j = 0 \quad \text{for } i \neq j \tag{4.43a}$$

$$a_i'\, a_j = 1 \quad \text{for } i = j \tag{4.43b}$$

Thus

$$f_i(x)\, w_i = z'\, a_i \tag{4.44}$$

Using equations (4.44) and (4.41), equation (4.42) can be written as

$$\epsilon_d(a) = \sum_{i=d+1}^{N} a_i' V a_i \tag{4.45}$$

where $V = E(zz')$ is the covariance matrix for x. Since $a_i' Va_i$ is positive definite, minimizing $\epsilon_d(a)$ is equivalent to minimizing each term of the form $a_i' Va_i$, $i = d + 1, \cdots, N$, subject to the condition given by equation (4.43a).

Introducing a Lagrange multiplier α_i, we form the synthetic function,

$$L(a_i) = a_i' Va_i - \alpha_i(a_i' a_i - 1)$$

Taking the partial derivative with respect to a_i and equating it to zero leads us to the condition

$$Va_i = \alpha_i a_i \tag{4.46}$$

This equation implies that a_i is an eigenvector of the covariance matrix V, and α_i are the corresponding eigenvalues. Since the covariance matrix V is symmetrical, we can always find a complete set of orthogonal eigenvectors, and thus the condition given by equation (4.43b) is automatically satisfied. Substitute equation (4.46) into equation (4.45); this yields the minimum expected square error as

$$\epsilon_d(a) = \sum_{i=d+1}^{N} \alpha_i \tag{4.47}$$

where α_i are the $(N - d)$ eigenvalues of V corresponding to the feature vector a_i, $i = d + 1, \cdots, N$. Hence the expected square error will assume a minimum value, given by equation (4.47), if we select the first d feature vectors corresponding to the largest eigenvalues of the matrix V. The features thus selected reflect the properties in the pattern, which tend to disperse the measured data, since the eigenvalues are the variances in the related problem.

8. Dimensionality and Sample Size

When the recognition machine is designed on the basis of a finite number of samples, pattern vector dimensionality is closely related to the effectiveness of the design. In statistical classification, estimation, and prediction, it has often been noted that, with finite samples, performance does not always improve as the number of variables is arbitrarily increased. Sometimes it may even deteriorate. In this section we shall discuss the relationship between dimensionality and sample size.

Suppose we have several design procedures applicable to a problem with a finite sample set. We may select the best design procedure based on a portion of the sample set and test the performance of the recognition machine using the remaining samples. This leads to the problem of optimum use of a sample set to maximize overall confidence in the design and testing of the system. Highleyman[27] suggested an optimum partitioning of the total sample set into disjoint design set and test set by minimizing the variance of the estimated error rate. The assumptions underlying the analysis are: (a) the error rate e can be expressed as a function of a finite number of estimated parameters; (b) it can be expanded into a Taylor series about the error rate, e_0, of the optimum system based on infinite design samples; and (c) the deviation $(e - e_0)$ is small so that those terms higher than the second order can be neglected in the series expansion. The result of the analysis is a set of curves showing the fractions of the available sample set, which should be used in the test, as a function of the total sample size, with the number of allowable pattern classes as a parameter. The optimum error rate e_0 is held constant.

The drawback of the analysis is that a large sample size is implied, so that approximation to the series expansion by terms up to the second order is valid. In practice, the sample size may be small and the analysis becomes too optimistic. Other works based on large sample size assumptions are available from references 22, 28, 29, and 30. Hughes[30] considers the relationship between dimensionality (number of quantized levels for each measurement) and sample size within the framework of a very general statistical model assuming practically no probability structure. The mean probability of correct recognition is calculated as an average of performances over all classification problems falling within the scope of the model and having a specified dimensionality and a priori class probabilities.

The reason for considering prior probabilities as a separate parameter is that some interesting phenomena occur for the case of unequal prior probabilities. Some clarifications of reference 30 are made in references 31 and 32. Let n_1 and n_2 be the number of samples available for estimating the parameters for classes 1 and 2 and let N be the dimension of a sample. Let r_i and s_i be the number of times out of n_1 and n_2 respectively, that a particular measurement value x_i (a quantized discrete value) occurred for classes 1 and 2. Let P_1 and P_2 be the a priori probabilities for classes 1 and 2 respectively. Then the Bayes decision rule[31] compares the quantities

$$\left(P_1 \frac{r_i + 1}{n_1 + N}\right) \quad \text{and} \quad \left(P_2 \frac{s_i + 1}{n_2 + N}\right)$$

and assigns x_i to class 1 if the first is greater than the second, and to class 2 otherwise.

When the a priori probabilities of the classes are equal, this decision rule leads

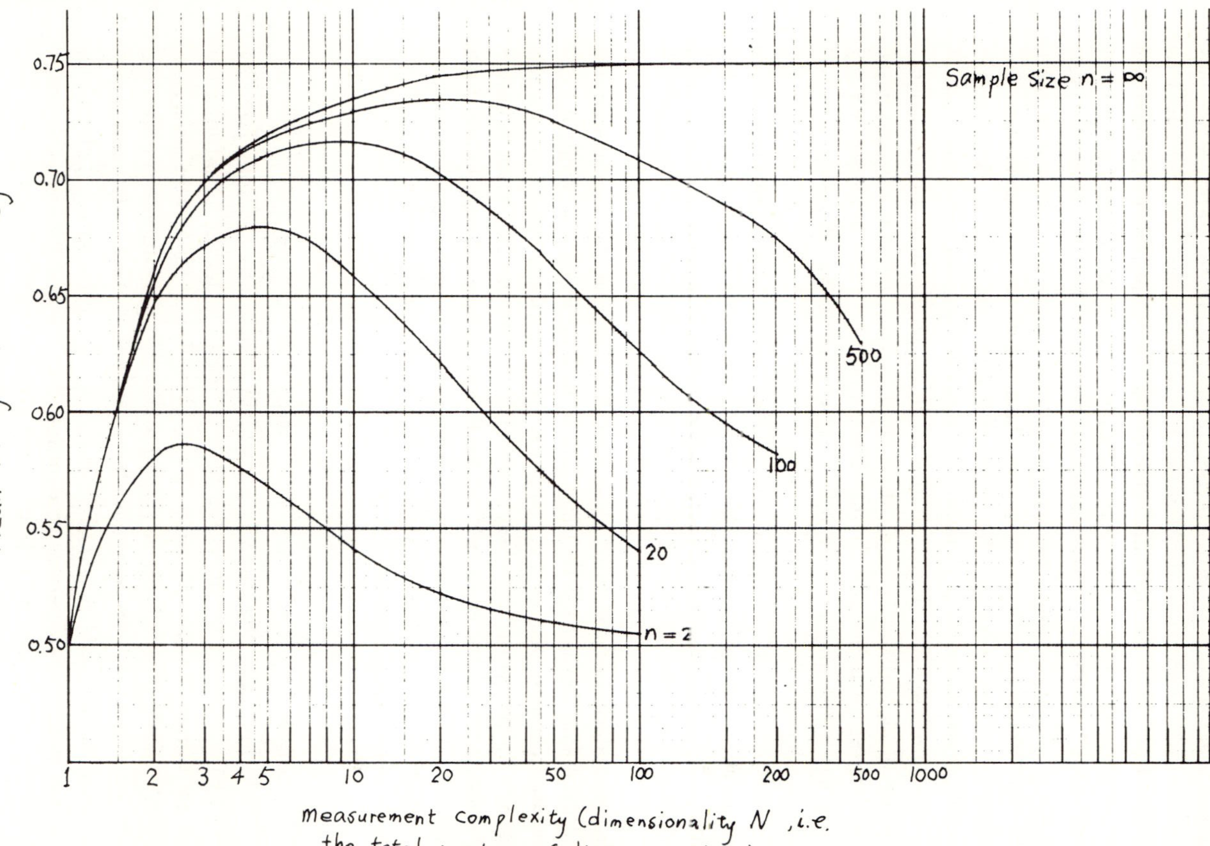

Fig. 4.4 Finite Data Set Accuracy (Taken from G. F. Hughes, "On the Mean Accuracy of Statistical Pattern Recognizers," *IEEE Transactions on Information Theory*, vol. IT-14, No. 1, pp. 55–63, January 1968)

to an average performance curve in which, for a fixed number of samples, the mean classification accuracy increases when the dimensionality is increased until an optimum value is reached. Beyond the optimum value, the performance falls off. At the infinite dimension, the performance is no better than that based on prior probabilities. As expected, the value of the optimum dimension increases with the number of samples. The values obtained are very pessimistic. Figure 4.4 is a typical plot[30] of mean recognition accuracy versus the dimensionality, i.e., the number of discrete values for each measurement, for various sample sizes. When 500 samples are available from each class, the optimum dimension is 23. For a vector of binary variables, this allows less than five variables. As shown in reference 32, some interesting variations on this behavior occur for the case of unequal prior probabilities. The existence of an optimum dimension is a likely characteristic of all statistical classification systems designed with a finite sample size. Performance as a function of the dimensionality of the variables and the sample size has been considered by Allais[33] and a tradeoff problem is examined by Kanal and Chandrasekaran.[34]

In the above discussion, we have examined the optimistic and pessimistic cases of dimensionality and sample size. Most recognition systems fall somewhere between these two extremes. A key factor is the probability structure assumed in each recognition system and the correspondence between the assumed structure and reality. Furthermore, optimal decision procedures differ from one another for different underlying probability structures. For instance, decision procedures involving estimated covariance matrices when nothing is known about the dependence or independence of the variables are nonoptimal while in fact the variables are independent. In many problems the probability structures are actually continuous. If the estimated probability structure is discontinuous such as obtained in the histogram method,[30] we may get a questionable conclusion regarding dimensionality and sample size. This might be an explanation of the conservative results given in reference 30.

9. Remarks

Feature selection and extraction is a problem which must be considered by every recognition system designer. We have focused on the use of information statistics to obtain computationally feasible methods of feature selection. Recently information statistics have played a key role in feature selection and a number of additional references are available (references 35–43). Other distance measures have been considered. The feature selection, of course, is closely related to other problems of pattern recognition. Wee[44] has considered the design of feature extractors and categorizers under a single, rather than separate performance criteria. Nonlinear and nonorthogonal projection techniques for feature extraction were examined by Calvert.[45] Nonparametric methods and sequential methods of feature selection will be presented in chapters 7 and 9 respectively.

Most feature selection methods considered thus far have been concerned with evaluating predetermined features and selecting the best ones. The features are predetermined by the human designer. Many features should be considered as mathematical features without physical meaning. The problem of automatic selection and extraction of features by the recognition machine itself remains unsolved. Another problem which does not yet have a satisfactory solution is the selection of a small feature subset from a very large feature set. A more immediate step toward feature selection via information statistics is probably to improve the performance bounds, because the exact performance evaluation is often not possible.

PROBLEMS

1. Show that for multivariate Gaussian distributions $p_i(x) \sim \eta(\mu_i, V_i)$ the Bhattacharyya distance is

$$B = \frac{1}{8}(\mu_1 - \mu_2)' V^{-1}(\mu_1 - \mu_2) + \frac{1}{2}\log\left(\frac{\det V}{\sqrt{\det V_1 \cdot \det V_2}}\right)$$

where $2V = V_1 + V_2$. Also show that the divergence is

$$J = \tfrac{1}{2}\, tr\, [V_1 - V_2]\, [V_2^{-1} - V_1^{-1}] + \tfrac{1}{2}\, tr \cdot [V_1^{-1} + V_2^{-1}]\, [\mu_1 - \mu_2]\, [\mu_1 - \mu_2]'$$

where tr denotes the trace of the matrix. Note that if the covariance matrices are equal, say $V_1 = V_2 = V$, we have $B = J/8$.

2. In problem 1 prove that in general $J \geqslant 8B$.
3. Prove that $P_E \leqslant \frac{1}{M} \sum_{i=1}^{m-1} \sum_{j=i+1}^{m} [1 - k_{ij}/2]$

REFERENCES

1. Lindley, D. "On a Measure of Information Provided by an Experiment." *Ann. Math. Stat.*, 27 (1956), 986–1005.
2. Kamentsky, L. A. and C. N. Liu. "A Theoretical and Experimental Study of a Model for Pattern Recognition." In *Proc. COINS Symposium.* Evanston, Ill., June 1963.
3. Liu, C. N. "A Programmed Algorithm for Designing Multifont Character Recognition Logics." *IEEE Trans. on Electronic Computers*, EC-13 (October 1964), 586–593.
4. Chen, C. H. "Information Theoretic Approach to Pattern Recognition." In *Second International Symposium on Information Theory.* Tsahkadsor, Armenian Republic, U.S.S.R., September 1971.
5. Lewis, P. M. "Character Selection Problem in Recognition Systems." *IRE Trans. on Information Theory,* IT-8 (February 1962), 171–178.

6. Blackwell, D. "Comparison of Experiments." In *Proc. Second Berkeley Symp. on Probability and Statistics*, vol. 1, pp. 93–102. Univ. of Calif. Press, Berkeley, 1951.
7. Karlin, S. and R. N. Bradt. "On the Design and Comparison of Dichotomous Experiments." *Ann. Math. Stat.*, 27 (1956), 390–409.
8. Ali, J. M. and S. D. Silvey. "A General Class of Coefficients of Divergence of One Distribution from Another. *J. Royal Stat.*, 28 (1966), 131–142.
9. Kullback, S. and R. A. Leibler. "On Information and Sufficiency." *Ann. Math. Stat.*, 22 (1951), 79–86.
10. Kullback, S. *Information Theory and Statistics.* Dover, New York, 1968.
11. Bhattacharyya, A. "On a Measure of Divergence Between Two Statistical Populations Defined by Their Probability Distributions." *Bull. Calcutta Math. Soc.*, 35 (1943), 99–109.
12. Kakutani, S. "On Equivalence of Infinite Product Measures." *Ann. Math. Stat.*, 49 (1948), 214–224.
13. Matusita, K. "Decision Rules, Based on the Distance, for Problems of Fit, Two Samples and Estimation." *Ann. Math. Stat.*, 26 (1955), 631–640.
14. Kailath, T. "The Divergence and Bhattacharyya Distance Measures in Signal Selection." *IEEE Trans. on Communication Technology*, COM-15 (February 1967), 52–60.
15. Kadota, T. T. and L. A. Shepp. "On the Best Finite Set of Linear Observables for Discriminating Two Gaussian Signals." *IEEE Trans. on Information Theory*, IT-13 (April 1967), 278–284.
16. Kobayashi, H. "Distance Measure and Related Criteria." In *Proc. of Fifth Annual Allerton Conference on Circuit and Systems Theory*, Univ. of Illinois, Urbana, October 1967.
17. Grettenberg, T. L. "Signal Selection in Communication and Radar Systems." *IEEE Trans. on Information Theory*, IT-9 (October 1963), 265–275.
18. Chen, C. H. "A Computer Searching Criterion for Best Feature Set in Character Recognition." *Proc. of IEEE* (correspondence), (December 1965).
19. Fu, K. S., P. J. Min, and T. J. Li. "Feature Selection in Pattern Recognition." *IEEE Trans. on Systems Science and Cybernetics*, SSC-6 (January 1970), 33–39.
20. Vajda, I. "Note on Discrimination Information and Variation." *IEEE Trans. on Information Theory* (correspondence), IT-16 (September 1970), 771–773.
21. Lainiotis, D. G. "A Class of Upper Bounds on Probability of Error for Multihypotheses Pattern Recognition." *IEEE Trans. on Information Theory* (correspondence), IT-15 (November 1969), 730–731.
22. Chu, J. T. and J. C. Chueh. "Inequalities Between Information Measures and Error Probability." *Journal of Franklin Institute*, 282 (August 1966), 121–125.
23. Hellman, M. E. and J. Raviv. "Probability of Error, Equivocation, and the Chernoff Bound." *IEEE Trans. on Information Theory*, IT-16 (July 1970), 368–372.
24. Kovalevsky, V. A. "The Problem of Character Recognition from the Point of View of Mathematical Statistics." In *Character Readers and Pattern Recognition*, edited by V. A. Kovalevsky. Spartan Books, New York, 1968.

25. Perez, A. "Information-theoretic Risk Estimates in Statistical Decisions." *Kybernetika*, 3 (1967), 1–21.
26. Tou, J. T. and R. P. Heydorn. "Some Approaches to Optimum Feature Extraction." In *Proc. Second Symp. on Computer and Information Sciences*, edited by J. T. Tou and R. Wilcox. Columbus, Ohio, August 1966.
27. Highleyman, W. H. "The Design and Analysis of Pattern Recognition Experiments." *Bell System Technical Journal*, (March 1962), 723–744.
28. Lachenbruch, P. A. and M. R. Mickey. "Estimation of Error Rates in Discriminant Analysis." *Technometrics* 10 (February 1968), 1–11.
29. Albrecht, R. and W. Werner. "Error Analysis of a Statistical Decision Method." *IEEE Trans. on Information Theory*, IT-10 (January 1968), 55–63.
30. Hughes, G. F. "On the Mean Accuracy of Statistical Pattern Recognizers." *IEEE Trans. on Information Theory*, IT-14 (January 1968), 55–63.
31. Abend, K. and T. J. Harley, Jr. "Comments on 'The Mean Accuracy of Statistical Pattern Recognizers'." *IEEE Trans. on Information Theory*, IT-15 (May 1969), 420–421.
32. Chandrasekaran, B. and T. H. Harley, Jr. "Comments on 'On the Mean Accuracy of Statistical Pattern Recognizers'." *IEEE Trans. on Information Theory*, IT-15 (May 1969), 421–423.
33. Allais, D. C. "The Problem of Too Many Measurements in Pattern Recognition and Prediction." In *IEEE International Convention Record.* New York, 1965.
34. Kanal, L. and B. Chandrasekaran. "On Dimensionality and Sample Size in Statistical Pattern Classification." In *Proc. of National Electronics Conference*. Chicago, 1968.
35. Barabash, Yu. L. "On Properties of Symbol Recognition." *Engineering Cybernetics*, 5 (1965), 71–77.
36. Chen, C. H. "Theoretical Comparison of a Class of Feature Selection Criteria in Pattern Recognition." *IEEE Trans. on Computers*, (September 1971).
37. Fukunaga, K. and T. F. Krile. "A Minimum Distance Feature Effectiveness Criterion." *IEEE Trans. on Information Theory*, (September 1968), 78–782.
38. Marill, T. and D. M. Green. "On the Effectiveness of Receptors in Recognition Systems." *IEEE Trans. on Information Theory*, IT-9 (January 1963), 11–17.
39. Silver, A. "Pattern Recognition and Classification: An Information Theory Approach." Martin Marietta Corp. Report, Denver, Colo., 1968.
40. Young, T. Y. "The Reliability of Linear Feature Extractors." *IEEE Trans. on Computers*, (September 1971).
41. Young, T. Y. and M. J. Yuschik. "On Minimax Feature Selection and Bhattacharyya Coefficients." In *IEEE Symposium on Adaptive Processes (9th), Decision and Control.* December 1970.
42. Paul, J. E., Jr., A. J. Goetze, and J. B. O'Neal, Jr. "A Modified Figure of Merit for Feature Selection in Pattern Recognition." *IEEE Trans. on Information Theory*, IT-16 (July 1970), 504–507.
43. Ryan, H. F. "The Information Content Measure as a Performance Criterion for Feature Selection." *IEEE Proc. 7th Symposium on Adaptive Processes*, Los Angeles, December 1968.
44. Wee, W. G. "On Feature Selection in a Class of Distribution-free Pattern

Classifiers." *IEEE Trans. on Information Theory*, IT-61 (January 1970), 47–55.

45. Calvert, T. W. "Nonorthogonal Projections for Feature Extraction in Pattern Recognition." *IEEE Trans. on Computers*, C-19 (April 1970).

Bibliography

1. Babu, C. C. "On the Application of Divergence for the Extraction of Features from Imperfectly Labeled Patterns." *IEEE Trans. on Systems, Man, and Cybernetics* (corresp.), vol. SMC-2, No. 2 (April, 1972), 290–292.
2. Babu, C. C. "On the Extraction of Pattern Features from Imperfectly Identified Samples." *IEEE Trans. on Computers* (corresp.) (April 1972), 410–411.
3. Butler, G. A. "Evaluating Feature Spaces for the Two-Class Problem." Submitted for the *Joint National Conference on Major Systems*, April 1971.
4. Caprihan, A. and R. J. P. DeFigueiredo. "On the Extraction of Pattern Features from Continuous Measurements." *IEEE Trans. on Systems Science and Cybernetics*, SSC-6 (April 1970).
5. Casey, R. G. "Linear Reduction of Dimensionality in Pattern Recognition." IBM Research Report RC-1431, March 1965.
6. Chandrasekaran, B. "Independence of Measurements and the Mean Recognition Accuracy." *IEEE Transactions on Information Theory*, IT-17, 4 (July 1971), 452–456.
7. Chen, C. H. "A Comparison Between Information Measure and Battachayya Distance in Feature Selection." *Proc. of IEEE International Symposium on Information Theory*, Pacific Grove, Calif., January 1972.
8. Couch, R. D. and D. C. Lai. "Computer-Aided Diagnosis–The Information Index for Laboratory Tests." *Data Acquisition and Processing in Biology and Medicine*, vol. 5, edited by K. Enslein. Pergamon Press, New York, 1968, 63–73.
9. Das, S. K. "Feature Selection with a Linear Dependence Measure." *IEEE Trans. on Computers*, C-20, No. 9 (September 1971), 1106–1109.
10. Estes, S. E. "Measurement Selection for Linear Discriminants Used in Pattern Classification." IBM Research Report RJ-331, April 1965.
11. Fu, K. S., ed. "Special Issue on Feature Selection and Extraction in Pattern Recognition." *IEEE Trans. on Computers*, C-20 (September 1971).
12. Fukunaga, K. and W. L. G. Koontz. "Application of the Karhunen-Loeve Expansion to Feature Selection and Ordering." *IEEE Trans. on Computers*, C-19 (1970), 311–318.
13. Gonzalez, R. C. and J. T. Tou. "Some Results in Minimum–Entropy Feature Extraction." *1968 IEEE Region III Convention*, Cocoa Beach, Florida, 1968.
14. Henderson, T. L. and D. G. Lainiotis. "Application of State–Variable Techniques to Optimal Feature Extraction–Multichannel Analog Data." *IEEE Trans. on Information Theory*, IT-16, 4 (July 1970), 396–406.
15. Henderson, T. L. and D. G. Lainiotis, "Comments on Linear Feature Extraction." *IEEE Trans. on Information Theory*, IT-15 (November 1969).

16. Knoll, A. L. "Experiments with 'Characteristic Loci' for Recognition of Handprinted Characters." *IEEE Trans. on Computers* (April 1969).
17. Koontz, W. L. G. and K. Fukunaga. "A Nonlinear Feature Extraction Algorithm Using Distance Transformation." *IEEE Transactions on Computers*, C-21, No. 1 (January 1972), 56–63.
18. Koontz, W. L. G. and K. Fukunaga. "A Nonparametric Valley-Seeking Technique for Cluster Analysis." *IEEE Transactions on Computers*, C-21, No. 2 (February 1972), 171–178.
19. Laemmel, A. E. "Machine Learning Processes Applied to Pattern Recognition." Polytechnic Institute of Brooklyn, Report PIB MRI-981-61, December 1961.
20. Lainiotis, D. G. and T. L. Henderson. "Application of State–Variable Techniques to Optimal Feature Extraction." *Proceedings of the IEEE*, vol. 56, No. 12 (December 1966), 2175–2176.
21. Lainiotis, D. G. and S. K. Park. "Probability of Error Bounds." *IEEE Transactions on Systems, Man, and Cybernetics* (corresp.), vol. SMC-1, No. 2 (April 1971), 175–178.
22. Lissack, T. and K. S. Fu. "A Separability Measure for Feature Selection and Error Estimation in Pattern Recognition." Purdue University Report TR-EE 72-15 (May 1972).
23. Mucciardi, A. N. and E. E. Gose. "A Comparison of Seven Techniques for Choosing Subsets of Pattern Recognition Properties." *IEEE Trans. on Computers*, C-20, No. 9 (September 1971), 1023–1031.
24. Nagy, G. "Feature Extraction on Binary Patterns." *IEEE Transactions on Systems Science and Cybernetics*, vol. SSC-5, No. 4 (October 1969) 273–278.
25. Rao, P. S. R. "On Selecting Variables for Pattern Classification." TR No. 11, Information Research Associates, Inc., June, 1967.
26. Swain, P. H., T. V. Robertson and A. G. Wacher. "Comparison of the Divergence and B-Distance in Feature Selection." *LARS Information Note 020871*, Purdue University, Lafayette, Indiana, 1971.
27. Toussaint, G. T. "On a Simple Minkowski Metric Classifier." *IEEE Trans. Systems Science and Cybernetics*, SSC-6 (October 1970).
28. Toussaint, G. T. "Some Functional Lower Bounds on the Expected Divergence for Multihypothesis Pattern Recognition, Communication, and Radar Systems." *IEEE Trans. on Systems, Man, and Cybernetics* (October 1971).
29. Toussaint, G. T. "Some Inequalities Between Distance Measures for Feature Evaluation." *IEEE Trans. on Computers* (corresp.) (April 1972), 409–410.
30. Vajda, I. "A Contribution to the Informational Analysis of Pattern." In *Methodologies of Pattern Recognition*, edited by S. Watanabe. Academic Press, New York, 1969.
31. Watanabe, S. et al. "Evaluation and Selection of Variables in Pattern Recognition." In *Proc. of Second Symp. on Computer and Information Sciences*, edited by J. T. Tou and R. Wilcox. Columbus, Ohio, August 1966.

CHAPTER V

Supervised and Unsupervised Parameter Estimations

1. Introduction

The probability density function of each pattern class is frequently unknown completely or partially. However, we can make an assumption of the probability density from the a priori knowledge with certain parameters unknown. Another way is to estimate the probability density function without assuming its parametric form, which is discussed in chapter 7.

The first approach is discussed in this chapter and the one following. The unknown parameters may be considered as random variables whose probability densities may or may not be available. We estimate the parameters from the present and all the past measurements. To estimate the parameters under the supervision of a teacher or trainer with correct classification information about the input measurements is called supervised estimation or learning with a teacher. If the parameter statistics are known, it has been shown by Braverman[1] that the average risk will be monotonically decreased as the parameters are estimated sequentially with the input measurements which may thus be called the learning samples. And the sequential estimation of the parameters may be considered as a machine learning process. On the other hand, learning without a teacher is called unsupervised estimation or the unsupervised learning process. If the classification information of input measurements is not available, it has been shown that performance improvement may still be available. This chapter emphasizes the Bayes method, i.e., the parameters are estimated by using the Bayes rule. The maximum likelihood estimates will also be discussed.

2. Bayesian Estimation for Gaussian Patterns

Let x denote the present measurement vector and let L_i be the set of n_i learning samples of the ith class. Assume that the probability density function of the ith class is known except some random parameter θ_i, whose a priori density $p(\theta_i)$ is available. The dominant quantity of the average risk is the probability density function $p(x, L_i/\omega_i)$ which can be written as

$$p(x, L_i/\omega_i) = \int p(x, \theta_i, L_i/\omega_i)\, p(\theta_i/\omega_i)\, d\theta_i \tag{5.1}$$

where $p(x, \theta_i, L_i/\omega_i) = p(x, \theta_i/L_i)\, p(L_i/\omega_i)$

$$p(x, \theta_i/L_i) = p(x/\theta_i, L_i)\, p(\theta_i/L_i) \tag{5.2}$$

and $p(x/\theta_i, L_i) = p(x/\theta_i)$

Hence the role of the learning samples is in the a posteriori probability density $p(\theta_i/L_i)$. If θ_i is known exactly with θ_{io} being the true parameter, then

$$p(\theta_i/L_i) = \delta(\theta_i - \theta_{io}) \tag{5.3}$$

a Dirac delta function, and we have exactly the same problem as in conventional decision theory. If θ_i is not known exactly, then a desirable convergent property is

$$\lim_{n_i \to \infty} p(\theta_i/L_i) = \delta(\theta_i - \theta_{io}) \tag{5.4}$$

The conditions for such convergence are listed in appendix B.

Consider the case that both measurements and random parameters are Gaussian distributed. Let x be a d-dimensional measurement vector with mean θ and covariance matrix K, denoted as $x \sim \eta(\theta, K)$, where θ is also Gaussian distributed, $\theta \sim \eta(\mu, \phi)$. Both K and ϕ are known covariance matrices. When a learning sample, denoted as x_1, is taken, the a posteriori parameters can easily be shown to be given by

$$\begin{aligned} \mu_1 &= \mu_0 + \phi_0(\phi_0 + K)^{-1}\,(x_1 - \mu_0) \\ \phi_1 &= \phi_0(\phi_0 + K)^{-1}\,K \end{aligned} \tag{5.5}$$

where the subscript 0 refers to the initial values which are known. As the sequence of learning samples x_1, and $x_2, \ldots, x_n$ are taken, the a posteriori parameters have exactly the same form as equation (5.5) except that the subscripts are changed,

$$\mu_n = E(\theta_{n+1}/x_1, x_2, \ldots, x_n) \tag{5.6a}$$

$$= \mu_{n-1} + \phi_{n-1}\,(\phi_{n-1} + K)^{-1}\,(x_n - \mu_{n-1}) \tag{5.6b}$$

$$\phi_n = \text{cov.}\,(\phi_{n+1}/x_1, x_2, \ldots, x_n) \tag{5.7a}$$

$$= \phi_{n-1}\,(\phi_{n-1} + K)^{-1}\,K \tag{5.7b}$$

Thus the estimation process is given by

$$\mu_0 \to \mu_1 \to \mu_2 \to \cdots \to \mu_n \to \cdots$$
$$\phi_0 \to \phi_1 \to \phi_2 \to \cdots \to \phi_n \to \cdots \tag{5.8}$$

or $p(x) \to p(x/x_1) \to p(x/x_1, x_2) \to \cdots \to p(x/x_1, x_2, \ldots, x_n) \to \cdots$

It is noted that the form of the probability density function is unchanged during the estimation process. The parameter density function $p(\theta)$ is called the reproducing density. The reproducing density of the mean vector of a Gaussian measurement is also Gaussian.

If the covariance matrix K is unknown instead, let $Q = K^{-1}$ be the random variable and for simplicity assume that the mean vector is zero, then the reproducing density of Q is the Wishart distribution.[2] Let α_0 be a positive definite matrix and ν_0 a real number, $\nu_0 > d$. Then the Wishart distribution is given by

$$p(q_{11}, q_{12}, \ldots q_{dd}) \propto (\det Q)^{[(\nu_0-d-2)/2]} \exp\left[-\tfrac{1}{2} \operatorname{tr} \nu_0 \alpha_0 Q\right] \tag{5.9}$$

where Q is a positive definite symmetric matrix,

$$Q = \begin{bmatrix} q_{11} & q_{12} & \cdots & q_{1d} \\ q_{12} & & & \\ \vdots & & & \vdots \\ q_{1d} & \cdots & & q_{dd} \end{bmatrix}$$

and $\det Q = |Q|$ is the determinant of the matrix Q.

For a sequence of n learning samples, the a posteriori parameter distribution is

$$p(q_{11}, q_{12}, \ldots, q_{dd}/x_1, x_2, \ldots, x_n) \propto (\det Q)^{[(\nu_n-d-2)/2]} \cdot \exp\left[-\tfrac{1}{2} \operatorname{tr} \nu_n Q \alpha_n\right] \tag{5.10}$$

where

$$\nu_n = \nu_0 + n \tag{5.10a}$$

$$\alpha_n = \frac{\nu_0 \alpha_0 + n \langle xx' \rangle}{\nu_0 + n} \tag{5.10b}$$

and

$$\langle xx' \rangle = \frac{1}{n} \sum_{i=1}^{n} x_i x_i'$$

Equation (5.10) has exactly the same form as equation (5.9) and the estimation process is

$$\alpha_0 \rightarrow \alpha_1 \rightarrow \alpha_2 \rightarrow \cdots \alpha_n \rightarrow \cdots$$

$$\nu_0 \rightarrow \nu_1 \rightarrow \nu_2 \rightarrow \cdots \nu_n \rightarrow \cdots \tag{5.11}$$

The parameters ν_0 and α_0 can be interpreted as: α_0 is a covariance matrix, and ν_0 is a confidence factor which measures how concentrated the density equation (5.9) is about α_0^{-1}. α_n reflects the weight attached to α_0 and $\langle xx' \rangle$ by taking a weighted sum with multipliers ν_0 and n respectively.

3. Comments on Supervised Bayesian Estimation

For the reproducing densities, the supervised parameter estimation is a straightforward recursive procedure. The reproducing density is, however, a very restricted class of probability densities.[3] The implementation of the Bayes decision rule for categorization becomes highly complex if the reproducing density is not available. The fundamental deficiency of the Bayesian method is the assumption of a priori statistics. Such assumption may not be justified. The subjective effect of the a priori knowledge can be partially removed by using sample statistics. The a priori parameters are estimated from the samples. In sequential decision making, the importance of the a priori statistics decreases as the number of measurements increases. This is a basic idea of the empirical Bayes approach to statistics,[4] which is an important departure from the classical Bayes approach.

There is no unique way to simplify the structure of the Bayes decision rule. Consider again the Gaussian measurement with unknown mean vector which is also Gaussian distributed, i.e., $x \sim \eta(\mu, K + \phi)$. Let $z = x - \mu$, the a posteriori probability density function is characterized by the determinant of the matrix $K + \phi$ and the quadrative form, $Q = z' (K + \phi)^{-1} z$ which requires matrix inverse. For a high-dimensional matrix, the computation of the matrix inverse may be a difficult task. The matrix inverse, however, may be expanded as a geometric series,

$$\begin{aligned}(K + \phi)^{-1} &= [(I + \phi K^{-1}) K]^{-1} = K^{-1} (I + \phi K^{-1})^{-1} \\ &= K^{-1} [I + \sum_{j=1}^{\infty} (-1)^j (\phi K^{-1})^j]\end{aligned} \tag{5.12}$$

Let $A = \phi K^{-1}$ be a $d \times d$ matrix and a_{ij} be the ith row and the jth column element of the matrix A. Then if $0 \leqslant a_{ij} < 1$ all i,j, $\Sigma_{i=0}\, a_{ij} < 1$, equation (5.12) will converge rapidly, the rate of convergence depending on the magnitude of

a_{ij}'s. The quadratic form can be rewritten as

$$Q = \sum_{j=0}^{\infty} (-1)^j \, z' K^{-1} \, [\phi K^{-1}]^j \, z \tag{5.13}$$

The matrix K usually takes the form $K = kI$ where k is a constant and I is an identity matrix. The system using truncated Q, denoted as Q_T, i.e., a finite number of terms in the series expansion, is a suboptimum system. Q_T is much easier to compute because it does not involve matrix inverses ϕ^{-1} and $(K + \phi)^{-1}$. It can be shown[5] that by properly choosing the number of terms in the series expansion, the performance of the suboptimum system is very close to the optimum one for the multiple pattern class.

4. Parameter Estimation of Slowly Varying Patterns

Let x_j, the jth learning measurement, be given by

$$x_j = \theta_j + N_j \tag{5.14}$$

where θ_j is the random mean vector and N_j is the noise vector which is independent from measurement to measurement. We specify the discrete-time parameter variation for θ_j be the recursive relation,[6]

$$\theta_j = a\theta_{j-1} + \Delta_{j-1} \tag{5.15}$$

where a is a constant scalar $(0 < a < 1)$ and Δ_j is a Gaussian vector with zero mean and covariance matrix ϕ_Δ. Δ_j is also independent from measurement to measurement. The problem is again the computation of the conditional mean and covariance of θ,

$$\mu_n = E[\theta_{n+1}/x_1, x_2, \ldots, x_n]$$

$$\phi_n = \text{cov.}\ [\phi_{n+1}/x_1, x_2, \ldots, x_n]$$

Let

$$\mu' = E[\theta_n/x_1, x_2, \ldots, x_n]$$

$$\phi' = \text{cov.}\ [\theta_n/x_1, x_2, \ldots, x_n]$$

From equation (5.15) we have

$$\mu_n = a\mu' \qquad \phi_n = a^2\phi' + \phi_\Delta \tag{5.16}$$

Now μ' and ϕ' can be obtained in the same manner as equation (5.8) because the information given in both cases is the same, viz., $x_1, x_2, \ldots, x_n$. Thus

$$\mu' = \mu_{n-1} + \phi_{n-1} (\phi_{n-1} + K)^{-1} (x_n - \mu_n)$$
$$\phi' = \phi_{n-1} (\phi_{n-1} + K)^{-1} K \tag{5.17}$$

and μ_n and ϕ_n are given by equation (5.16). For large n, $\phi_n \simeq \phi_{n-1}$, we may solve equation (5.16) for ϕ_n with slowly varying mean, i.e., $a \simeq 1$; the solution is

$$\phi_n \simeq [\phi_\Delta K^{-1}]^{1/2} K \tag{5.18}$$

Expanding $[I + (\phi_\Delta K^{-1})^{1/2}]^{-1}$ in power series, we have

$$\mu_n \simeq [I - (\phi_\Delta K^{-1})^{1/2}]\, \mu_{n-1} + (\phi_\Delta K^{-1})^{1/2} x_n \tag{5.19}$$

Equation (5.19) indicates that the new mean μ_n is a weighted sum of the old mean and the new measurement.

Consider a special case that $\phi_\Delta = \beta^2 K$, where β is a constant. β^2 may be called the drift-to-noise ratio. Then we have, from equations (5.18) and (5.19),

$$\phi_n = \beta K \tag{5.20}$$

$$\mu_n = (1 - \beta)\, \mu_{n-1} + \beta x_n \tag{5.21}$$

Equation (5.21) states that the new estimate is obtained by adding βx_n onto an attenuated version of the previous estimate of the pattern. In this manner we follow, i.e., track, the slowly varying pattern as new learning measurements arrive.

For a more general parameter variation, we may consider a second-order polynomial expression for the random parameter,

$$\theta_{n+1} = \alpha_n + n\beta_n + n^2 \gamma_n \tag{5.22}$$

where α_n, β_n, and γ_n are independent random parameters whose a priori distributions are available. The joint conditional estimation of α_n, β_n, and γ_n can be made from the sequence of input measurements.[5]

5. Bayes Solutions to Unsupervised Estimation

Let θ be the random parameter, $x_1, x_2, \ldots, x_n$ be a sequence of n unclassified learning samples, and x be the measurement to be classified. Then according to the argument of equations (1) and (2), the Bayes solution requires the computation of the a posteriori parameter distribution $p(\theta/x_1, x_2, \ldots, x_n)$, denoted as $p_n(\theta)$. From the Bayes rule,

$$p_n(\theta) = \frac{p(x_n/\theta, x_1, x_2, \ldots, x_{n-1})}{p_{n-1}(x_n)} p_{n-1}(\theta) \tag{5.23}$$

where the subscript n or $n - 1$ indicates that the probability density is conditioned on the past n or $n - 1$ samples. It is assumed that here the measurements are conditionally independent. This implies that if θ is known, then

$$p(x/\theta, x_1, \ldots, x_n) = p(x/\theta) \tag{5.24}$$

Thus it is not necessary to store all the past samples $x_1, x_2, \ldots, x_n$ because of the conditional independence assumption. Although all past information is in $p_k(\theta)$, realization of the system requires that θ takes on only a finite number of values. This will be the assumption made in the subsequent analysis.

To synthesize the system,[7] we consider first the two pattern class case in which only one class is characterized by the random parameter. The $(n + 1)$th vector measurement, x, arises from either class ω_1 or from class ω_2. Hence the numerator of equation (5.23) can be written as

$$p(x_n/\theta, x_1, x_2, \ldots, x_{n-1}) = p(x_n/\theta, \omega_1) P(\omega_1) + p(x_n/\omega_2) P(\omega_2) \tag{5.25}$$

and the denominator is

$$p_{n-1}(x_n) = P(\omega_1) \int p(x_n/\theta, \omega_1) p_{n-1}(\theta) d\theta + P(\omega_2) p(x_n/\omega_2) \tag{5.26}$$

The forms of $p(x_n/\theta, \omega_1)$ and $p(x_n/\omega_2)$ being given, equation (5.23) can be computed recursively for every quantized value of θ.

The method can be easily extended to the multiple pattern class case. Assume that each class has one random parameter, θ_i. Then

$$p_n(x_{n+1}/\omega_i) = \int p(x/\theta_i, \omega_i) p_n(\theta_i) d\theta \tag{5.27}$$

$$p_n(\theta_i) = p_{n-1}(\theta_i) \left[\frac{p(x_n/\theta_i, \omega_i) P(\omega_i) + \sum_{j \neq i} p_{n-1}(x_n/\omega_j) P(\omega_j)}{\sum_j p_{n-1}(x_n/\omega_j) P(\omega_j)} \right] \tag{5.28}$$

Equation (5.28) has the same recursive form as obtained for the two pattern class case. If all $P(\omega_i)$, $i = 1, \ldots, m$ are assumed equal, then $p_0(\theta_i)$ must be different, otherwise $p_n(\theta_i)$ would be the same for all classes and the system will learn nothing.

For a slowly time-varying random parameter, delete the subscript i and assume $\theta_{n+1} = \theta_n + \Delta_n$, where Δ_n is a random increment, then by the convolutional integral,

$$p_n(\theta_{n+1}) = \int p(\theta_{n+1} - \theta_n) p_n(\theta_n)\, d\theta_n \tag{5.29}$$

the required a posteriori parameter density can be computed. The above discussion can be easily extended to the case that the successive measurements are Markov-dependent.[7]

6. Estimation of Mixture Parameters

If the a priori parameter statistics are not considered, the maximum likelihood estimate may be used. For supervised estimation, the maximum likelihood estimates of parameters, which generally are not in recursive form, are the same as those discussed in mathematical statistics. We consider in this section the unsupervised maximum likelihood estimate. Although the samples are not classified, each sample belongs to the mixture of probability densities,

$$p(x) = \sum_{i=1}^{m} P(\omega_i) p(x/\omega_i) \tag{5.30}$$

which is generally a multimodal distribution. The decision boundaries among all pattern classes may be estimated. This amounts to the estimation of the parameters of the decision rule and requires the decomposition of the mixture into m component probability densities. Alternately, the parameters of certain classes may be estimated from the unclassified samples.

Consider two pattern classes and the one-dimensional measurement of Gaussian densities with the same variances but different means. The two probability densities are

$$p(x/\omega_i) = \eta(\mu_i, \sigma^2) = \frac{1}{\sqrt{2\pi}\,\sigma} \exp - \frac{(x - \mu_i)^2}{2\sigma^2}, i = 1, 2$$

Let n_1 and n_2 be the number of unclassified samples belonging to class 1 and class 2 respectively and let $n = n_1 + n_2$. In the supervised estimation, the means are estimated from the samples of a known classification,

$$\hat{\mu}_i = \frac{1}{n_i} \sum_{k=1}^{n_i} x_k, \quad i = 1, 2 \tag{5.31}$$

and the threshold is estimated from $\hat{\mu} = \frac{1}{2}(\hat{\mu}_1 + \hat{\mu}_2)$. The estimator $\hat{\mu}$ is unbiased with variance σ_s^2 given by

$$\sigma_s^2 = \frac{\sigma^2}{n}\left[\frac{n^2}{4n_1(n-n_2)}\right] \tag{5.32}$$

which has a minimum value σ^2/n. Now assume we have merely n samples without knowing their classification. Expressed in terms of its component (unimodal) Gaussian densities, the resultant bimodal distribution is

$$p(x) = \frac{1}{2}\left[\eta(\mu_1, \sigma^2) + \eta(\mu_2, \sigma^2)\right] = \frac{1}{\sqrt{2\pi}}\, e^{-(\alpha^2/2\sigma^2)}\, e^{-[(x-\mu)^2/2\sigma^2]} \cdot \cosh\left[\frac{\alpha}{\sigma^2}(x-\mu)\right] \tag{5.33}$$

where $\mu = \mu_2 - \alpha = \mu_1 + \alpha$. Note that the bimodal form of the distribution does not become evident unless $|\mu_2 - \mu_1| > 2\sigma$. The sample mean,

$$\hat{\mu}_n = \frac{1}{n}\sum_{k=1}^{n} x_k \tag{5.34}$$

is an unbiased estimate of the overall mean. Note that equation (5.31) is the maximum likelihood estimate of the mean of each class but equation (5.34) is not a maximum likelihood estimate. The distribution for this unbiased estimator is asymptotically Gaussian, and for any n its variance is

$$\sigma_u^2 = \frac{1}{n}(\sigma^2 + \alpha^2) = \frac{\sigma^2}{n}(1 + \gamma^2) \tag{5.35}$$

Here γ^2 is the "signal-to-noise" ratio. The sample mean given by equation (5.34) converges for all values of γ^2 and is especially effective for the small values. It is interesting to note that for the finite n, small γ, and $n_1 = n_2$, σ_s^2 could be larger than σ_u^2. As $\gamma \to 0$, the sample mean given by equation (5.34) is the best estimator. The sample mean can be easily updated by writing

$$\hat{\mu}_{n+1} = \frac{n\hat{\mu}_n + x_{n+1}}{n+1} \tag{5.36}$$

The decision rule is to decide on class 1 if $x_{n+1} > \hat{\mu}_{n+1}$ and class 2 otherwise. The maximum likelihood estimator of the overall mean can be obtained by setting to zero the partial derivatives of the logarithm of the likelihood function, i.e., the probability density given by equation (5.33) with respect to the parameter μ. The result can be closely approximated[8] by

$$\hat{\mu}' = \frac{1}{n} \sum_{k=1}^{n} x_k - \frac{|\alpha|}{n} H \tag{5.37}$$

where H is the difference between the number of x_k greater than $\hat{\mu}'$ and the number less than $\hat{\mu}'$. H can be estimated by comparing all x_k with $\hat{\mu}_n$ given by equation (3). When α is not known, it can be estimated from

$$|\hat{\alpha}| = \frac{1}{n-1} \sum_{k=1}^{n} |x_k - \hat{\mu}_n| \tag{5.38}$$

The above discussion has been extended to the case of multidimensional measurement with Gaussian densities.[8,9]

Generally there are three basic problems confronting the mixture approach to the unsupervised estimation. Having given the overall probability density of the mixture, under what conditions is it possible to break the mixture apart into its component distributions or to estimate the parameters of the decision rule? This is the identifiability problem discussed in appendix C. The second problem is concerned with the representation of the actual desired parameters in terms of suitable parameters of the overall distribution. For a multivariate Gaussian distribution, for example, the problem is to establish the relationships among the mean vectors and covariance matrices of the individual Gaussian distributions and the moments of the overall distribution. The third problem is concerned with obtaining good estimators for the parameters. The maximum likelihood estimate is most frequently used. Some ad hoc procedures such as to reduce the problem to an essentially supervised one will simplify the procedure, although the optimality is not guaranteed.

7. Decision-Directed Estimation

The performance of the supervised estimation is generally better than that of the unsupervised estimation. The recognition machine may use the samples classified by the machine itself and the supervised estimation is obtained as if the samples were correctly classified. This is called the decision-directed estimation, which has exactly the same structure as the supervised estimation. The main difference between these two systems is in the classifications of the learning measurements, which may not be correct in the decision-directed estimation because the system is likely to make errors. While in supervised estimation, such classifications are all correct. Since the decision-directed system makes mistakes, the estimated parameters do not necessarily converge to their true values. The condition for convergence and the performance are the two major considerations for the decision-directed system. The supervised estimation provides a lower bound for the probability of misclassification of the decision-directed system.

In comparison with the other unsupervised estimations, the decision-directed method requires the least amount of implementation. The method does not depend on the number of pattern classes and is not restricted to the Bayesian system. Various decision-directed methods have been examined: Scudder,[10] Chen,[11] Patrick and Costello,[12] and Agrawala[13] considered the performances of Bayesian systems and examined the convergence problem.† Davisson and Schwartz[14] obtained the probability of runaway or divergence of the estimation process. Kashyap,[15] Duda and Singleton[16] considered the decision-directed method in the deterministic classification problem. The possibility of switching from supervised estimation to unsupervised estimation using the decision-directed method has also been examined.[5]

8. Remarks

The supervised estimations discussed in this chapter fall primarily on the Bayes framework. This subject is closely related to Kalman filtering[17] which plays an important role in control theory. Several other Bayesian estimations have also been examined (see, e.g., references 18 and 19). The problems that remain are the required a priori statistics and the rate of convergence.

The unsupervised estimation is a relatively new area of research which is now also useful in cluster analysis. A comparison of some unsupervised estimation methods is made by Spragins.[20] Patrick and Hancock[21] considered the estimation of mixture densities by using a multidimensional histogram method. Some experimental self-correcting results were reported by Nagy and Shelton.[22] The unsupervised estimation requires more restrictive conditions for convergence as compared with the supervised estimation. There may still be some asymptotic bias even if the unsupervised estimate converges. Again the rates of convergence of the unsupervised estimates remain to be examined theoretically.

PROBLEMS

1. Write an expression of the a posteriori likelihood function $p(x/\omega_i)$ when only the mean vector is unknown and updated by equation (5.8).
2. For multivariate Gaussian density with zero mean vector and unknown covariance matrix as discussed in section 2, prove that the a posteriori likelihood function is given by

$$\log p(x, x_1, x_2, \ldots, x_n) = -\frac{d}{2}\log 2\pi - \frac{1}{2}\log|\alpha_n|$$

$$-\frac{\nu_n}{2}\log\left(1 + \operatorname{tr}\frac{xx'}{\nu_n}\alpha_n^{-1}\right) + \log\frac{\Gamma\left(\frac{\nu_n}{2}\right)}{\Gamma\left(\frac{\nu_{n-d}}{2}\right)\left(\frac{\nu_n}{2}\right)^{d/2}} \qquad \text{(P.1)}$$

†It is agreed that the convergence is assumed with a good initial knowledge of the parameters.

Obtain an asymptotic expression of equation (P.1) by using Stirling's approximation to the last term of equation (P.1).

3. The result of problem 1 as applied to a two-pattern class recognition problem is an optimum threshold recognition system which can be realized by an adjustable threshold function. Let $\bar{x}$ and $\bar{y}$ be the sample averages of the learning samples of the two classes and x be an unclassified sample. Assume $\mu_0 = 0, K = I$, and $\phi_0 = kI$ where k is a constant.
   a. Determine the threshold function.
   b. Evaluate the asymptotic probability of misrecognition and interpret the result. See reference 27.
4. Consider the Bayesian estimation with the unknown mean vector updated by equation (5.8). Construct a new sequence of measurements $z_1, z_2, \ldots$, etc. given by

$$z_1 = x_1$$

$$z_2 = \tfrac{1}{2}(x_2 + x_3)$$

$$z_3 = \tfrac{1}{3}(x_4 + x_5 + x_6)$$

$$\cdots$$

$$z_k = \frac{1}{k}\left[\frac{x_{k(k-1)}}{2} + 1 + \cdots + \frac{x_{k(k+1)}}{2}\right]$$

Compare the mean-squared errors using the sequence $x_i, i = 1, 2, \ldots$ and the sequence $z_i, i = 1, 2, \ldots$.

5. Consider two pattern classes of the multivariate Gaussian densities with unequal covariance matrices. The individual mean vectors are $\mu_1 = \mu - \alpha$, $\mu_2 = \mu + \alpha$ and the covariance matrices are $\Sigma = [\sigma_{ij}]$ and $\Omega = [\omega_{ij}]$. Obtain the relationships among the means and covariance matrices of the individual densities and various moments of the overall mixture of the two densities for the following cases:
   a. Diagonal matrices—all unknown
   b. General matrices—one mean known
   c. General matrices—equal but unknown matrices
   d. General matrices—unknown and unequal matrices, equal means

REFERENCES

1. Braverman, D. "Machine Learning and Automatic Pattern Recognition." Stanford Electronics Laboratories Technical Report 2003-1, February 1961.
2. Keehn, D. G. "A Note on Learning for Gaussian Properties," *IEEE Trans. on Information Theory,* IT-11 (January 1965), 126–132.
3. Spragins, J. D., Jr. "Reproducing Distributions for Machine Learning." Stanford Electronics Laboratories Technical Report 6103-7, November 1963.

4. Robbins, H. "The Empirical Bayes Approach to Statistical Decision Problems." *Ann. Math. Stat.*, 35 (1964), 1–20.
5. Chen, C. H. "A Theory of Bayesian Learning Systems." *IEEE Trans. on Systems Science and Cybernetics*, SSC-5 (January 1969), 30–37.
6. Abramson, N. and D. Braverman. "Learning to Recognize Patterns in a Random Environment." *IRE Trans. on Information Theory*, IT-8 (September 1962), 558–563.
7. Fralick, S. C. "Learning to Recognize Patterns Without a Teacher." *IEEE Trans. on Information Theory*, IT-13 (January 1967), 57–64.
8. Cooper, D. B. and P. W. Cooper. "Nonsupervised Adaptive Signal Detection and Pattern Recognition." *Information and Control*, 7 (1964), 416–444.
9. Cooper, P. W. "Some Topics on Nonsupervised Adaptive Detection for Multivariate Normal Distributions." In *Computer and Information Sciences*, vol. II. Academic Press, New York, 1967.
10. Scudder, H. J., III. "Probability of Error of Some Adaptive Pattern-Recognition Machines." *IEEE Trans. on Information Theory*, IT-11 (July 1965), 363–371.
11. Chen, C. H. "A Note on Sequential Decision Approach to Pattern Recognition and Machine Learning." *Information and Control*, 9 (1966), 549–562.
12. Patrick, E. A. and J. P. Costello. "Asymptotic Probability of Error Using Two Decision-Directed Estimators for Two Unknown Mean Vectors." *IEEE Trans. on Information Theory* (correspondence), IT-14 (January 1968), 160–162.
13. Agrawala, A. K. "Learning with a Probabilistic Teacher." *IEEE Trans. on Information Theory*, IT-16 (July 1970), 373–379.
14. Davisson, L. D. and S. C. Schwartz. "Analysis of a Decision-Directed Receiver with Unknown Priors." *IEEE Trans. on Information Theory*, IT-16 (May 1970), 270–276.
15. Kashyap, R. L. "Recursive Algorithms for Classification Using Pattern Misclassified Samples." *IEEE Proc. 7th Symposium on Adaptive Processes*, Los Angeles, December 1968.
16. Duda, R. O. and R. C. Singleton. "Training a Threshold Logic Unit with Imperfectly Classified Patterns." Presented at the WESCON Convention, Los Angeles, California, August 1964.
17. Kalman, R. E. "A New Approach to Linear Filtering and Prediction Problems." *Journal of Basic Engineering*, 82-D: 35 (1960).
18. Beisner, H. M. "A Recursive Bayesian Approach to Pattern Recognition." *Pattern Recognition Journal*, Pergamon Press, 1 (1968), 13–31.
19. Lin, T. T. and S. S. Yau. "Bayesian Approach to the Optimization of Adaptive Systems." *IEEE Trans. on Systems Science and Cybernetics*, SSC-3 (November 1967).
20. Spragins, J. "Learning Without a Teacher." *IEEE Trans. on Information Theory*, IT-12 (April 1966), 223–229.
21. Patrick, E. A. and J. C. Hancock. "Nonsupervised Sequential Classification and Recognition of Patterns." *IEEE Trans. on Information Theory*, IT-12 (July 1966), 362–372.

22. Nagy, G. and G. L. Shelton, Jr. "Self-Corrective Character Recognition Systems." *IEEE Trans. on Information Theory,* IT-12 (April 1966), 215–222.
23. Berk, R. H. "Asymptotic Properties of Sequential Probability Ratio Test." Ph.D. dissertation, Department of Statistics, Harvard Univ., Cambridge, Mass., April 1964.
24. Berk, R. H. "Limiting Behavior of Posterior Distributions when the Model is Incorrect." *Ann. Math. Stat.*, 37 (February 1966), 51–58.
25. Teicher, H. "Identifiability of Finite Mixtures." *Ann. Math. Stat.,* 34 (1963), 1265–1269.
26. Yakowitz, S. J. and J. D. Spragins. "On the Identifiability of Finite Mixtures." *Ann. Math. Stat.,* 39 (1968), 209–214.
27. Braverman, D. J. "Theories of Pattern Recognition." In *Advances in Communication Systems,* vol. 1, edited by A. V. Balakieshnan. Academic Press, New York, 1964.

Bibliography

1. Braverman, D. "Learning Filters for Optimum Pattern Recognition." *IRE Trans. on Information Theory,* IT-8 (July 1962).
2. Chien, Y. T. and K. S. Fu. "On Bayesian Learning and Stochastic Approximation." *IEEE Trans. on Systems Science and Cybernetics,* SSC-3 (June 1967), 28–38.
3. Cooper, D. B. and J. H. Freeman. "On the Asymptotic Improvement in the Outcome of Supervised Learning Provided by Additional Nonsupervised Learning." *IEEE Trans. on Computers,* C-19 (November 1970), 1055–1063.
4. Cunningham, D. R. and A. M. Breipohl. "Empirical Bayesian Learning." *IEEE Trans. on Systems, Man, and Cybernetics,* SMC-1 (January 1971), 19–33.
5. Daly, R. F. "Adaptive Binary Detectors." Stanford Electronic Laboratories Technical Report 2003-2, June 1961.
6. Daly, R. F. "The Adaptive Binary-Detection Problem on the Real Line." Stanford Electronics Laboratories Technical Report 2003-3, February 1962.
7. Gaarder, N. T. "Recursive Relation for the Inverse of the Covariance Matrix in Optimal Pattern Classifiers." *IEEE Trans. on Information Theory*, Vol. IT-11, January 1965.
8. Hasselblad, V. "Estimation of Parameters for a Mixture of Normal Distributions." *Technometrics*, 8, August 1966.
9. Hilborn, C. G., Jr. and D. G. Lainiotis. "Optimal Estimation in the Presence of Unknown Parameters." *IEEE Trans. on Systems Science and Cybernetics*, SSC-5 (January 1969), 38–43.
10. Hilborn, C. G., Jr. and D. G. Lainiotis. "Optimal Unsupervised Learning Multicategory Dependent Hypotheses Pattern Recognition." *IEEE Trans. on Information Theory*, IT-14 (May 1968), 468–470.
11. Hilborn, C. G., Jr. and D. G. Lainiotis. "Recursive Computations for the Optimal Tracking of Time-Varying Parameters." *IEEE Trans. on Information Theory*, IT-14 (May 1968), 514–515.

12. Ho, Y. C. and A. K. Agrawala. "On the Self–Learning Scheme of Hagy and Shelton." *Proceedings of IEEE* (letter), 55 (October 1967), 1764–1765.
13. Kailath, T. "Sequential Detection of Gaussian Signals in Gaussian Noise." JPL Space Program Summary 36-13, pp. 38–42, 1963.
14. Klinger, A. "Prior Information and Bias in Sequential Estimation." *IEEE Trans. on Automatic Control* (1969).
15. Lainiotis, D. G. "Sequential Structure and Parameter-Adaptive Pattern Recognition. Part I: Supervised Learning." *IEEE Trans. on Information Theory,* IT-16 (September 1970), 548–556.
16. Lainiotis, D. G. "Supervised Learning Sequential Structure and Parameter Adaptive Pattern Recognition: Discrete Data Case." *IEEE Trans. on Information Theory,* IT-17 (January 1971), 106–110.
17. Morishita, I. and R. Takanuki. "Steady-State Behavior of a Nonsupervised Learning Algorithm for Multicategory Pattern Classification." *IEEE Trans. on Systems, Man, and Cybernetics,* SMC-2 (January 1972), 49–58.
18. Patrick, E. A. "On a Class of Unsupervised Estimation Problems." *IEEE Trans. on Information Theory,* IT-14 (May 1968), 407–415.
19. Patrick, E. A., J. P. Costello, and F. C. Monds. "Decision-Directed Estimation of a Two Class Decision Boundary." *IEEE Trans. on Computers,* C-19 (March 1970), 197–205.
20. Patrick, E. A. and J. P. Costello. "On Unsupervised Estimation Algorithms." *IEEE Trans. on Information Theory,* IT-16 (September 1970), 556–569.
21. Pugachev, V. S. "A Bayes Approach to the Theory of Learning Systems." Preprints, *Proc. IFAC Conference, 3rd.* June 1966.
22. Rajasekaran, P. K. and M. D. Srinath. "Structure and Parameter Adaptive Pattern Recognition with Supervised Learning: A New Formulation." *IEEE Trans. on Information Theory,* IT-17 (July 1971), 499–500.
23. Sammon, J. W. "An Adaptive Technique for Multiple Signal Detection and Identification." In *Pattern Recognition,* edited by L. Kanal. Thompson, Washington, D.C., 1968.
24. Shanmugam, K. "A Parametric Procedure for Learning with an Imperfect Teacher." *IEEE Trans. on Information Theory,* IT-18 (March 1972), 300–302.
25. Shanmugam, K. and A. M. Breipohl. "An Error Correcting Procedure for Learning with an Imperfect Teacher." *IEEE Trans. on Systems, Man, and Cybernetics,* SMC-1 (July 1971), 223–229.
26. Stanat, D. F. "Nonsupervised Pattern Recognition through the Decomposition of Probability Functions." Sensory Intelligence Laboratory Technical Report, Univ. of Michigan, April 1966.
27. Tamura, S., S. Higuchi, and K. Tanaka. "On the Recognition of Time-Varying Patterns Using Learning Procedures." *IEEE Trans. on Information Theory,* IT-17 (July 1971), 445–452.
28. Yakowitz, S. J. "Unsupervised Learning and the Identification of Finite Mixtures." *IEEE Trans. on Information Theory,* IT-16 (May 1970), 330–338.

CHAPTER VI

Recursive Algorithms Using Stochastic Approximation

1. Introduction

In statistical pattern recognition, the measurement or observation error is considered as due to the stochastic nature of the problem. Our best knowledge about the measurement or observation is expressed in terms of the probability density function. The unknown parameters are then estimated by using all available measurements and the probability density function. The estimates so obtained may or may not be recursive. Computationally recursive estimates would be feasible as long as they are rapidly convergent. Stochastic approximation approach starts with a recursive expression for successive estimation of a sought quantity, which may be the unknown parameters or an unknown function. This recursive expression, which is subject to certain constraints, provides improved approximation or estimation of the quantity to be determined.

Let x be a random variable depending on a parameter θ. Denote the nth estimate of θ by $\hat{\theta}_n$. Let $f(x_n)$ be a function of x_n such that

$$E\,[f(x_n)] = \theta;\;\; E\,[\hat{\theta}_n - \hat{\theta}\,]^2 < \infty \tag{6.1}$$

are satisfied. The following stochastic approximation algorithm is proposed for the estimation of θ:

$$\hat{\theta}_{n+1} = \hat{\theta}_n + a_{n+1}\,[f(x_n) - \hat{\theta}_n] \tag{6.2}$$

When $\{a_n\}$ is chosen such that

$$0 < a_n < 1, \;\; \sum_{n=1}^{\infty} a_n = \infty, \;\; \text{and} \;\; \sum_{n=1}^{\infty} a_n^2 < \infty, \tag{6.3}$$

the successive estimate $\hat{\theta}_{n+1}$ approaches the quantity θ in the mean square sense and with probability 1.

The use of stochastic approximation to determine the supervised and the unsupervised estimations will be discussed in this chapter. Mathematical background on stochastic approximation will be introduced as needed. For a more detailed treatment of stochastic approximation algorithms, the reader is referred to Albert and Gardner,[1] Sakrison,[2] and Fu.[3] The stochastic approximation method was first proposed by Robbins and Monro[4] for estimating the zero of an unknown regression function given by

$$M(\theta) = \int x\, p(x \mid \theta) dx = \text{constant} \tag{6.4}$$

Following Robbins and Monro's formulation, Kiefer and Wolfowitz[5] considered the estimation of the extremum of an unknown regression function, which is equivalent to estimate the unique root of the equation

$$M'(\theta) = 0 \tag{6.5}$$

Dvoretzky[6] suggested a generalized stochastic approximation procedure for patterns perturbed by an "additive noise." Methods of improving the convergence rate were proposed by Kesten,[7] Fabian,[8] and others. Dynamic stochastic approximation was considered by Dupac[9] for estimating the unknown parameter which was time-varying.

2. Supervised Parameter Estimation Using Stochastic Approximation

A. Estimating the a priori probability $P(\omega_i)$

Let $x_1, x_2, \ldots, x_n$ be a sequence of classified learning samples and n_i be the number of times that the samples are from class ω_i,

$$\sum_{i=1}^{m} n = n$$

and

$$\sum_{i=1}^{m} P(\omega_i) = 1$$

If the initial estimate of $P(\omega_i)$ is $P_0(\omega_i)$,

$$0 \leqslant P_0(\omega_i) \leqslant 1, \quad \sum_{i=1}^{m} P_0(\omega_i) = 1$$

then the successive estimates of $P(\omega_i)$ can be formed by the following stochastic approximation algorithm:

$$P_{n+1}(\omega_i) = P_n(\omega_i) + a_{n+1}\left[\frac{n_i}{n} - P_n(\omega_i)\right], \quad i = 1, 2, \ldots, m \tag{6.6}$$

where a_{n+1} satisfies the conditions given by equation (6.3).

Since $E(n_i) = nP(\omega_i)$, the conditions given by equation (6.1),

$$E\left(\frac{n_i}{n}\right) = P(\omega_i)$$

and

$$E\,[P_n(\omega_i) - P(\omega_i)]^2 \leqslant 2E\left[P_n(\omega_i) - \frac{n_i}{n}\right]^2 + 2E\left[\frac{n_i}{n} - P(\omega_i)\right]^2 < \infty$$

are satisfied. It is noted that, in general, the unknown parameter is a vector and conditions somewhat stronger than those given by equation (6.1) are required for convergence. According to Dvoretzky's theorem, the following conditions must be satisfied for convergence:

$$\lim_{n\to\infty} E\,\{\|\hat{\theta}_n - \theta\|^2\} = 0 \tag{6.7}$$

and

$$P\,\{\lim_{n\to\infty} \hat{\theta}_n = \theta\} = 1 \tag{6.8}$$

B. *Estimating the mean vector θ of a Gaussian distribution*

Consider a special case when $\phi_0 = \alpha^{-1}K$. The following is a stochastic approximation algorithm for estimating the mean vector:

$$\mu_n = \mu_{n-1} + a_n(x_n - \mu_{n-1}) \tag{6.9}$$

where a_n is chosen as $a_n = \phi_{n-1}(\phi_{n-1} + K)^{-1} = (n + \alpha)^{-1} < 1 \sum_{n=1}^{\infty} a_n = \infty$, $\sum_{n=1}^{\infty} a_n^2 < \infty$; thus equation (6.3) is satisfied. Also

$$E\,\{\|\mu_n - \theta\|^2\} \leqslant 2E\,\{\|\mu_n - x_n\|^2\} + 2E\,\{\|x_n - \theta\|^2\}$$

where the second term on the right-hand side of the above equation is bounded above by a constant and the first term is

$$E\,\{\|x_n - \mu_n\|^2\} = E\,\{(1 - a_1)(1 - a_2)\cdots(1 - a_n)\|x_n - \mu_0\|^2\} < \infty$$

Thus equation (6.1) is satisfied. Similarly equations (6.7) and (6.8) can be shown to be satisfied.[10]

C. *Estimating the covariance matrix ϕ of a Gaussian distribution*

The following is a stochastic approximation algorithm for estimating ϕ,

$$\phi_n = \phi_{n-1} + a_n (x_n x_n' - \phi_{n-1}) \tag{6.10}$$

where $a_n = (n + \nu_0)^{-1}$ satisfies the conditions for convergence and ν_0 is a constant.

D. *Estimating the parameter p of a binomial distribution*

Consider the binomial distribution $b(n, p)$ with parameter p being unknown. Let $x_1, x_2, \ldots, x_n$ denote the measurements where each x (1 or 0) is drawn from a distribution $b(1, p)$, $0 < p < 1$. If $r = \sum_{i=1}^{n} x_i$, then r is the number of ones (success) at the nth measurement which has the binomial distribution $b(n,p)$. That is, the conditional density function of r, given p, is

$$p(r/p) = \binom{n}{r} p^r (1 - p)^{n-r}, \quad r = 0, 1, 2, \ldots, n \tag{6.11}$$

The reproducing distribution for p is the beta probability density function

$$p_0(p) = [B(r_0, n_0 - r_0]^{-1} p^{r_0 - 1} (1 - p)^{n_0 - r_0 - 1} \tag{6.12}$$

where $B(r_0, n_0 - r_0)$ is the beta function with parameters r_0 and n_0, which are assigned positive constants reflecting the initial knowledge about the unknown parameter p. A stochastic approximation algorithm for estimating p is

$$p_n = p_{n-1} + a_n \left(\frac{r}{n} - p_{n-1}\right) \tag{6.13}$$

where $a_n = (n + n_0)^{-1}$ satisfies the conditions for convergence.

It is noted that by selecting the sequence $\{a_n\}$ properly, the stochastic approximation algorithms equations (6.9), (6.10), and (6.13) are consistent with the Bayesian estimations discussed in chapter 5. The stochastic approximation algorithm, however, has a much larger flexibility in selecting $\{a_n\}$ as long as a rapid convergence is possible.

3. Estimation of the Probability Density Function

The probability distribution function or the probability density required for categorization is frequently unknown. They can be approximated by a finite series of M terms,

$$f(x) = \sum_{i=1}^{M} \alpha_i \psi_i(x) = \alpha' \phi(x) \tag{6.14}$$

where $f(x)$ denotes the probability distribution, the probability density function, or the a posteriori probability, α is the unknown vector parameter, and $\phi(x)$ is the vector of functions, $\phi(x) = [\psi_1(x), \psi_2(x), \ldots, \psi_M(x)]$, where $\psi_i(x)$, $i = 1, 2, \ldots, M$, is a system of orthonormal functions, i.e.,

$$\begin{aligned} \int \psi_i(x) \psi_j(x) dx &= 0, \quad i \neq j \\ &= 1, \quad i = j \end{aligned} \tag{6.15}$$

A stochastic approximation algorithm for estimating α is

$$\alpha_{n+1} = \alpha_n + a_n \, [\phi(x) - \alpha_n] \tag{6.16}$$

where $\{a_n\}$ satisfies the conditions, equation (6.3), for convergence. If $f(x)$ denotes the a posteriori probability for a two pattern class problem, then two stochastic approximation algorithms minimizing the mean square error, $E[f(x) - \alpha' \phi(x)]^2$ can be stated as follows.[11]

ALGORITHM I. $\alpha_{n+1} = \alpha_n + a_n \phi_n(x) \, [z_n - \alpha_n' \phi_n(x)]$ (6.17)

where a_n satisfies equation (6.3) and

$$\begin{aligned} z_n = 1;\ & x_n \in \omega_A \text{ (class A)} \\ 0;\ & x_n \notin \omega_A \end{aligned}$$

ALGORITHM II. $\alpha_{n+1} = \alpha_n + R_{n+1} \, \phi_n(x) \, [z_n - \alpha_n' \, \phi_n(x)]$ (6.18)

where $R_{n+1}^{-1} = R_n^{-1} + \phi_n(x) \, \phi_n(x)'$ (6.19)

Equation (6.19) can also be written as

$$R_{n+1} = R_n - R_n \, \phi_n(x) \, [\phi_n(x)' R_n \, \phi_n(x) + I]^{-1} \, \phi_n(x)' R_n \tag{6.20}$$

and the initial matrix can be chosen as $R_0 = \beta I$ where β is a constant. Algorithms I and II say that the $(n + 1)$th approximation of α consists of two terms; (a) the nth approximation of α and (b) a correction term that is proportional to the difference between the ideal probability of classification (i.e., 1 or 0) and the estimated probability of classification [i.e., $\alpha_n' \, \phi_n(x)$]. The factors $a_n \phi_n(x)$ and $R_{n+1} \phi_n(x)$ specify how the correction is to be distributed and weighted. Initially, when the approximation $\alpha_n' \, \phi_n(x)$ is not expected to be good, considerable weight is attached to the correction (i.e., both a_n and R_{n+1} are large). As the estimate improves, less and less weight is attached to the difference between z_n and $\alpha_n' \phi_n(x)$ since $[a_n - \alpha_n' \phi_n(x)]$ is now close to the irreducible difference between the ideal classification probability (i.e., 1 or 0) and the true probability of $P(A/x)$. Here we denote $f(x) = P(A/x)$.

Another way to look at both algorithms is to note that the differential square error with respect to α_n is given by

$$\nabla_{\alpha_n} [z_i - \alpha_n' \phi_n(x)]^2 = -2\, \phi_n(x)\, [z_n - \alpha_n' \phi_n(x)] \tag{6.21}$$

Then both algorithms can be regarded as descent schemes which proceed in the direction to reduce the current difference between the ideal performance and the actual performance in classification. Alternatively, we may look upon z_n as the nth noisy measurement of the linear functional $\alpha' \phi_n(x)$ for which we are interested in estimating its parameter α. Algorithm II can be seen as a recursive least square fit to the parameter α, using the measurements z_n. Algorithm I can be interpreted directly as a stochastic approximation sequence satisfying the conditions of Dvoretzky's theorem[6] for the convergence sequence. Algorithm II has a better convergence property since it minimizes the mean-squared error $E\,[f(x) - \alpha' \phi(x)]^2$ at *each* stage, whereas algorithm I merely follows the gradient of equation (6.21) at each stage.

4. Unsupervised Estimation Using Stochastic Approximation

The stochastic approximation procedures can be applied to estimate the parameters in a mixture distribution. It is assumed that there exist unbiased estimates of certain statistics $H = \{H(x)\}$ for the mixture (e.g., first moment, second moment, etc.). The functional relationship between H and the parameter sets is known. Additional equations relating the parameter sets are available to give a unique solution for the unknown parameter. An example is presented in the following to illustrate this so-called moment estimator method.

Consider two pattern classes. Let $P(\omega_1) = P$, and $P(\omega_2) = 1 - P$. Each component density function $p(x/\omega_i)$ is characterized by its mean m_i and variance σ_i^2, $i = 1, 2$. The mixture density function characterized by $\theta = \{m_1, \sigma_1^2, m_2, \sigma_2^2\}$ and P is given by

$$p(x/\theta, P) = Pp(x/m_1, \sigma_1^2, \omega_1) + (1 - P)p(x/m_2, \sigma_2^2, \omega_2) \tag{6.22}$$

The problem is to estimate the unknown parameters θ and P from the unclassified learning samples $x_1, x_2, \ldots, x_n$.

Let the first, second, and third moment of x with respect to $p(x/\theta, P)$ be computed from equation (6.22),

$$E(x) = Pm_1 + (1 - P)m_2 = P(m_1 - m_2) + m_2 \tag{6.23}$$

$$E(x^2) = P(m_1^2 + \sigma_1^2) + (1 - P)(m_2^2 + \sigma_2^2) \tag{6.24}$$

$$E(x^3) = P(m_1^3 + 3m_1\sigma_1^2) + (1 - P)(m_2^3 + 3m_2\sigma_2^2) \tag{6.25}$$

Case I. Consider that $\sigma_1^2 = \sigma_2^2 = \sigma^2$ and P are fixed and known. Let $m_2 = 0$ and m_1 be the parameter to be estimated. From equation (6.23), m_1 can be solved directly,

$$m_1 = \frac{E(x)}{P} \tag{6.26}$$

where an asymptotically unbiased estimate of $E(x)$ can be obtained from the following stochastic approximation algorithm,

$$E_n(x) = E_{n-1}(x) + a_n\,[x_n - E_{n-1}(x)] \tag{6.27}$$

where a_n satisfies equation (6.3). The true value of m_1 is estimated in the mean square sense and with probability 1, i.e.,

$$\lim_{n\to\infty} E\left\{\left[\frac{E_n(x)}{P} - m_1\right]^2\right\} = 0 \tag{6.28}$$

$$P\left\{\lim_{n\to\infty} \frac{E_n(x)}{P} = m_1\right\} = 1 \tag{6.29}$$

Case II. Let $\sigma_1^2 = \sigma_2^2 = \sigma^2$ be known and $m_2 = 0$. The problem is to estimate P and m_1. Equations (6.23) and (6.24) give

$$m_1 = \frac{[E(x^2) - \sigma^2]}{E(x)} \tag{6.30}$$

$$P = \frac{E(x)}{m_1} \tag{6.31}$$

The stochastic approximation procedure can be applied as in case I to give asymptotically unbiased estimates of the moments $E(x)$ and $E(x^2)$, which in turn will give the unbiased estimates of m_1 and P.

Case III. Let $m_2 = 0$ and let m_1, P, and $\sigma^2 (= \sigma_1^2 = \sigma_2^2)$ be the parameters to be estimated through the first three moments. Equations (6.23), (6.24), and (6.25) become

$$E(x) = Pm_1 \tag{6.32}$$

$$E(x^2) = Pm_1^2 + \sigma^2 \tag{6.33}$$

$$E(x^3) = P(m_1^3 + 3m_1\sigma^2) \tag{6.34}$$

Solving equations (6.32), (6.33), and (6.34) simultaneously for m_1 gives

$$m_1^2 - 3E(x)m_1 + 3E(x^2) - \frac{E(x^3)}{E(x)} = 0 \tag{6.35}$$

which is a second-order equation in m_1. In order that m_1 has a unique solution, the discriminant,

$$9E^2(x) - 12E(x^2) + \frac{4E(x^3)}{E(x)} = m_1^2\,(3P - 2)^2$$

must be zero. Since $m_1 \neq 0$, $P = \frac{2}{3}$. For $P = \frac{2}{3}$, σ^2 and m_1 can be estimated through equations (6.32), (6.33), and (6.34) by defining the stochastic approximation algorithm to give asymptotically unbiased estimates of $E(x)$, $E(x^2)$, and $E(x^3)$. If $P \neq \frac{2}{3}$, P must also be estimated and the problem will have multiple solutions.

5. Comparison of Three Stochastic Approximation Algorithms

In this section we compare the performance of three stochastic approximation algorithms of the Dvoretzky type given by equation (6.2). The pattern x_n is given by

$$x_n = \theta + \xi_n \tag{6.36}$$

where ξ_n is a random component of zero mean noise. Here x_n is a scalar and x_n's can be considered as elements of a random process with a fixed but unknown signal parameter θ to be estimated. Algorithms I and II are given by Fu[3] and algorithm III is given by Sinha and Griscik.[12] The three algorithms are stated as follows and their convergence has been proved in references 3 and 12.

For ***algorithm I***, $f_1(x_n) = x_n$, $a_n = 1/(n + \alpha)$, where α is a constant. The selection of the constant α is arbitrary, but if a priori statistics are known and the process is known to have a noise component of finite variance, denoted as σ^2, then

$$\alpha = \frac{V_0^2}{\sigma^2} \tag{6.37}$$

provides the best convergence, where V_0^2 is the initial value of the expected mean square error.

For ***algorithm II,*** $f_2(x_n) = \frac{1}{n} \sum_{i=1}^{n} x_n$ is the sample mean and

$$a_n = \frac{n}{n(n+1)/2 + \alpha} \tag{6.38}$$

provides the best convergence, where α is again dependent upon a priori statistics given by equation (6.37).

For ***algorithm III,*** the function f is chosen as

$$f_3(x_n) = |\hat{R}_{x_n}(l)|^{1/2}$$

where $\hat{R}_{x_n}(l)$ is an estimate of the sample autocorrelation function of the samples $x_1, x_2, \ldots, x_n$ with $l - 1 \leqslant n$ and where $|\hat{R}_{x_n}(l)|$ is the absolute value of $\hat{R}_{x_n}(l)$. A large class of noise has the autocorrelation function given by

$$\hat{R}_{\xi_n}(l) = \sum_i \sigma_i^2 e^{-\alpha_i |l|} \tag{6.39}$$

where $|l|$ represents the magnitude of l. As the spectrum of the noise becomes wider, i.e., as it approaches white noise, the autocorrelation function becomes an impulse,

$$\hat{R}_{\xi_n}(l) = \sigma^2 \delta(l)$$

Two sequences of a_n satisfying the convergence condition are:[12]

$$a_n = \frac{1}{n} \tag{6.40a}$$

and

$$a_n = 1 - \left(\frac{1}{n}\right) \tag{6.40b}$$

The expected mean square errors for the three algorithms after $n + 1$ iterations, V_{n+1}, are as follows,

For ***algorithm I,*** $$V_{n+1}^2 = (1 - a_{n+1}) V_n^2 + a_{n+1}^2 \sigma^2 \tag{6.41}$$

For ***algorithm II,*** $$V_{n+1}^2 = (1 - a_{n+1})^2 V_n^2 + a_{n+1}^2 \left(\frac{\sigma^2}{n}\right) \tag{6.42}$$

For *algorithm III*, $V_{n+1}^2 = V_0^2 \left\{ \prod_{i=1}^{n+1} (1 - a_i) \right\}^2$ (6.43)

A plot of these three equations against n for the sequence $a_n = 1/n$ is shown in figure 6.1. In addition, a plot for the sequence $a_n = 1 - (1/n)$ is also shown for the new algorithm. It is seen that the performance (especially the rate of convergence) of algorithm III is better than that of algorithms I and II, particularly if the sequence $a_n = 1 - (1/n)$ is used. It may be noted that for algorithms I and II, the sequence $a_n = 1/n$ may be regarded as optimal in the absence of a priori statistical information.

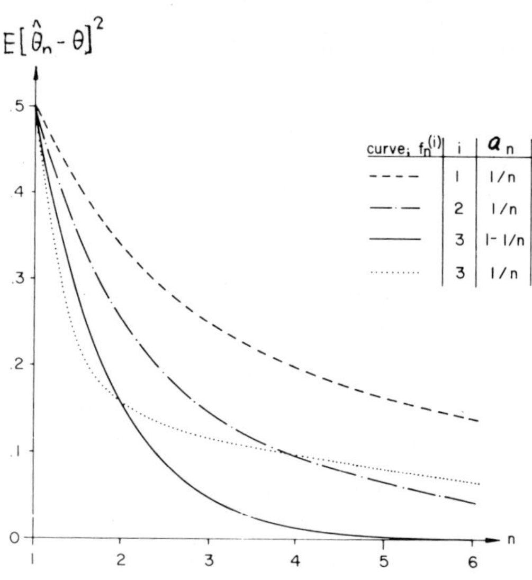

Fig. 6.1 The Expected Mean-Square Error (Normalized at $N = 1$) as a Function of n (Taken from N. K. Sinka and M. P. Griscik, "A Stochastic Approximation Method," *IEEE Transactions on Systems, Man, and Cybernetics*, vol. SMC-1, No. 4, pp. 338–344, October, 1971)

6. Remarks

We have introduced in this chapter the use of stochastic approximation procedures to estimate the unknown parameters and the probability distribution functions (or probability density functions). Providing the convergent sequence $\{a_n\}$ can be found, the desired estimates can be obtained by a stochastic approximation procedure very efficiently and conveniently. The rate of convergence, which is of major concern in practical applications, depends considerably upon the initial guess as well as the sequence $\{a_n\}$.

Probably the most important application of stochastic approximation in pattern recognition is the estimation of probability density functions. The potential function method has been proposed[13,14] so that the potential function itself or its related function will converge to the true probability density function. There is always the unknown parameter involved, which is estimated through the stochastic approximation procedure. The unknown probability density function may also be approximated by the mixture of Gaussian densities. Then the mixture parameters can be estimated by using the stochastic approximation.[15] In addition to minimizing the mean square error as discussed in this chapter, stochastic approximation algorithms may be obtained to minimize an information criterion[15] or the integral square error[11] defined as

$$I(\alpha) = \int [f(x) - \alpha'\phi(x)]^2 \, dx \tag{6.44}$$

where the integration is over the measurement space. $I(\alpha)$ may be transformed into a regression function whose zero crossing point corresponds to the minimum of $I(\alpha)$. The stochastic approximation procedure can be applied to search for such zero crossing point.

PROBLEMS

1. Show that the sequence of the vector parameter α_n defined by equation (6.17) (algorithm I) satisfies the mean square convergence

   $$\lim_{n\to\infty} E\,\{\|\alpha_n - \alpha\|^2\} \to 0$$

   if the following conditions hold:

   a. $E[\phi(x)\phi(x)']$ exists and is positive definite

   b. $\sum_{n=1}^{\infty} a_n = \infty, \quad \sum_{n=1}^{\infty} a_n^2 < \infty$

   c. x_n are sampled independently with the same sampling distribution for all n

2. Show that the sequence of the vector parameter α_n defined by equations (6.18) and (6.19) (algorithm II) satisfies

   $$\lim_{n\to\infty} \alpha_n = \alpha \text{ with probability 1}$$

   if a. $E[\phi(x)\phi(x)']$ exists and is positive definite

   b. $\phi(x_n)$ are independently drawn from the same distribution

REFERENCES

1. Albert, A. and L. A. Gardner, Jr. *Stochastic Approximation and Nonlinear Regression.* M.I.T. Press, Cambridge, Mass., 1966.
2. Sakrison, D. "Stochastic Approximation: A Recursive Method for Solving Regression Problems." In *Advances in Communication Systems, Theory and Applications*, vol. 2, edited by A. V. Balakrishnan, pp. 51–106. Academic Press, New York, 1966.
3. Fu, K. S. *Sequential Methods in Pattern Recognition and Machine Learning*, Academic Press, New York, 1968. Chapter 7 and Appendix F.
4. Robbins, H. and S. Monro. "A Stochastic Approximation Method." *Ann. Math. Stat.*, 22 (1951), 400–407.
5. Kiefer, J. and J. Wolfowitz. "Stochastic Estimation of the Maximum of a Regression Function." *Ann. Math. Stat.*, 23 (1952), 462–466.
6. Dvoretzky, A. "On Stochastic Approximation." In *Proc. Symp. Math. Stat. and Probability 3rd*, vol. 1. Univ. of Calif. Press, Berkeley, 1956.
7. Kesten, H. "Accelerated Stochastic Approximation." *Ann. Math. Stat.*, 29 (1958), 41–59.
8. Fabian, V. "Stochastic Approximation Methods." *Czechoslovak Math. J.* 10 (1960), 123–159.
9. Dupač, V. "A Dynamic Stochastic Approximation Method." *Ann. Math. Stat.*, 26 (1965), 1695–1702.
10. Chien, Y. T. and K. S. Fu. "On Bayesian Learning and Stochastic Approximation." *IEEE Trans. on Systems Science and Cybernetics*, SSC-3 (June 1967), 28–38.
11. Blaydon, C. and Y. C. Ho. "On the Abstraction Problem in Pattern Classification." In *Proc. NEC*, pp. 857–862. October 1966.
12. Sinha, N. K. and M. P. Griscik. "A Stochastic Approximation Method." *IEEE Trans. on Systems, Man, and Cybernetics*, SMC-1 (October 1971), 338–344.
13. Aizerman, M. A., E. M. Braverman, and L. I. Rozonoer. "Theoretical Functions of the Potential Function Method in Pattern Recognition Learning." *Automation and Remote Control*, 25 (June 1964).
14. Aizerman, M. A., E. M. Braverman, and L. I. Rozonoer. "The Probability Problem of Pattern Recognition Learning and the Method of Potential Functions." *Automation and Remote Control*, 25 (September 1964).
15. Young, T. Y. and G. Coraluppi. "Stochastic Estimation of a Mixture of Normal Density Functions Using and Information Criterion." *IEEE Trans. on Information Theory*, IT-16 (March 1970), 258–263.

Bibliography

1. Arkadev, A. G. and E. M. Braverman. *Computers and Pattern Recognition.* Translated from Russian. Thompson, Washington, D.C., 1967.
2. Bashikirov, O. A., E. M. Braverman, and I. B. Muchnik. "Potential Function Algorithms for Pattern Recognition Learning Machines." *Automation and Remote Control*, 25 (May 1964).

3. Blaydon, C. C. "Approximation of Distribution and Density Functions." *Proc. of IEEE* (February 1967), 231–232.
4. Blum, J. A. "Multidimensional Stochastic Approximation." *Ann. Math. Stat.*, 25 (1965), 737–744.
5. Braverman, E. M. "Potential Function Method in the Problem of Learning Pattern Recognition without a Teacher." *Automat. i Telemeh*, 27 (1966), 1748–1770.
6. Chien, Y. T. "Linear and Nonlinear Stochastic Approximation Algorithms for Learning Systems." In "Pattern Recognition and Machine Learning," K. S. Fu, ed., Plenum Press, New York, 1971.
7. Chien, Y. T. and K. S. Fu. "Stochastic Learning of Time-Varying Parameters in Random Environment." *IEEE Trans. on Systems Science and Cybernetics*, SSC-5 (July 1969), 237–246.
8. Cooper, D. B. "Adaptive Pattern Recognition and Signal Detection Using Stochastic Approximation." *IEEE Trans. on Electronic Computers*, EC-13 (June 1964), 306–307.
9. Davisson, L. D. "Convergence Probability Bounds for Stochastic Approximation." *IEEE Trans. on Information Theory*, IT-16 (November 1970), 680–685.
10. DeFigueiredo, R. J. P. "Convergent Algorithms for Pattern Recognition in Nonlinearly Evolving Nonstationary Environment." *Proc. of IEEE*, 56 (February 1968), 188–189.
11. Devyaterikov, I. P., A. I. Propoi, and Y. Z. Tsypkin. "Iterative Learning Algorithms for Pattern Recognition." *Automation and Remote Control*, 1 (January 1967).
12. Fu, K. S. et al. "On the Stochastic Approximation and Related Learning Techniques." Purdue Univ. TR-EE66-6, April 1966.
13. Ho, Y. C. "On Stochastic Approximation Method and Optimal Filtering Theory." Cruft Laboratory Technical Report 387, Harvard Univ., October 1962.
14. Kac, M. "A Note on Learning Signal Detection." *IEEE Trans. on Information Theory* (February 1962), 126–128.
15. Kashyap, R. L. and C. C. Blaydon. "Estimation of Probability Density and Distribution Functions." *IEEE Trans. on Information Theory*, LT-14 (July 1968), 549–556.
16. Kashyap, R. L. and C. C. Blaydon. "Recovery of Function from Noisy Measurements Taken at Randomly Selected Points." *Proc. of IEEE*, 54 (1966), 1127–1128.
17. Nikolic, Z. J. and K. S. Fu. "A Mathematical Model of Learning in an Unknown Random Environment." In *Proc. National Electronics Conference.* Chicago, 1966.
18. Patrick, E. A. and G. Carayannopoulos. "Codes for Unsupervised Learning of Source and Binary Channel Probabilities." *Information and Control*, 14 (1969), 358–376.
19. Patrick, E. A. and L. A. Liporace. "Quasi-Bayes Averaging of Stochastic Approximation Estimators." *Information and Control*, 18 (1971), 168–182.
20. Saridis, G. N., Z. J. Nikolic, and K. S. Fu. "Stochastic Approximation

Algorithms for System Identification, Estimation and Decomposition of Mixtures." *IEEE Trans. on Systems Science and Cybernetics*, SSC-5 (January 1969), 8–15.

21. Tsypkin, Ya. Z. "Use of the Stochastic Approximation Method in Estimating Unknown Distribution Densities from Observations." *Automat. i Telemeh*, 27 (1966), 432–434.
22. Wagner, T. J. "The Rate of Convergence of an Algorithm for Recovering Functions from Noisy Measurements taken at Randomly Selected Points." *IEEE Trans. on Systems Science and Cybernetics*, SSC-4 (July 1968), 151–154.
23. Wolverton, C. T. and J. T. Rawgen. "A Counterexample to Dvoretzky's Stochastic Approximation Theorem." *IEEE Trans. on Information Theory* (January 1968).
24. Wolverton, C. T. and T. J. Wagner. "Asymptotically Optimal Discriminant Functions for Pattern Recognition," TR No. 45, Lab. for Electronics and Related Science Research, University of Texas at Austin, February 1968.
25. Yau, S. S. and J. M. Schumpent. "Design of Pattern Classifiers With the Updating Property Using Stochastic Approximation Techniques." *IEEE Transactions on Computers*, C-17 (Sept. 1968), 861–872.

CHAPTER VII

Nonparametric Methods and Compound Decision Theory

1. Introduction

For any statistical pattern recognition problem, it is clear that partial knowledge of the probability density function or the decision function is essential for pattern classification. Such knowledge may be expressed as a parametric form of the underlying probability density function. The parameters are estimated from the available samples as discussed in chapters 5 and 6. The fundamental difference of the nonparametric or distribution-free methods from the parametric methods is that the parametric form of the underlying probability density function is not assumed or used. The nonparametric methods are important because the a priori parametric information is usually not available or the assumption of it is not justified. Having introduced some basic concepts and tools in nonparametric statistics, we shall discuss the construction of sample sets, the nearest-neighbor decision rule, nonparametric estimation of the probability density function, and the compound decision approach. Selection of features without using the parametric form of the probability density function is also examined.

The compound decision approach *assumes* the parametric form of the probability density function. As the decision is made by considering the collection of component decision problems as a totality, the approach is much less dependent upon the parametric form of the probability density function than classical decision theory.

2. Some Basic Concepts and Tools

A. *Empirical distribution function*

For a one-dimensional measurement, a function $t(u)$ is defined as

$$t(u) = \begin{cases} 1 & \text{if } u \geqslant 0 \\ 0 & \text{if } u < 0 \end{cases} \tag{7.1}$$

Let $X_1, X_2, \ldots, X_N$ be a set of N samples from a pattern class with the probability distribution function $F(x)$. The empirical distribution function is defined as

$$F_N(x) = \frac{1}{N} \sum_{k=1}^{N} t(x - X_k) = \frac{1}{N} \# (X_k \leqslant x), \quad k = 1, 2, \ldots, N \tag{7.2}$$

where the symbol # ( ) stands for the number of times the relationship stated within parentheses is satisfied for the indicated range of subscripts. It is noted that $F_N(x)$ converges in probability to $F(x)$ for all values of x according to the Glivenko-Cantelli theorem which states that

$$\sup_{-\infty < x < \infty} |F_N(x) - F(x)| \to 0 \quad \text{with probability 1}$$

The construction of the empirical density function for multidimensional measurements requires the partitioning of the measurement space into a number of cells and counting the number of samples falling in each cell. Let d be the dimension of a measurement vector. The multidimensional empirical distribution function can be defined as

$$F_N(x_1, x_2, \ldots, x_d) = \frac{1}{N} \# (X_{k_1} \leqslant x_1, X_{k_2} \leqslant x_2, \ldots, X_{k_d} \leqslant x_d)$$

$$k = 1, 2, \ldots, N \tag{7.3}$$

where X_{k_i} denotes the ith dimension of the kth vector.

B. Order statistics and probability integral transformation

Let $X_1, \ldots, X_N$ be a set of N one-dimensional samples with the probability distribution function $F(x)$. The samples can be arranged according to increasing size using the notation

$$X_{(1)} \leqslant \cdots \leqslant X_{(N)} \tag{7.4}$$

For $k = 1, \ldots, N$, the quantity $X_{(k)}$ defined in this way is called the kth-order statistic of the sample of size N.

If $F(x)$ is continuous, we can define a probability integral transformation,

$$U = F(X) \tag{7.5}$$

The probability distribution of U is $P(U \leqslant u) = P(X \leqslant x) = F(x) = u$. Thus the random variable U has the uniform (or rectangular) distribution on the interval [0, 1]. Furthermore, if $X_1, \ldots, X_N$ are independent random variables each with continuous distribution $F(x)$, then the joint density function of the variables $U_1 = F(X_1), \ldots, U_N = F(X_N)$ is 1 on the unit cube.

$$0 \leqslant u_k \leqslant 1, \quad k = 1, \ldots, N \tag{7.6}$$

and 0 elsewhere. The probability integral transformation of equation (7.3) is

$$U_{(1)} < \cdots < U_{(N)} \tag{7.7}$$

which corresponds to one of $N!$ different permutations of the original sample values. The joint density function of the N order statistics, $U_{(1)}, \ldots, U_{(N)}$ is equal to $N!$ on the part of the unit cube equation (7.6) that satisfies equation (7.7) and equals 0 elsewhere.

C. Ranks

Many nonparametric methods in current use are based on ranks rather than on actual measurements. Ranks are obtained by arranging the available measurements according to size and assigning to them numbers that correspond to their positions in such an ordering or "ranking." If there are N objects in a ranking and if no two objects are "tied" for the same position, it is customary—though not necessary—to use the positive integers from 1 to N as ranks. The rank $r(x_k)$ of x_k among measurements $x_1, \ldots, x_N$ can be expressed as

$$r(x_k) = \sum_{h=1}^{N} t(x_k - x_h) = 1 + \sum_{h \neq k}^{N} t(x_k - x_h), \quad k = 1, \ldots, N \tag{7.8}$$

where $t(u)$ is defined by equation (7.1). Many statistical procedures are "invariant" under order-preserving transformation of the measurements. The rank methods are particularly useful in this case because of their relative simplicity. In situations where quantitative measurements are unobtainable, rank methods may still be applicable if the subject matter under investigation allows for qualitative comparisons.

For additional concepts and basic techniques in nonparametric statistics, readers are referred to Noether[1] and Fraser.[2]

3. Sample Set Construction

To obtain the empirical density function, it is desirable to have a simple alogorithm that sequentially establishes the density function which converges to the true density function as the number of samples becomes infinite. Several methods of sample set construction that provide an empirical density function have been examined. It is instructive to consider an adaptive sample set construction method due to Sebestyen.[3] The samples are of known classifications.

To begin with, the memory of the recognition system is empty. When the first sample is taken, construct a sphere around the sample with the standard deviation σ as the radius, assuming for simplicity that the sample has equal variance in all directions. When the second sample is taken, if it is inside the sphere constructed for the first sample, then the mean vector is updated from the sample mean around which a new sphere is constructed with radius σ. If the new sample is outside the first sphere and within some threshold distance, say T, from the center of the sphere, then the sample is stored and used later. If it is of distance greater than T from the center of the first sphere, then a new sphere is constructed around the new sample. For every new sample falling in one of the existing spheres, such sphere will be updated and the number of samples for updating the sample set is counted. The conditional probability density of a pattern class is the sum of component probability densities of all sample sets. Each set is weighted by the number of samples forming the set. The maximum likelihood method can then be used to classify an unknown sample.

Instead of constructing spheres, d-dimensional histograms can be constructed[4] such that the interior of the nth cell is defined by an ellipsoid of d-dimension,

$$Q_m(x, n) = \sum_{k=1}^{d} \left(\frac{x_k - S_{mk}(n)}{\sigma_{mk}(n)} \right)^2 \leqslant \tau_d^2 \tag{7.9}$$

Here n is the number of samples belonging to the mth cell up to the present time, x_k is the kth dimension of the nth measurement vector x, $S_{mk}(n)$ is the stored center of the mth cell at the kth dimension based on n samples, and $\sigma_{mk}(n)$ is the "scale factor" or the radius of the ellipsoid, which determines the shape of the mth cell. The interior of an arbitrary cell m is readily defined as the locus of points "nearer" to $S_m = (S_{m_1}, \ldots, S_{m_d})$ than any other stored point. τ_d is the threshold control parameter. The cell radius is properly chosen such that it will not shrink to its initial value. Except for a constant that depends on the number of dimensions, the volume of the cell is expressed by the product of the standard deviations in the quadratic form (7.9) used to define the boundaries of the cell. The volume is an estimate of the probability density,

$$p(S_m, n) \propto \frac{n}{N} \left[\prod_{k=1}^{d} \sigma_{mk}(n) \right]^{-1} \tag{7.10}$$

where N denotes the total number of input samples to the present and $\propto$ and Π stand for "proportional to" and "product of" respectively. The procedures of generating new cells, updating old cells, or storing cells temporarily for later use are identical to the sample set construction discussed earlier in this section. It is noted that no assumption is made that the probability density is Gaussian, because only in a small neighborhood does a Gaussian function form sufficiently well approximate the actual probability density. Proof of the convergence of the sample set construction method is not available. If the method is considered as an estimation of the probability density, some statistical results[5,6] may be used to interpret the convergence property of the method.

4. Nearest-Neighbor Decision Procedure

Let $x_1, x_2, \ldots, x_n$ be a sequence of n independent measurements of known classifications, and x be the measurement to be classified. Among $x_1, x_2, \ldots, x_n$, let the measurement with the smallest distance from x be denoted as x', i.e.,

$$d(x, x') = \min_{x' \epsilon \{x_1, \ldots, x_n\}} |x_i - x|, \quad i = 1, \ldots, n \tag{7.11}$$

Then the nearest-neighbor (*NN*) decision rule assigns the classification of x' to x. Here one nearest-neighbor is used in decision making. Figure 7.1 illustrates the *NN* rule for two classes in a two-dimensional measurement space.

The *NN* rule appears to have been first formulated and analyzed by Fix and

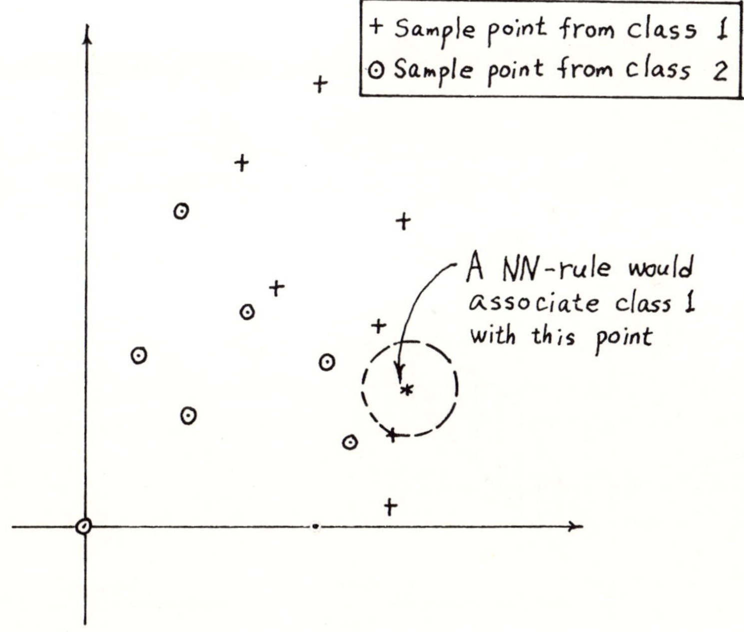

Fig. 7.1 The Nearest-Neighbor Rule for Two Classes in a Two-Dimensional Sample Space

Hodges.[7,8] They investigated a rule which might be called the k_n-*NN* rule. It assigns to an unclassified sample point the class most heavily represented among its k_n nearest neighbors to x (in some appropriate metric). Fix and Hodges established the consistency of the rule for $k_n \to \infty$, $n \to \infty$ such that $k_n/n \to 0$. Loftsgaarden and Quesenberry[5] have shown that a simple modification of the k_n-*NN* rule gives a consistent estimate of a probability density function. Important results of the *NN* rule were obtained by Cover and Hart.[9,10] Let R_n be the risk incurred when the classification based on the *NN* rule and n samples is incorrect, and R^* be the Bayes risk when the statistics are known exactly. As before, let m be the number of pattern classes. Cover and Hart[9] showed that as $n \to \infty$, R_n is tightly upper and lower bounded as (figure 7.2)

$$R^* \leqslant R_n \leqslant R^* \left(2 - \frac{m}{m-1} R^*\right) \tag{7.12}$$

and for $m = 2$,

$$R^* \leqslant R_n \leqslant 2R^* (1 - R^*) \leqslant 2R^* \tag{7.13}$$

Thus for any number of pattern classes, the risk (or the probability of error) of the *NN* rule is bounded above by twice the Bayes risk (or the probability of error). In this sense, it may be said that half of the classification information in an infinite sample set is contained in the nearest neighbor. The same conclusion

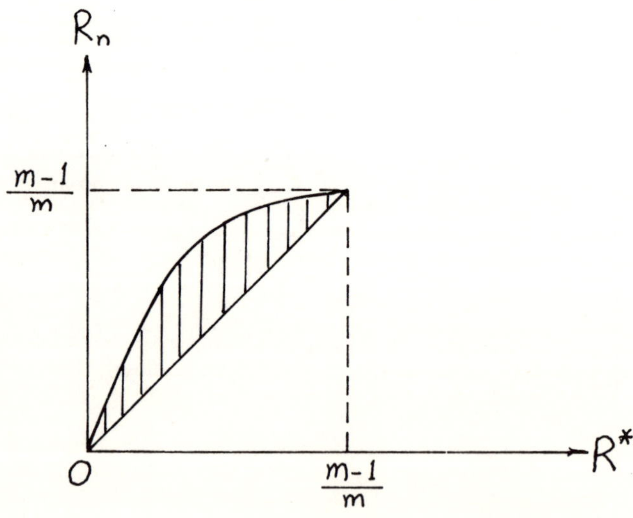

Fig. 7.2 Bounds on the NN Risk

as in equation (7.13) can be drawn essentially for the estimation problem using the *NN* rule.[10] It is noted that the *NN* rule is nonparametric or distribution-free, in the sense that it does not depend on any assumptions about the underlying statistics for its application. The Bayes risk serves merely as a reference indicating the best possible performance available.

For any number n of samples, the 1-*NN* rule has a strictly lower probability of error than any other k_n-*NN* rule against certain classes of distributions, and hence is "admissible" among the k_n-*NN* rule. The convergence of the probability of error based on k neighbors and n samples, denoted as $P_e(k, n)$ may be written as

$$
\begin{aligned}
&P_e(k; n) \uparrow \tfrac{1}{2} \quad \text{in } k, \text{ for any } n \\
&P_e(k; n) \downarrow 0 \quad \text{in } n, \text{ for any } k > 0
\end{aligned}
\tag{7.14}
$$

The *NN* rule in the $(n + 1)$th sample case makes a different classification from the n-sample case only if the $(n + 1)$th sample is the closest. Since this occurs with probability $1/(n + 1)$, we have $| R_n - R_{n+1} | \leqslant 1/(n + 1)$, and in general, $| R_n - R_{n+1} | \leqslant k/(n + 1)$. This bound on the fluctuations of the small-sample risk is rather conservative. The actual difference $| R_n - R_{n+1} |$ for large n, i.e., the rate of convergence, is shown by Cover[11] to be of the order of $1/n^2$. Using the risk itself instead of the expected (average) risk discussed above, Peterson[12] showed that in nearly any reasonable case, limit on the risk can be selected arbitrarily and a data size n selected sufficiently large to insure that the *NN* risk associated with any particular decision is within the specified limit with high probability.

The near optimum (Bayes) performance and the relative simplicity of the *NN* rule makes it an attractive decision procedure. Figure 7.3 shows typical computer recognition results by using both the maximum likelihood decision rule (a standard parametric approach) and the *NN* decision rule. The features are those selected in chapter 4. The disadvantages of the *NN* rule are the storage requirements for a large number of samples of known classifications and the computations involved in distance comparisons. Various modifications of the rule are possible to reduce the storage requirements with certain small degradation in performance. Some experimental methods of reducing the large sample set to a much smaller set were reported by Hart.[13]

5. Compound Decision Approach

Classical decision theory is applicable when only a single decision must be made. A compound decision problem arises when one is confronted with the same decision problem, called the component problem, not only once, but N times. Advantages might be gained by considering the whole collection of prob-

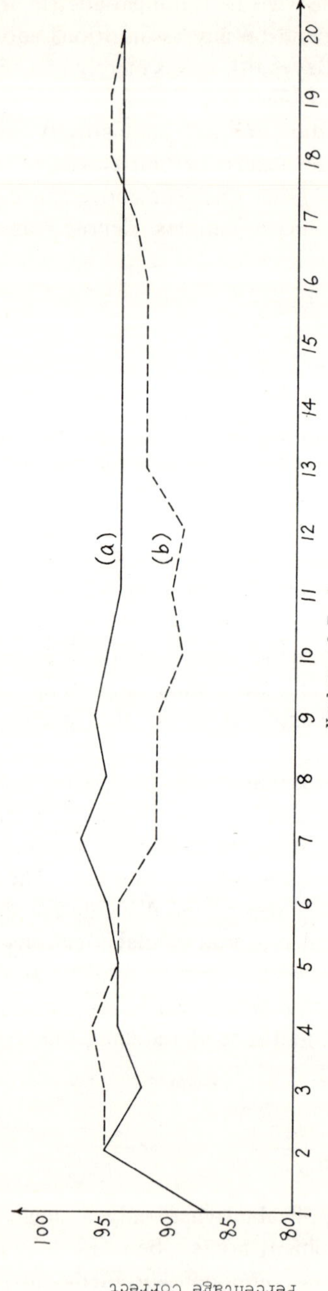

Fig. 7.3 Percentage Correct Recognition of (a) Maximum Likelihood Decision Rule and (b) Nearest-Neighbor Decision Rule for Highleyman's Data Samples "P" and "Q." (50 test samples are used for each class [character]). The non-monotonic behavior of curves may be caused by the small test sample size.

lems as a totality. Compound decision theory is powerful as a general theoretical framework into which to embed pattern recognition. It can lead to methods of threshold adjustment and to methods for taking context into account. The compound decision approach is useful for both known and unknown distribution cases.

In classical decision theory, the Bayes risk can be defined as follows. Let $L_{ij} = L(\omega_i, dj)$ be the loss when ω_i is true, i.e., the state of nature, but the decision is to select ω_j. Also introduce the action probability $t(j/x)$ as $t(j/z) = 1$ when ω_j is selected for given x and $t(j/x) = 0$ otherwise. Here $j = 1, 2, \ldots, m'$ and m' may differ from m. For example, we can let $m' = m + 1$ and the $(m + 1)$th action is to reject, i.e., make no decision. The Bayes risk as averaged over all pattern classes and actions is given by

$$R(P, t) = \int \sum_{j=1}^{m'} \sum_{i=1}^{m} L_{ij} P_i \, p(x/\omega_i) \, t(j/x) \, dx \tag{7.15}$$

where $P_i = P(\omega_i)$ is the a priori probability of the ith class and the integration is over the space of x. Here the essential quantity is $\Sigma_{i=1}^{m} L_{ij} P_i \, p(x/\omega_i)$. A decision rule t^P which minimizes the Bayes risk $R(P, t)$ is said to be Bayes against P. Thus a Bayes procedure t^P has $t(j/x) = 1$ for that j which minimizes $\Sigma_{i=1}^{m} L_{ij} P_i \, p(x/\omega_i)$. The function

$$R(P) = \min_t R(P, t) = R(P, t^P) \tag{7.16}$$

is called the Bayes envelope.

For a compound decision problem, there exists a vector $\theta^N = (\theta_1, \ldots, \theta_N)$ of states of nature, and a corresponding vector $x^N = (x_1, \ldots, x_N)$ of measurements (random variables), where θ_k denotes the state in the kth problem. For a given θ_k, x_k is independent of the other x's and θ's. We do not assume that the θ's are necessarily independent. The loss in the compound decision problem is taken to be the average of losses incurred at each of the N decisions and the risk is defined correspondingly. If all measurements x^N are available before the individual decisions must be made, one can use *a compound decision rule* $t^N = (t_1, \ldots, t_N)$ where $t_k = t_k \, (j/x^N)$. If only the measurements x^k are at hand when the kth decision must be made, one can use a *sequential* compound decision rule, where $t_k = t_k \, (j/x^k)$. A simple rule is one where $t_k = t_k \, (j/x_k)$, that is, one where the decision about θ_k depends on x_k alone. For a simple *symmetric* rule, $t_k = t(j/x_k)$. Classical decision theory is restricted to using only simple symmetric rules. The risk for the compound rule t^N is

$$R(\theta^N, t^N) = \frac{1}{N} \sum_{k=1}^{N} R(\theta^k, t_k) \tag{7.17}$$

where

$$R(\theta^N, t_k) = \int_{\text{space of } x^N} \sum_{j=1}^{m'} L_{\theta_{kj}} t_k(j/x^N) p(x^N/\theta^N) dx^N \tag{7.18}$$

is the risk for the kth problem (the kth component risk) with

$$p(x^N/\theta^N) = \prod_{k=1}^{N} p_{\theta_k}(x_k)$$

One can also talk about a compound Bayes risk $\bar{R}(G, t^N)$ with respect to an a priori distribution $G(\theta^N)$. Since

$$\bar{R}(G, t^N) = \sum_{\text{space of } \theta^N} R(\theta^N, t^N)\ G(\theta^N) = \frac{1}{N} \sum_{k=1}^{N} \bar{R}(G, t_k) \tag{7.19}$$

where

$$\bar{R}(G, t_k) = \sum_{\text{space of } \theta^N} R(\theta^N, t_k) G(\theta^N), \tag{7.20}$$

a procedure is compound Bayes against G if it minimizes $\bar{R}(G, t_k)$ for each k.

For known densities $p_i(x)$ and $G(\theta^N) = \Pi_{k=1}^{N} q_k(\theta_k)$, i.e., when the states of nature are independently distributed as $q_k(i)$ which is unknown, a simple rule will be compound Bayes against G. If, furthermore, the states of nature are also identically distributed, i.e., $q_k(i) = q(i)$, one may use an empirical Bayes decision procedure whereby one employs a "simple" procedure which is Bayes against a consistent estimate of q. Since the estimate of q is based upon measurements associated with the component problems, such a procedure is really compound. An estimate of $q(i)$ is the fraction of the $N\theta$'s that are equal to i.

Consider two pattern classes with zero-one loss function. The problem is to decide for each $k = 1, \ldots, N$ whether $\theta_k = 0$ or 1. For a simple symmetric rule with $t_k = t(x_k)$, equation (7.17) becomes

$$R(\theta^N, t^N) = \frac{1}{N} \sum_{k=1}^{N} R(\theta_k, t) = \bar{\theta}_N R(1, t) + (1 - \bar{\theta}_N) R(0, t)$$

$$= \bar{R}(\theta_N, t) \tag{7.21}$$

where

$$\bar{\theta}_N = \frac{1}{N} \sum_{k=1}^{N} \theta_k \tag{7.22}$$

Thus the simple symmetric procedure which is Bayes against the empirical a priori distribution $\bar{\theta}_N$, minimizes the compound risk. If we know in advance the proportion $\bar{\theta}_N$ of 1's among $\theta_1, \ldots, \theta_N$, we could, by using a simple symmetric rule,

$$t_{\bar{\theta}_N}(x_k) = \begin{cases} 1 & \text{if } \dfrac{p_i(x_k)}{p_0(x_k)} > \dfrac{1 - \bar{\theta}_N}{\bar{\theta}_N} \\ 0 & \text{otherwise} \end{cases} \tag{7.23}$$

obtain the Bayes envelope $R(\bar{\theta}_N)$. If $\bar{\theta}_N$ is not known, it must be estimated or a minimax procedure can be used.[14]

For unknown densities $p_i(x)$ as well as unknown G, the nonparametric empirical Bayes approach of Johns[15] assumes that the θ's are independent and identically distributed and examines the convergence of the component Bayes risk to its minimum value, $R(q)$. It has been assumed in the nonparametric problem that when the kth decision must be made there are at hand the true values of all the previous states of nature, and a sequential compound decision rule with $t_k = t_k(j/\theta^{k-1}, x^k)$ is used. One may use θ^{k-1} and x^{k-1} to obtain consistent estimates of $p_i(x)$ for all i and act as if these were the true densities to define a procedure "Bayes" against the known empirical a priori distribution q^{k-1}. Such a procedure is asymptotically optimum in the empirical Bayes sense.

6. Nonparametric Estimation of Multivariate Density Function

Let $X_i = (X_{i1}, \ldots, X_{id})$, $i = 1, 2, \ldots, N$ be independent and identically distributed d-dimensional random vectors with probability distribution function $F(x) = F(x_1, \ldots, x_d)$ and density function $p(x)$. The empirical (sample) distribution function defined by equation (7.3) is a binomially distributed random variable whose mean and variance are given by

$$E[F_N(x)] = F(x) \tag{7.24}$$

$$\operatorname{Var}[F_N(x)] = \frac{1}{N} F(x)[1 - F(x)] \tag{7.25}$$

As an estimate of $p(x)$, one might take the weighted average over the sample distribution function:

$$p_N(x, \ldots, x_d) = \int_{-\infty}^{\infty} \cdots \int_{-\infty}^{\infty} \frac{1}{h_1 \ldots h_d} K\left(\frac{x_1 - y_1}{h_1}, \ldots, \cdot \frac{x_d - y_d}{h_d}\right) dF_N(y_1, \ldots, y_d) = \frac{1}{Nh_1 \ldots h_d} \sum_{i=1}^{N} \cdot K\left(\frac{x_1 - x_{i1}}{h_1}, \ldots, \frac{x_n - x_{id}}{h_d}\right) \tag{7.26}$$

where $K(x_1, \ldots, x_d)$ is a d-dimensional "window," or weighting function, and the constants $h_j = h_j(N), j = 1, \ldots, d$, are positive functions of N approaching zero as $N \to \infty$. Let the window $K(x)$ satisfy the conditions

$$\begin{aligned}
&(1)\ K(x) \geqslant 0 \\
&(2)\ K(x_1, \ldots, x_d) = K(|x_1|, \ldots, |x_d|) \\
&(3)\ K(x_1) \leqslant K(x_2) \quad \text{if} \quad |x_1| \geqslant |x_2| \\
&(4)\ \int_{-\infty}^{\infty} \cdots \int_{-\infty}^{\infty} K(x_1, \ldots, x_d)\, dx_1, \ldots dx_d = 1
\end{aligned} \tag{7.27}$$

At all points x at which $p(x)$ is continuous, $p_N(x)$ is asymptotically unbiased,

$$\lim_{N \to \infty} E[p_N(x)] = p(x) \tag{7.28}$$

and also

$$\lim_{N \to \infty} Nh_1 \ldots h_d \operatorname{Var}[p_N(x)] = p(x) \int_{-\infty}^{\infty} \cdots \int_{-\infty}^{\infty} K^2(y_1, \ldots, y_d) \cdot dy_1 \ldots dy_d \tag{7.29}$$

If in addition to

$$\lim_{N \to \infty} h_j(N) = 0$$

the positive constants $h_j = h_j(N), j = 1, \ldots, d$ also satisfy

$$\lim_{N \to \infty} Nh_1(N) \ldots h_d(N) = \infty$$

then $p_N(x)$ is a consistent and asymptotically normal estimate of $p(x)$ at all points of continuity of $p(x)$.

For the case $h_1 = h_2 = \cdots = h_d = h$, the estimate of $p(x)$ may be written more compactly as

$$p_N(x) = \frac{1}{Nh^d} \sum_{i=1}^{N} K\left(\frac{x - X_i}{h}\right) \tag{7.30}$$

with $h \to 0$ and $Nh^n \to \infty$ as $N \to \infty$. For $d = 1$, equation (7.30) is the probability density estimation first considered by Parzen,[16] who examined different weighting functions. The more general case as described in this section is due to Murthy.[17] Van Ryzin[18] considered the rate of convergence by taking $h(n) = 0(n^{-1/d+2})$.

7. Nonparametric Feature Selection

When the features are selected without using the parametric form of probability densities, we have the nonparametric feature selection problem. The probability of misrecognition may be estimated directly by using the Parzen-Murthy estimation of a probability density function.[19] A feature that results in a smaller probability of misrecognition than any other features is then selected. The probability of misrecognition or risk may also be estimated directly by using the nearest-neighbor risk; the feature that has the least nearest-neighbor risk is then selected.[20] Consider one nearest-neighbor case ($k = 1$). The bounds given by equation (7.13) can be rewritten as

$$\frac{1}{2}\left[1 - \sqrt{1 - 2R_n}\right] \leqslant R^* \leqslant R_n \tag{7.31}$$

When the upper bound is very close to the lower bound, the nearest-neighbor risk R_n is a good estimate of the Bayes risk R^*. The first method obviously requires a large amount of computer time for an exhaustive search of features. The second method is suboptimum but computationally simpler. Let

$$\rho_{d-1}(x,y) = \left[\sum_{i=1}^{d-1} (x_i - y_i)^2\right]^{1/2} \tag{7.32}$$

be the Euclidean distance between the $d - 1$ dimensional vectors x and y with components x_i and y_i respectively. To evaluate the dth feature, the square of the distance can easily be obtained as

$$[\rho_d(x,y)]^2 = [\rho_{d-1}(x,y)]^2 + (x_d - y_d)^2 \tag{7.33}$$

where $[\rho_{d-1}(x,y)]^2$ is stored from the previously selected subset. It is noted that both direct methods require a "teacher" to count the number of errors as an estimate of the probability of misrecognition. Furthermore, it would be desirable that the samples for classification be different from those for density estimation in the first method and for reference use in the second method.

A third method selects the features indirectly.[21] To reduce a D-dimensional measurement x to a d-dimensional ($d < D$) measurement x', there is usually a unique linear transformation matrix A such that $Ax = x'$, where x' is a sample vector in the d-dimensional measurement space M. The Parzen-Murthy estimation of the probability densities in the original and the transformed spaces can be written, from equation (7.26), as

$$p(x/\omega_i) = \frac{1}{N_i} \frac{1}{(h(N_i))^D} \sum_{j=1}^{N_i} K\left(\frac{x - x_j^i}{h(N_i)}\right) \tag{7.34}$$

and

$$p(x/\omega_i, M) = \frac{1}{N_i} \frac{1}{(h(N_i))^d} \sum_{j=1}^{N_i} K\left(A\left(\frac{x - x_j^i}{h(N_i)}\right)\right) \tag{7.35}$$

respectively. Here N_i is the number of samples of the ith class and $h(N_i)$ is a positive valued function of N_i that tends to 0 as N_i increases, and $K(x)$ is a weighting function. Now consider two pattern classes and define the separation of the two probability densities as

$$d(p_1, p_2) = \left\{\int_M [P_1\, p(x/\omega_1, M) - P_2\, p(x/\omega_2, M)]^2\, dx\right\}^{1/2} \tag{7.36}$$

Substituting equation (7.35) in (7.36) and expanding the integrand, we have

$$d(A) = d(p_1, p_2) = \left[\int_M \sum_{r=1}^{2} \sum_{s=1}^{2} \sum_{j=1}^{N_1} \sum_{k=1}^{N_2} \xi_{rs} \frac{P_r P_s}{N_r N_s} \cdot \left(\frac{1}{h(N_r)} \frac{1}{h(N_s)}\right)^d K\left(A\left(\frac{x - x_j^r}{h(N_r)}\right)\right) \cdot K\left(A\left(\frac{x - x_k^s}{h(N_s)}\right)\right) dx\right]^{1/2} \tag{7.37}$$

where

$$\xi_{rs} = \begin{cases} 1, & r = s \\ -1, & r \neq s, \end{cases}$$

or

$$d(A) = \left[\sum_{j=1}^{N_1} \sum_{k=1}^{N} C_{jk}^{1,1} + \sum_{j=1}^{N_2} \sum_{k=1}^{N_2} C_{jk}^{2,2} - 2\sum_{j=1}^{N_1} \sum_{k=1}^{N_2} C_{jk}^{1,2}\right]^{1/2} \tag{7.38}$$

where

$$C_{jk}^{r,s} = \frac{P_r P_s}{N_r N_s} \left(\frac{1}{h(N_r)} \frac{1}{h(N_s)} \right)^d \int_M K \left(A \left(\frac{x - x_j^r}{h(N_r)} \right) \right) \cdot K \left(A \left(\frac{x - x_k^s}{h(N_s)} \right) \right) dx \qquad (7.39)$$

$C_{jk}^{r,s}$ can be interpreted as a non-Euclidean measure of proximity between x_j^r and x_k^s. For example, if $K(\cdot)$ is a Gaussian function, $C_{jk}^{r,s}$ increases as the distance $|x_j^r - x_k^s|$ decreases. If $r = s$, this distance is called an intraclass distance, while if $r \neq s$ it is called an interclass distance. The best M for a given K is defined to be the one maximizing $d(A)$. The corresponding projection map A is the best linear transformation from a D-dimensional space to a d-dimensional space M.

There is no closed form solution, however, for the best transformation A. The solution requires hill-climbing[21] or computer search. Again a large amount of computer time may be necessary. The advantages of the method are that the class densities can be multimodal or otherwise nonunimodal and that the classified samples are used for density estimation only.

8. Remarks

As the assumption of the parametric form of a probability density is not justified† for most patterns, nonparametric methods should play an important role in density estimation, pattern classification, and feature selection. Although there is an extensive literature in nonparametric statistics, the corresponding work in statistical pattern recognition is much less. The methods presented in this chapter, however, are only a few important ones. Most researchers have now recognized the importance of nonparametric methods and designed recognition procedures without relying on the parameter statistics.

Most sample set construction methods may be considered as engineering approaches without rigorous mathematical justification. Some use of the order statistics such as the distribution-free tolerance region[22,23] may provide sample set construction methods fully justified in statistics. It is also possible to evaluate the average risk which approaches the Bayes risk asymptotically. However, the resulting methods may not be flexible (they are not recursive) and computationally feasible in terms of storage and the amount of computation; and the methods would be of only theoretical interest. Such disadvantages, which are typical in many nonparametric statistical methods, remain to be overcome.

The nearest-neighbor decision and estimation rule and the Parzen-Murthy

†A convenient assumption of Gaussian density, for example, may lead to pessimistic or even incorrect results.

density estimation method have been most widely used in statistical pattern recognition. Recently, Wagner[24] considered the convergence and the rate of convergence of the probability of error for the nearest-neighbor rule conditioned on the n known samples. Specht[25] has employed the exponential weighting function for Parzen-Murthy density estimation in constructing the polynomial discriminant function for each class. Section 5 is based on chapter 7 of reference 26. It is included in this chapter to emphasize the fact that the compound decision approach can easily become nonparametric (consider, for example, the binary measurements[27]). Some further discussion of nonparametric methods, including the compound approach, is available in reference 28.

More feasible nonparametric feature selection methods besides those presented in section 7 remain to be examined. For example, the "teacher" should be removed and a closed form solution, at least for certain important cases, should be available. The nonparametric feature selection appears to be an important and unresolved problem in the statistical pattern recognition field.

PROBLEMS

1. Design a computer recognition experiment as follows. Obtain handprinted character samples of symbols A and B in the manner described by Marill and Green (*IRE Trans. on Electronic Computers*, EC-9, no. 4, 1960). Take 200 samples for each symbol.
   a. Use 100 samples of each symbol to calculate the mean vector. Then use 200 samples (100 of each symbol) to compute the common covariance matrix of the two symbols. A Gaussian density function is assumed for each symbol.
   b. Perform the maximum likelihood decision on each of the 200 samples of both symbols which were not used in part a. Count the number of errors made. It is the percentage of misrecognition. Parts a and b may be called the design and test, respectively, of the recognition system.
   c. Use the nearest-neighbor decision rule to determine the percentage of misrecognition. For each symbol (class), again 100 samples are for design (reference) use and the remaining 100 samples are for testing. Compare the result with part b.
   d. Partition the design and test samples such that there is only one test sample and the remaining samples are for reference use. Classify the test sample by using the nearest-neighbor rule. Repeat the procedure with other partitions each containing only one test sample. Compare the result with part c. For a discussion of such partition see P. A. Lachenbruch and M. R. Mickey. "Estimation of Error Rates in Discriminant Analysis." *Technometrics*, 10 (February 1968), 1-11.
2. Write the Parzen-Murthy density estimate for each of the following weighting functions. Assume $h_1 = h_2 = \cdots = h_d = \sigma_{(N)}$.

a. Uniform weighting function with

$$K(x, \ldots, x_d) = \prod_{i=1}^{d} U(x_i)$$

where

$$U(x_i) = \begin{cases} \frac{1}{2} & \text{if } |x_i| < 1 \\ 0 & \text{if } |x_i| \geqslant 1 \end{cases}$$

b. Gaussian weighting function

$$K(x) = \left(\frac{1}{\sqrt{2\pi}}\right)^d \exp\left(-\frac{1}{2}|x|^2\right)$$

REFERENCES

1. Noether, G. E. *Elements of Nonparametric Statistics.* Wiley, New York, 1967.
2. Fraser, D. A. S. *Nonparametric Methods in Statistics.* Wiley, New York, 1957.
3. Sebestyen, G. S. *Decision Making Processes in Pattern Recognition.* Macmillan, New York, 1962.
4. Sebestyen, G. S., and J. Edie. "An Algorithm for the Nonparametric Pattern Recognition." *IEEE Trans. on Electronic Computers*, EC-15 (December 1966), 908–915.
5. Loftsgaarden, D. O., and C. P. Quesenbury. "A Nonparametric Estimate of a Multivariate Density Function." *Ann. Math. Stat.* (June 1965).
6. Parzen, E. "On Estimation of a Probability Density Function and Mode." *Ann. Math. Stat.* (1962), 1065–1076.
7. Fix, E. and J. L. Hodges, Jr. "Discriminatory Analysis, Nonparametric Discrimination: Consistency Properties." USAF School of Aviation Medicine, Randolph Field, Tex., Project 21-49-004, Report 4, Contract AF 41(128)-31, February 1951.
8. Fix, E. and J. L. Hodges, Jr. "Discriminatory Analysis: Small Sample Performance." USAF School of Aviation Medicine, Randolph Field, Tex., Project 21-49-004, Report 11, August 1952.
9. Cover, T. M. and P. E. Hart. "Nearest Neighbor Pattern Classification." *IEEE Trans. on Information Theory*, IT-13 (January 1967), 21–27.
10. Cover, T. M. "Estimation by the Nearest Neighbor Rule." *IEEE Trans. on Information Theory*, IT-14 (January 1968), 50–55.
11. Cover, T. M. "Rates of Convergence for Nearest Neighbor Classification." In *Proc. First Annual Hawaii Conference on System Theory*, pp. 413–415. January 1968.
12. Peterson, D. W. "Some Convergence Properties of a Nearest Neighbor De-

cision Rule." *IEEE Trans. on Information Theory*, IT-16 (January 1970), 26–31.

13. Hart, P. E. "The Condensed Nearest Neighbor Rule." *IEEE Trans. on Information Theory*, IT-14 (January 1968), 50–51.
14. Robbins, H. "Asymptotically Subminimax Solutions of Compound Statistical Decision Problems." In *Proc. Second Berkeley Symposium on Mathematical Statistics and Probability*, pp. 131–148, Univ. of Calif. Press, Berkeley, 1951.
15. Johns, M. V., Jr. "An Empirical Bayes Approach to Non-Parametric Two-Way Classification." In *Studies in Item Analysis and Prediction*, edited by H. Solomon, pp. 221–232. Stanford University Press, Stanford, Calif., 1961.
16. Parzen, E. "On Estimation of a Probability Density Function and Mode." *Ann. Math. Stat.*, 33 (September 1962), 1065–1076.
17. Murthy, V. K. "Estimation of Probability Density." *Ann. Math. Stat.*, 36 (June 1965), 1027–1031.
18. Van Ryzin, J. R. "Non-Parametric Bayesian Decision Procedures for (Pattern) Classification with Stochastic Learning." In *Fourth Prague Conference on Information Theory, Statistical Decision Functions, and Random Processes.* September 1965.
19. Fu, K. S., P. J. Min, and T. J. Li. "Feature Selection in Pattern Recognition." *IEEE Trans. on Systems Science and Cybernetics*, SSC-6 (January 1970), 33–39.
20. Whitney, A. W. "A Direct Method of Nonparametric Measurement Selection." In *IEEE Conference Record of the Symposium on Feature Extraction and Selection in Pattern Recognition.* Argonne National Laboratory, October 1970.
21. Patrick, E. A. and F. P. Fischer II. "Nonparametric Feature Selection." *IEEE Trans. on Information Theory*, IT-15 (September 1969), 577–584.
22. Patrick, E. A. "Distribution-free, Minimum Conditional Risk Learning Systems." In *Proc. of the First Annual Princeton Conference on Information Science and Systems.* Princeton, N.J., March 1967.
23. Patrick, E. A. and F. P. Fischer II. "Class of Decision Rules using Distribution Free Tolerance Regions." In *International Symposium on Artificial Intelligence.* Washington, D.C., May 1969.
24. Wagner, T. J. "Convergence of the Nearest Neighbor Rule." *IEEE Trans. on Information Theory*, IT-17 (September 1971), 566–571.
25. Specht, D. F. "Generation of Polynomial Discriminant Functions for Pattern Recognition." In *Pattern Recognition*, edited by L. N. Kanal, pp. 291–322. Thompson, Washington, D.C., 1968.
26. Kanal, L. N. et al. "Adaptive Modelling of Likelihood Classification–1." Technical Report RADC-TR-66-190, June 1966. Also AD036519.
27. Robbins, H. "Some Numerical Results on a Compound Decision Problem." In *Recent Developments in Information and Decision Processes*, edited by R. E. Machol and P. Gray. Macmillan, New York, 1962.
28. Cover, T. M. "Learning in Pattern Recognition." In *Methodologies of Pattern Recognition*, edited by S. Watanabe, pp. 111–132. Academic Press, New York, 1969.

Bibliography

1. Abend, K. "Compound Decision Procedures for Pattern Recognition: Tutorial Introduction and Summary." In *Proc. National Electronics Conference.* Chicago, 1966.
2. Abend, K. "Compound Decision Procedures for Unknown Distributions and for Dependent States of Nature." In *Pattern Recognition*, edited by L. N. Kanal, pp. 207–249. Washington, D.C., 1968.
3. Alens, N. "Compound Bayes Learning without a Teacher." Stanford Univ. SU-SEL-67-019 (TR No. 6151-2), August 1967.
4. Anderson, M. W. and R. D. Benning. "A Distribution-Free Discrimination Procedure Based on Clustering." *IEEE Trans. on Information Theory*, vol. IT-16, No. 5 (September 1970), 541–548.
5. Anderson, T. W. "Some Nonparametric Multivariate Procedures Based on Statistically Equivalent Blocks." In *Proc. International Symposium on Multivariate Analysis.* Wright Patterson Air Force Base, Ohio, June 1965.
6. Babu, C. C. "On the Distance Criterion of Patrick and Fischer." *IEEE Trans. on Information Theory* (corresp.), IT-18 (May 1972), 428.
7. Becker, P. W. "Recognition of Patterns Using the Frequencies of Occurrence of Binary Words." Ph.D. thesis, Technical University of Denmark, Chapters 2, 3, 4, Polyteknisk Forlag, Copenhagen, 1968.
8. Cacoullos, T. "Estimation of a Multivariate Density." *Ann. Inst. Statist. Math.*, 18 (1966), 179–190.
9. Chen, C. H. "Sequential Sample Set Construction for Pattern Recognition." In *IEEE International Symposium on Information Theory.* Ellenville, New York, January 1969.
10. Cover, T. M. "A Survey of Nonparametric Statistical Pattern Recognition." In *IEEE Northeast Electronic Research and Engineering Meeting (NEREM) Record.* Boston, Mass., November 1968.
11. Fukunaga, K. and D. L. Kessell. "Estimation of Classification Error." *IEEE Trans. on Computers*, C-20 (December 1971).
12. Gates, G. W. "The Reduced Nearest Neighbor Rule." *IEEE Trans. on Information Theory* (corresp.), IT-18 (May 1972), 431–433.
13. Henrichon, E. G. "An Algorithm for Nonparametric Pattern Recognition." Information Research Associates Technical Report 14, November 1967.
14. Henrichon, E. G. and K. S. Fu. "Calamity Detection using Nonparametric Statistics." Purdue Univ. TR-EE 68-31, September 1968.
15. Lebo, J. A. "On the Selection of Decision Criteria and the Estimation of Probabilities in Pattern Recognition." Ph.D. dissertation, Purdue University, January 1965.
16. Meisel, W. S. "Comments on Nonparametric Feature Selection." *IEEE Trans. on Information Theory*, IT-17 (January 1971).
17. Rosenblatt, M. "Remarks on Some Nonparametric Estimates of a Density Function." *Ann. Math. Stat.*, 27 (1956), 832–837.
18. Samuel, E. "Asymptotic Solutions of the Sequential Compound Decision Problem." *Ann. Math. Stat.*, 34 (September 1963).
19. Schwartz, S. C. "Estimation of Probability Density by an Orthogonal Series." *Ann. Math. Stat.*, 1967.

20. Shubert, B. O. "Learning with a Lack of Prior Data." Center for Systems Research, Stanford Univ., Technical Report 6151-4, December 1967.
21. Swain, P. H. and K. S. Fu. "Nonparametric and Linguistic Approaches to Pattern Recognition." Purdue Univ. TR-EE 70-20, June 1970.
22. Watson, G. S. and M. R. Leadbetter. "On the Estimation of the Probability Density." *Ann. Math. Stat.*, 34 (1963), 480–491.
23. Whitney, A. W. and S. J. Dwyer III. "Performance and Implementation of the *k*-nearest Neighbor Decision Rule with Incorrectly Identified Training Samples." In *Allerton Conference on Circuit and System Theory*, Monticello, Ill., 1966.
24. Wilson, D. L. "Asymptotic Properties of Nearest Neighbor Rules Using Edited Data." *IEEE Trans. on Systems, Man, and Cybernetics*, SMC-2, 3 (July 1972), 408–421.

CHAPTER VIII

Cluster and Mode-Seeking Techniques

I. Introduction

So far we have discussed assigning patterns to predetermined classes. In some problems, however, even the number and nature of the classes, if any, are unknown. A large amount of data may often be analyzed by a digital computer in such a way as to give an understanding of the structure of the data and useful numerical measurements of certain characteristics of the data. For example, different types of clouds may be determined from a number of satellite photographs. From the accumulated electrocardiac records of thousands of patients, a clue to the possible varieties of heart disease may be sought. These and similar problems form the object of the range of techniques known as cluster analysis, numerical taxonomy, mode seeking, and unsupervised adaptation.

A cluster of patterns can be loosely defined as a set of patterns contained in a high-dimensional space where the density of patterns is large as compared to the surrounding volumes. In statistics, a mode is the most frequently observed value of a random variable. In this chapter we consider a mode as a cluster of patterns that belong to the same class. The object of cluster analysis is to classify experimental data in a certain number of sets where the samples of each set should be as similar as possible and dissimilar from those of other sets. This implies the existence of a measure of distance or similarity between the samples to be classified. The number of such classes must be fixed beforehand or may be a consequence of some constraints imposed on them.

The need for cluster analysis is evident if we consider the inadequacy of conventional statistical data analysis in which much use is made of the covariance and the correlation matrix.† Ball[1] showed three sets of data which appear to be quite different but with identical covariance matrices. As expected, there are also some difficulties in cluster analysis as illustrated by Nagy[2] and shown in figure 8.1. The problem of misclassifications originated in (1) "bridges" or

†For example, the correlation matrix is used in a central way in principal components analysis, in factor analysis, and in canonical correlation analysis.

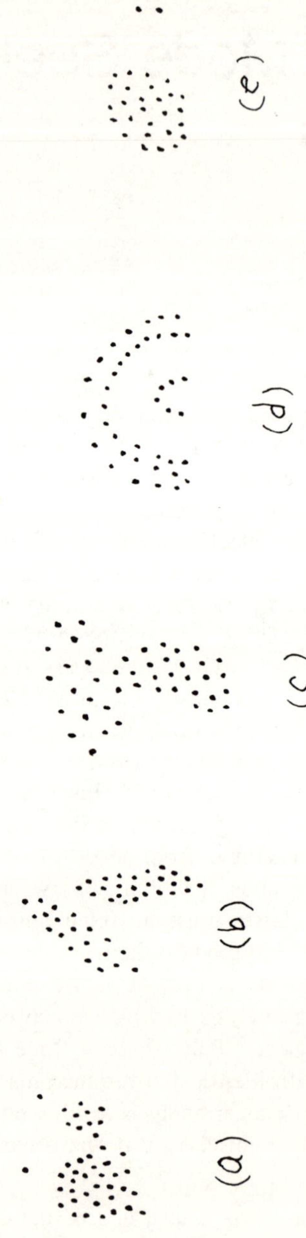

Fig. 8.1 Major Difficulties Found in Cluster Analysis; (a) and (c) Bridges Between Clusters; (b) Nonspherical Clusters; (d) Linearly Nonseparable Clusters; (e) Unequal Cluster Populations (Taken from E. H. Ruspini, "A New Approach to Clustering," *Information and Control*, 15, pp. 22–32, 1969)

strays between sets and (2) pairs classified in different classes having a greater similarity than some pairs within the same set. A survey of the methods and techniques of clustering may be found in Ball.[1]

In this chapter, various distance and similarity measures and information measures are presented, which will be followed by a discussion of important cluster and mode-seeking algorithms. Some operational pattern (data) analysis and recognition systems including those with on-line and interactive capability are also described.

2. Distance and Similarity Measures

For patterns with numerical components, a simple distance measure is the unweighted Euclidean distance

$$d_{ij}^2 = (x_i - x_j)' (x_i - x_j) = \sum_{k=1}^{D} (x_{ik} - x_{jk})^2 \tag{8.1}$$

where x_i and x_j are vectors of dimension D. The Euclidean distance is considerably affected by the scale factor associated with each pattern component. For binary patterns, the most common measure is the correlation $x_i'x_j$ which is often normalized by the geometric mean of the number of ones in both vectors, i.e., the normalized correlation

$$\rho_{ij} = \frac{x_i'x_j}{\sqrt{(x_i'x_i)\,(x_j'x_j)}} \tag{8.2}$$

which can also be used for numerical measurements.[3]

Another similarity measure[4] for binary variables which takes pairwise correlation into account is given by

$$S_{\alpha\beta} = \sum_{i=1}^{D} \sum_{j=1}^{D} r_{ij}[1 - |x_{\alpha i} - x_{\beta i}|]\ [1 - |x_{\alpha j} - x_{\beta j}|]\ [1 - 2|x_{\alpha i} - x_{\beta j}|] \tag{8.3}$$

where $S_{\alpha\beta}$ is the similarity between patterns α and β and r_{ij} is the correlation coefficients for features i and j.

A weighted Euclidean distance may take into account the dispersion of samples within a cluster. Let C_k be the weighting coefficient, then the weighted distance[4,5] is

$$D_{ij}^2 = \sum_{k=1}^{D} C_k(x_{ik} - x_{jk})^2 \tag{8.4}$$

A somewhat more complicated measure with some desirable information theoretic properties but without all the properties of a metric is given by[6]

$$d_{ij} = -\log \frac{x_i' x_j}{x_i' x_i + x_j' x_j - x_i' x_j} \tag{8.5}$$

The argument of the logarithm is a similarity measure,[6]

$$S_{ij} = \frac{x_i' x_j}{x_i' x_i + x_j' x_j - x_i' x_j} \tag{8.6}$$

By representing each pattern vector with a code word, Wallace and Boulton[7] have used an information measure to optimize the length of the codes, subject to some restrictions of each pattern vector. For each code, the first element represents the number of the class to which the sample (pattern vector) x belongs, the next r elements where r is variable are the parameters of the class to which x belongs, and the next S elements are devoted to specify the position of x with respect to the class (e.g., distance of x to the mean in some units in normal distributions). The length of the code vector is then variable depending on the class selected and the amount of information needed to specify that class and the position of x within the cluster.

Distance, correlation, and information functions are most commonly used for clustering. A number of other similarity measures are cataloged by Ball.[1]

3. Remarks on Cluster and Mode-Seeking Methods

It is evident that classification information is very useful in finding the most economical cluster description. The classification information is particularly important in mode seeking. Consider, for example, two classes. If two modes of class 2 are remote from samples of class 1, then the two modes may be considered as one. If, however, a third class is introduced with samples located between the two modes of class 2, then the two modes of class 2 cannot be combined into one.

Cluster analysis almost always involves a large amount of data. The amount of computation required to process all the data at the same time may be excessive for most computers. Iterative techniques allow the examination of iteratively selected subsets of patterns where the selection of one subset depends on the results obtained from a previous selection. The amount of computation can be reduced although the selection of data is very much dependent on the nature and structure of the data.

From the above discussion, the applicability of a given cluster-seeking method is determined by five factors: (1) computational complexity, (2) memory requirement, (3) sample size requirement, (4) nature of the data, and (5) availability of classification information.

4. Three Clustering Methods

Three different clustering methods are presented in this section to illustrate the techniques of constructing clusters.

(1) Bonner. Bonner[4] considers binary measurements for patterns and computes the similarity measure S_{ij} by using equation (8.6). He assumes that the number of samples is the same as the number of features, viz., D. Then a $D \times D$ matrix is constructed with elements S_{ij}, $i, j = 1, \ldots, D$. Each element is compared with a threshold T where $0 < T < 1$. If the threshold is exceeded, the element is replaced by 1; otherwise by 0. Tight clusters are formed such that all samples in a cluster have the largest similarity measures. Then, using the clusters so identified, a set of clusters is formed where no sample is in more than one cluster and all samples in a cluster are similar to each other. This step is to find a set of "core" clusters. Then a cluster adjustment program is written to integrate the members of the smaller core clusters into the larger and to relocate misplaced members of the larger. This step is accomplished by using a measure of interaction between a pair of clusters, x and y, given by

$$I_{xy} = \frac{1}{N_x N_y} \sum_{\alpha=1}^{N_x} \sum_{\beta=1}^{N_y} S_{\alpha\beta} \tag{8.7}$$

where N_x is the number of members in cluster x, N_y is the number of members in cluster y, $S_{\alpha\beta}$ is 1 if member α of cluster x is similar to member β of cluster y; is 0 if they are not similar. I_{xy} is the percentage of possible similarity "links" which are actually present between the members of cluster x and the members of cluster y.

To test the validity of a cluster, let $\bar{x}_{ik}$ and σ_{ik}^2 be the kth components of the sample mean and the sample variance respectively of the ith cluster with N_i samples. Also let $\bar{x}_k$ be the kth component of the sample mean based on N samples in the total given population. A test statistic G_i is then computed as

$$G_i = \sum_{k=1}^{D} \frac{(\bar{x}_{ik} - \bar{x}_k)^2}{\sigma_{ik}^2 / N_i} \tag{8.8}$$

The given population is a hypothetical one, where G has a chi-square distribution. The probability that $G \geqslant G_k$ can be estimated. If such probability is high, the set of samples for the proposed cluster belongs to the population. If such probability is small, then the given cluster is not valid.

(2) Ball and Hall. Ball and Hall[8] considered an iterative self-organizing data analysis (ISODATA) and pattern classification technique. Initially, several patterns are selected as trial cluster points. The patterns are sorted, one by one, on the basis of unweighted Euclidean distance from the initial cluster points which are modified only after all patterns considered have been clustered. Each pattern goes into that subset (cluster) having the closest clustering point. After all patterns have been sorted, the average of each of the subsets of patterns is computed and subset standard deviations in each dimension are determined. Small clusters, with fewer than k_1 samples, are discarded. Splitting or lumping of clusters takes place next. Splitting takes place if the standard deviation in any dimension is greater than k_2, and also if the cluster (1) has enough members to split and (2) has high average distance between its mean and the patterns in its subset. Lumping occurs between a controlled number of pairs of cluster centers that are less than k_3 apart. The process parameters k_1 (the minimum allowable size of a cluster), k_2 (the allowable maximum standard deviation in the cluster), and k_3 (the minimum distance between two cluster points), as well as others, are supplied by the data analyst. After each lumping or splitting, the updated set of average points is used as the set of cluster points for the next iteration. Several properties of the data structure such as the average distance of the patterns in the cluster from the average point of the cluster along with the number and identity of patterns in the cluster are printed out. At the termination of the program, the cluster points should adequately fit the data.

The gross structure of the data in data space is obtained by examining the vector relationships between the average points. It is noted that the number of average points is small enough to allow comparison of each average point with every other average point. A most useful way of comparing these average points is by means of various forms of graphic plots. An example of 225 data samples analyzed by Ball and Hall[8] is shown in figure 8.2. The data were artificially generated from nine approximately Gaussian parent distributions. The marginal distributions on the two axes are approximately uniform and the overall average of this complete data set is at the center of the figure. This is taken as the initial cluster center. After the first iteration, the single cluster point is split at right angles to the dimension having maximum standard deviation. Ball and Hall proposed an error of fit as a measure of clustering. Each stage of splitting and clustering reduces and minimizes the error of fit. Figure 8.2 also illustrates the fit of four and six clusters to the data samples. If the cost involved with every addition of a cluster must be considered, then the optimum number of clusters can be determined.

(3) Ruspini. Ruspini[9] considered numerical classification as the process of assigning to each data sample a certain degree of belongingness to each cluster $S_i, \ldots, S_m$. In that sense, the S_j's are "fuzzy sets" in the sense of Zadeh[10]. However, the degree of belongingness is considered as probabilistic. Let N be the

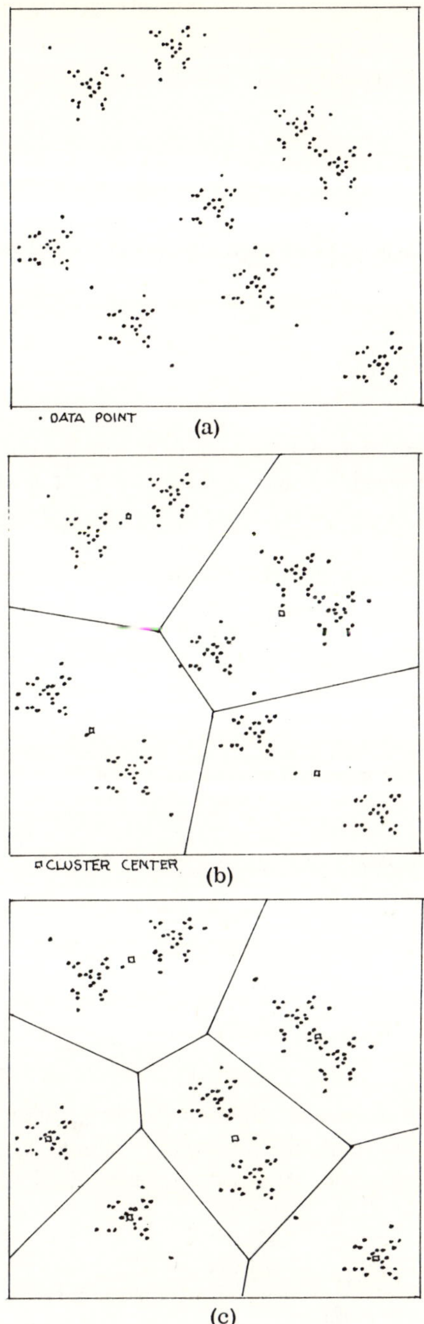

Fig. 8.2 Data Samples; (a) Original Data, (b) Four Clusters, (c) Six Clusters (Taken from G. H. Ball and D. J. Hall, "ISODATA, An Iterative Method of Multivariate Data Analysis and Pattern Classification," *IEEE Transactions on International Communications Conference*, June 1966)

total number of samples. Then

$$P(S_j) = \sum_{i=1}^{N} p(x_i)\, P(S_j|x_i) \tag{8.9}$$

is a measure of the relative size of each cluster; $P(S_j) \geqslant 0$ and $\Sigma_{j=1}^{m} P(S_j) = 1$. It is also noted that

$$p(x) = \sum_{j=1}^{m} P(S_j)\, p(x\,|\,S_j) \tag{8.10}$$

and so the clustering process may be seen as the decomposition of the density function $p(x)$ into the weighted sum of the component cluster densities $p(x\,|\,S_j)$ with weights $P(S_j)$. This concept is similar to the unsupervised learning described in chapter 5.

We now define $\delta(x_i, x_k)$ as the distance function with the properties: $\delta(x, x) = 0$ and $\delta(x, y) = \delta(y, x)$. Also define

$$M(x_i) = \sum_{k=1}^{N} p(x_k)\, \delta(x_i, x_k) \tag{8.11}$$

as the mean density of the population around x_i and

$$M_j(x_i) = \sum_{k=1}^{N} p(x_k\,|\,S_j)\, \delta(x_i, x_k) \tag{8.12}$$

as the mean density of the cluster S_j around x_i. Note that

$$\sum_{j=1}^{m} P(S_j)\, M_j(x_i) = M(x_i) \tag{8.13}$$

To insure that the decomposed density function, $p(x\,|\,S_j)$, really represent clusters, optimality conditions and constraints should be imposed. Two optimality conditions considered by Ruspini are to minimize the functional I defined as

$$\text{(1)}\quad I = \sum_{i=1}^{N} \left[p(x_i) \frac{P(S_{(i)}\, M_{(i)}\,(x_i)}{M(x_i)} \right]^2 \quad \text{(clustering I)} \tag{8.14}$$

$$\text{(2)}\quad I = \sum_{i=1}^{N} p(x_i) \sum_{j=1}^{m} P(S_j) \left[\frac{P(S_j)\, M_j(x_i)}{M(x_i)} \right] P(S_j|x_i) \quad \text{(clustering II)} \tag{8.15}$$

The parenthetical subscript notation introduced in equation (8.14) is used to indicate the cluster to which the sample x most likely belongs. Clustering I tries to minimize the average mean distance of each sample to the cluster to which it most likely belongs. Clustering II is based on the fact that when

$$\frac{P(S_j)\,M_j(x_i)}{M(x_i)}$$

is small, $P(S_j|x_i)$ should be large and vice versa. The methods to minimize I as well as the constraints and numerical results are described in detail at reference 11.

5. Other Methods in Clustering, Clumping, and Data Grouping

(1) Okajima, Stark, Whipple, and Yasui.[3] Patterns are selected in random order, weighted, and compared with a set of "typical" patterns, using a normalized correlation measure of similarity. The typical pattern correlation that is maximum is compared with a threshold. If the threshold is exceeded, then the pattern is added to that filter (cluster). If the threshold is not exceeded, then a a new filter is created. A smoothness of convergence parameter as well as a similarity threshold is used to control the program. Clusters are not destroyed in the process. Cluster points are the average of all of the patterns associated with that cluster point. The clustering is dependent on the order in which the individual patterns are presented to the program.

(2) Sebestyen and Edie.[5] This is the same as the sample set construction method described in chapter 7. The technique is specifically pointed toward establishing a probability density function.

(3) Rogers and Tanimoto.[6] The information theoretic entropy described in equation (8.5) is computed and minimized. This selects the pattern point nearest the centroid of the system of patterns. This most typical pattern is designated "a prime mode" and a clump of cases very similar to it are clustered around it. Patterns are added to this clump until the inhomogeneity measure suddenly takes a large jump in value, indicating that the last pattern added was not truly a member of this clump.

(4) Michener and Sokal.[12] The nucleus of a cluster is established using those two patterns having the highest pairwise coefficient of correlation. Then patterns are added to this nucleus one at a time, always adding first the pattern with the highest average correlation with the members of the group. The limit of the groups could be found by decreases in the level of the average correlation. A "significant" drop was empirically determined. Correlations between small clusters were used to group these small clusters into larger clusters. An obvious disadvantage of this method is the large number of comparisons to be made. This technique is best suited to taxonomic applications.

(5) Friedman and Rubin.[13] Let $x_1, x_2, \ldots, x_N$ be N D-dimensional samples which are to be divided into M groups, $G_1, G_2, \ldots, G_M$, with $N_1, N_2, \ldots, N_M$ samples respectively: $N = N_1 + N_2 + \cdots + N_M$. Define scatter matrices as follows:

$$\text{Total scatter:} \quad T = \sum_{k=1}^{N} x_k x_k^T \tag{8.16}$$

$$\text{Intragroup scatter:} \quad W_j = \sum_{x_k \epsilon G_j} (x_k - C_j)(x_k - C_j)^T \tag{8.17}$$

where C_j is the sample mean of G_j, $C_j = \dfrac{1}{N_j} \sum_{x_k \epsilon G_j} x_k$

$$\text{Total intragroup scatter:} \quad W = \sum_{j=1}^{M} W_j \tag{8.18}$$

$$\text{Intergroup scatter:} \quad B = \sum_{j=1}^{M} N_j C_j C_j^T \tag{8.19}$$

The superscript T denotes transposition. It is easily shown that

$$T = W + B \tag{8.20}$$

regardless of the partition. Furthermore, the eigenvalues of $W^{-1}B$, $\lambda_1, \lambda_2, \ldots, \lambda_d$ are invariant under nonsingular linear transformations of the x_k's.

The intragroup scatter is a measure of the degree of association of the members of the group. A simple criterion for grouping is to use J_0, defined as

$$J_0 = t_r W = \sum_{j=1}^{M} \sum_{x_k \epsilon G_j} |x_k - C_j|^2 \tag{8.21}$$

where $t_r W$ is the trace of the matrix W. J_0 may be interpreted as the mean-squared distance to the group center. The optimum is taken as the one which minimizes J_0. J_0 is not invariant under nonsingular linear transformation of the x_k's. This means that by changing the coordinate system of the original data, one may alter the optimum partition. Friedman and Rubin[13] then introduced a family of invariant criteria of the form

$$J = f(\lambda_1, \ldots, \lambda_D) \tag{8.22}$$

Two such criteria are

$$J_1 = \frac{\det T}{\det W} = \prod_{i=1}^{D} (1 + \lambda_i) \tag{8.23}$$

and

$$J_2 = t_r\, W^{-1} B = \sum_{i=1}^{D} \lambda_i \tag{8.24}$$

Several numerical examples were used to show that J_1 and J_2 are superior to J_0 in the sense of the performance requirement.

(6) Fukunaga and Kootz.[14] One drawback with J_1 and J_2 given by equations (8.23) and (8.24) respectively is the required time-consuming computation of W^{-1} and $\det W$. If the coordinate system is suitably chosen, J_0 can become a function of $\lambda_1, \ldots, \lambda_D$. For a two group problem, the authors were able to show that J_0, J_1, and J_2 are equivalent.

6. On-Line Pattern Analysis and Recognition Systems

A common drawback to all clustering algorithms is that their performance is highly dependent upon the user setting various parameters. In fact, the "proper" setting usually can only be determined by a trial and error method. Because of this, many researchers have found that the effective use of clustering algorithms necessitates their execution on an on-line system. This on-line evaluation can be used to dictate any parameter changes which may be required.

Some operational on-line or interactive computer facilities reported in the literature are as follows:

(1) Sammon,[15,16,17,18] The on-line pattern analysis and recognition system (OLPARS) employs two distinct on-line methods for performing cluster analysis. The first is ISODATA for cluster detection and identification, data compression, and measurement reduction (feature selection) when large numbers of vector samples (i.e., greater than 200 vectors) are involved. For smaller numbers of vectors, the second method is used. It is called the Similarity Matrix Method and is based on a clumping technique proposed by Needham, Parker-Rhodes, and Abraham. Reports by the three authors may not be readily available. A brief discussion of the Similarity Matrix Method is presented in appendix D. As an aid in solving the general problem of "structure" analysis, an effective algorithm called "nonlinear mapping" is provided in the OLPARS system. A D-dimensional vector space is mapped into a two-dimensional vector space under the criterion that points which are close in the D-space remain close in the two-space and points which are far apart in the D-space be mapped far apart in the two-space.

The results of this mapping are then presented to the user as a scatter diagram displayed on the cathode-ray tube.

Suppose that we have N vectors in a D-space designated as x_i, $i = 1, 2, \ldots, N$, and corresponding to these we have N vectors in a two-space designated as y_i, $i = 1, 2, \ldots, N$. Let d_{ij}^* be the Euclidian distance between vectors x_i and x_j in the D-space and d_{ij} be the Euclidian distance in the two-space. We can obtain an initial configuration for the y vectors by projecting the x vectors onto the two-coordinate space possessing the largest variance. An error function is then defined by

$$\text{Error} = \frac{\sum\limits_{i<j} f(d_{ij}^*)\,[d_{ij}^* - d_{ij}]^2}{\sum\limits_{i<j} [d_{ij}^{*2}]} \tag{8.25}$$

where $f(d_{ij}^*)$ is a weighting function which may be a monotonic decreasing function of d_{ij}^*. A gradient-seeking method is then used to solve for the configuration of y vectors which minimizes the error. A nonlinear mapping of four-dimensional Iris data† onto the two-dimensional space is shown in figure 8.3.

(2) Ball, Hall, and Evans.[19,20] They reported the interactive graphic computer facilities, PROMENDADE and ENVIRON at Stanford Research Institute and SARF (Signature Analysis Research Facility; Stanley et al.[21]) at the AC Electronics-Defense Research Lab. SARF is programmed for an IBM 360/50 computer with 2250 display unit. SARF includes a diffraction-pattern-sampling system that can be controlled from the interactive console. This allows the user to modify the characteristics of the transducer and to see the effects of this modification in all parts of the system.

(3) Walter.[22] The interactive facility for signal analysis was designed mainly for both speech and cardiograph bandwidth compression.

Other research activities are described by Dixon,[23] Engelbart and English,[24] Fukunaga and Olsen,[25] and others.

7. Remarks

As clustering methods are concerned with a broad class of data including those from social, behavioral, biological, and physical sciences, the potential development of cluster analysis is very great. Recently, the availability of interactive computer facilities adds an important dimension to cluster analysis as

†The Iris data set was used by Kendall in several statistical experiments. The data was originally obtained by making four measurements on Iris flowers. These measurements were then used to classify three different species of Iris flowers. Fifty sample vectors were obtained from each of the three species. Thus the data set consists of the 150 points in a four-dimensional space. See appendix E.

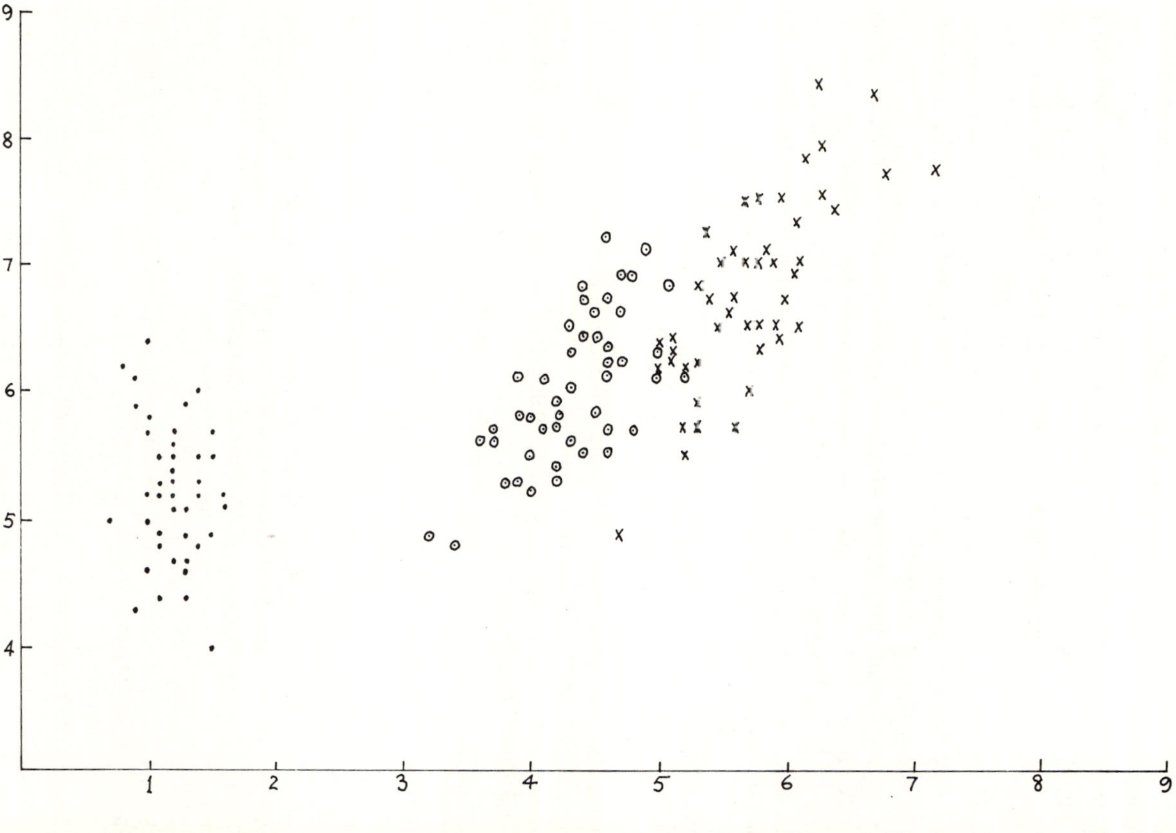

Fig. 8.3 Nonlinear Mapping Algorithm as Applied to Iris Data (Taken from J. W. Sammon, Jr., "On-Line Pattern Analysis and Recognition System (OLPAS)," RADC-TR68-263, Aug. 1968)

well as pattern classification. A number of clustering techniques have been introduced in this chapter. In spite of the fact that the process parameters for a particular set of data must be selected by trial and error or experience, the techniques presented in this chapter should be helpful for the user to select a technique for his specific application. The required amount of computation may be determined from the number of samples and the number of operations that each sample has to go through. The optimum number of clusters is highly dependent on the data at hand and no mathematical relationship has been available. A measure of the goodness of fit or a test of validity of a cluster should be useful to determine the suitable number of clusters. The cost of constructing a cluster may be taken into account also. The convergence of clusters is another topic of the analytical study.

The paper by Ball[1] provides an excellent survey of cluster and mode-seeking methods up to 1965. Although many developments since 1965 have been incorporated in this chapter, there are still a number of important clustering techniques which are not mentioned or only briefly discussed. The reader is referred to the bibliography at the end of this chapter for such techniques.

PROBLEMS

1. For the data shown in figure 8.2, obtain two clusters and nine clusters by using the ISODATA method.
2. Determine the amount of computation for the clustering techniques due to (1) Ball and Hall,[8] (2) Sebestyen and Edie,[5] (3) Okajima, Stark, Whipple, and Yasui,[3] (4) Bonner,[4] (5) Rogers and Tanimoto,[6] (6) Michener and Sokal,[12] (7) Ruspini[9] Clustering I.

REFERENCES

1. Ball, G. H. "Data Analysis in the Social Sciences: What About the Details?" *Proc. of Fall Joint Computer Conference,* (1965), 533–559.
2. Nagy, G. "State of the Art in Pattern Recognition." *Proceedings of IEEE,* 56 (1968), 836–882.
3. Okajima, M., L. Stark, G. Whipple, and S. Yasui. "Computer Pattern Recognition Techniques: Some Results with Real Electrocardiographic Data." *IEEE Trans. on Bio-Medical Electronics,* BME-10 (July 1963).
4. Bonner, R. E. "On Some Clustering Techniques." *IBM Journal of Res. and Dev.,* (January 1964), 22–32.
5. Sebestyen, G. S. and J. Edie. "An Algorithm for the Nonparametric Pattern Recognition." *IEEE Trans. on Electronic Computers,* EC-15 (December 1966), 908–915.
6. Rogers, D. J. and T. T. Tanimoto. "A Computer Program for Classifying Plants." *Science,* 132 (October 21, 1960).
7. Wallace, C. S. and D. M. Boulton. "An Information Measure for Classification." *Computer Journal,* 11 (1968), 185–194.
8. Ball, G. H. and D. J. Hall. "ISODATA, An Iterative Method of Multivariate Data Analysis and Pattern Classification." In *IEEE International Communications Conference.* Philadelphia, June 1966.

9. Ruspini, E. H. "A New Approach to Clustering." *Information and Control,* 15 (1969), 22–32.
10. Zadeh, L. A. "Fuzzy Sets." *Information and Control,* 8 (1965), 338–353.
11. Ruspini, E. H. "Numerical Methods for Fuzzy Clustering." *Information Sciences,* 2 (1970), 319–350.
12. Michener, C. D. and R. R. Sokal, "A Quantitative Approach to a Problem in Classification." *Evolution,* 11 (June 1957), 130–162.
13. Friedman, H. P. and J. Rubin. "On some Invariant Criteria for Group Data." *Amer. Stat. Assoc. J.,* 62 (December 1967), 1159–1178.
14. Fukunaga, K. and W. L. G. Koontz. "A Criterion and an Algorithm for Grouping Data." *IEEE Trans. on Computers,* C-19 (October 1970), 917–923.
15. Sammon, J. W., Jr. "On-line Pattern Analysis and Recognition System." Technical Report RADC-TR-68-263, August 1968.
16. Sammon, J. W., Jr. "A Nonlinear Mapping for Data Structure Analysis." *IEEE Trans. on Computers,* C-18 (May 1969), 401–409.
17. Sammon, J. W., Jr. "Iterative Pattern Analysis and Classification." *IEEE Trans. on Computers,* C-19 (July 1970), 594–616.
18. Sammon, J. W., Jr. "An Optimal Discriminant Plane." *IEEE Trans. on Computers,* C-19 (September 1970), 826–829.
19. Ball, G. H., D. J. Hall, and D. A. Evans. "Implications of Interactive Graphic Computers for Pattern Recognition Methodology." In *Methodologies of Pattern Recognition,* edited by S. Watanabe. Academic Press, New York, 1969.
20. Ball, G. H., D. J. Hall, and D. A. Evans. "Some Implications of Interactive Computer Systems for Data Analysis and Statistics." Presented at the American Statistical Association Meeting, Pittsburgh, August 1968.
21. Stanley, G. L., G. G. Landaris, and W. C. Nienow. "Pattern recognition program." AC Electronics-Defense Research Laboratory Technical Report 569-16, Santa Barbara, Calif., November 1967.
22. Walter, C. M. "On-Line Computer-Based Aids for the Investigation of Sensor Data Compression, Transmission and Display Problems." In *Proc. of 1966 National Telemetry Conference.* Boston, 1966.
23. Dixon, W. J. "Use of Displays with Packaged Statistical Programs." In *Proc. AFIPS Fall Joint Computer Conference,* vol. 31, pp. 481–484. Thompson, 1967.
24. Engelbart, D. C. and W. K. English. "A Research Center for Augmenting Human Intellect." In *Proc. AFIPS Fall Joint Computer Conference,* vol. 33, pp. 395–410. Thompson, 1968.
25. Fukunaga, K. and D. R. Olsen. "A Two-Dimensional Display for the Classification of Multivariate Data." *IEEE Trans. on Computers,* C-20 (August 1971), 917–923.

Bibliography

1. Bennett, R. S. "The Intrinsic Dimensionality of Signal Collections. *IEEE Trans. on Information Theory,* IT-15 (September 1969), 517–525.
2. Butler, G. A. "A Vector Field Approach to Cluster Analysis." *Pattern Recognition,* vol. 1, No. 4 (July 1969), 291–299.

3. Casey, R. G. and G. Nagy. "An Autonomous Reading Machine." *IEEE Trans. on Computers,* C-17 (May 1968), 492–503.
4. Firschein, O. and M. Fischler. "Automatic Subclass Determination for Pattern Recognition Application." *Trans. of PGEC,* EC-12 (April 1963).
5. Fukunaga, K. and D. R. Olsen. "An Algorithm for Finding Intrinsic Dimensionality of Data." *IEEE Trans. on Computers,* C-20 (February 1971), 176–183. Comments by G. V. Trunk, *IEEE Trans. on Computers* (December 1971).
6. Hall, D. J., G. H. Ball, and D. E. Wolf. "Applications of the Promenade Data Analysis System." In *IEEE Computers and Communications Conference Record.* Rome, New York, October 1969.
7. Haralick, R. M. and I. Dinstein. "An Iterative Clustering Procedure." *IEEE Trans. on Systems, Man, and Cybernetics,* SMC-1 (July 1971), 374–389.
8. Henrichon, E. G. and K. S. Fu. "On Mode Estimation in Pattern Recognition." *IEEE Proceedings of Seventh Symposium on Adaptive Processes,* UCLA, December 1968.
9. Hyvarinen, L. "Classification of Qualitative Data." *British Information Theory Journal* (1962), 83–89.
10. Kaskey, G. et al. "Cluster Formation and Diagnostic Significance in Psychiatric Symptom Evaluation." In *Proc. Fall Joint Computer Conference,* p. 285, 1962.
11. Kochen, M. and E. Wong. "Concerning the Possibility of a Cooperative Information Exchange." *IBM Journal of Res. and Dev.*, 6 (April 1962), 270–271.
12. Koontz, W. L. G. and K. Fukunaga. "A Nonparametric Valley-seeking Technique for Cluster Analysis." *IEEE Trans. on Computers*, C-21, (February 1972), 171–178.
13. Kruskal, J. B. "Comments on 'A Nonlinear Mapping for Data Structure Analysis'." *IEEE Trans. on Computers*, (December 1971).
14. Kruskal, J. B. "Multidimensional Scaling by Optimizing Goodness of Fit to a Nonmetric Hypothesis." *Psychometrika*, 29 (1964), 1–27.
15. Lance, C. N. and W. T. Williams. "A General Theory of Classificatory Sorting Strategies II Clustering Systems." *Computer Journal*, 10 (1967), 271–277.
16. Ling, R. F. "Cluster Analysis." Ph.D. dissertation, Technical Report No. 18, Dept. of Statistics, Yale University, 1971.
17. MacQueen, J. "Some Methods for Classification and Analysis of Multivariate Observations." In *Proc. Fifth Berkeley Symposium on Probability and Statistics*, pp. 281–297. 1967.
18. Masson, C. G. "Hierarchical Clustering of Data with a Mutual Entropy Criterion: Its Structural Feature Extraction Ability." In *IEEE Conference Record of the Symposium on Feature Extraction and Selection in Pattern Recognition*. Argonne National Laboratory, October 1970.
19. Mattson, R. L. and J. E. Dammann. "A Technique for Determining and Coding Subclasses in Pattern Recognition Problems." *IBM Journal of Res. and Dev.*, 9 (July 1965), 294–302.
20. Mucciardi, A. N. and E. E. Gose. "An Automatic Clustering Algorithm and Its Properties in High-Dimensional Spaces." *IEEE Trans. on Systems, Man, and Cybernetics*, vol. SMC-2, No. 2 (April 1972), 247–254.

21. Nunnally, J. "The Analysis of Profile Data." *Psychological Bulletin*, 59 (1962), 311–319.
22. Rubio, J. E. "The Clustering and Recognition of Patterns." *International Journal of Control*, 4 (1966), 459–485.
23. Shepard, R. N. "The Analysis of Proximities: Multidimensional Scaling with an Unknown Distance Function." *Psychometrika*, 29, part I, 125–140, part II, 219–246, 1962.
24. Shepard, R. N. and J. D. Carroll. "Parametric Representation of Nonlinear Data Structures." In *Proc. International Symposium on Multivariate Analysis*, edited by P. R. Krishnarah. Academic Press, New York, 1966.
25. Shepard, R. N., J. B. Kruskal, J. D. Carroll, L. R. Tucker, et al. "Workshop on Multidimensional Scaling: Lecture Notes." University of Pennsylvania, Philadelphia, June 7–10, 1972.
26. Smith, J. W. "The Analysis of Multiple Signal Data." *IEEE Trans. on Information Theory*, IT-10 (July 1964), 208–214.
27. Sokal, R. R. and P. H. A. Sneath. *Principles of Numerical Taxonomy*. Freeman, San Francisco, 1963.
28. Trunk, G. V. "Parameter Identification Using Intrinsic Dimensionality." *IEEE Trans. on Information Theory*, IT-18 (January 1972), 126–133.
29. Tryon, R. C. and D. E. Bailey. *Cluster Analysis*. McGraw-Hill, New York, 1970.
30. Tukey, J. W. and M. B. Wilk. "Data Analysis and Statistics: An Expository Overview." In *Proc. Fall Joint Computer Conference*, pp. 695–709. 1966.
31. Watanabe, S. M. *Knowing and Guessing*. Wiley, New York, 1969.
32. Wee, W. G. "Generalized Inverse Approach to Clustering, Feature Selection, and Classification." *IEEE Trans. on Information Theory*, IT-17 (May 1971), 262–269.
33. Whitney, A. W., W. E. Blasdell, and S. Giulieri. "Study of Computer Graphics and Signal Classification Applications." General Electric Electronics Laboratory Report R70ELS-80, September 1970.
34. Wilde, D. J. *Optimum Seeking Methods*. Prentice-Hall, Englewood Cliffs, N.J., 1964.

CHAPTER IX
Sequential Pattern Recognition Systems

1. Introduction

In previous chapters we have assumed that each pattern vector has a finite and fixed number of measurements (features) and that an infinite number of learning samples are available in the learning or estimation problems. The fact that the measurements or learning samples are costly has not been considered. In this chapter, the concept of sequentially taking observations (measurements or samples) and making decisions is applied to problems in pattern recognition and learning.

It is evident that an insufficient number of observations will not lead to satisfactory results in pattern recognition. An infinite number of observations, on the other hand, is impractical. A tradeoff between the error and the number of observations can be made by taking observations sequentially and terminating the sequential procedure, i.e., making a final decision, when sufficient or desirable accuracy has been achieved. In other words, a decision is not made until the recognition system has sufficient confidence to do so. An observation with very high dimension may not necessarily describe the measurement space in an optimal manner. The sequential decision procedure automatically determines, on the average, the smallest dimension feature set which truly characterizes the pattern class in pattern recognition or the smallest number of learning samples for a learning problem.

Another important advantage is the availability of feature ordering and sample selection. By ordering the features in a predetermined manner or in an on-line process, the sequential classification procedure can be terminated much faster for a given recognition accuracy. Similarly, the best learning samples can be processed earlier than the bad ones and the required number of learning samples can be much reduced for a specified estimation accuracy. Thus sequential decision theory adds an important dimension to statistical pattern recognition. The difficulty with this approach is to determine the stopping rule, i.e., where to discontinue the sequential recognition or learning procedure. The development of sequential decision theory[1,2,3] in recent years has provided many useful answers to this problem.

A block diagram of the sequential recognition system is shown in figure 9.1. As compared with figure 1.2, the sequential recognition system enables us to consider the problems of receptor and categorizer jointly. The stopping bounds may be adjusted to improve the performance. In this chapter we shall start with the optimal sequential decision procedure, the generalized sequential probability ratio test, and sequential Bayesian learning. We shall then proceed with the feature ordering and selection, nonparametric sequential ranking procedures and applications to medical diagnosis. A number of computer results will be included. The term "sequential" in this chapter implies the existence of a stopping rule.

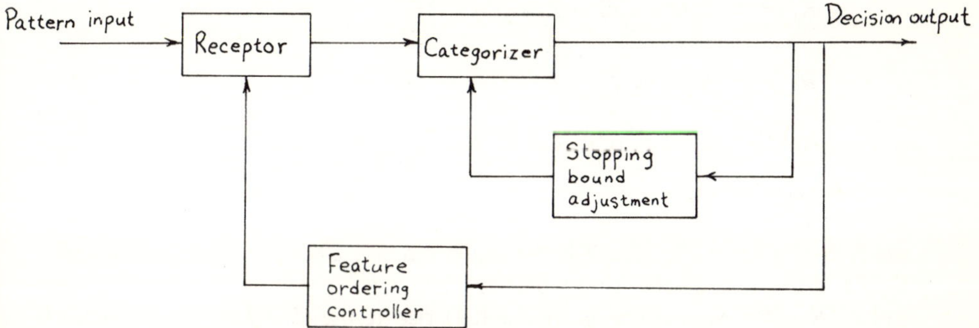

Fig. 9.1 The Sequential Pattern Recognition System

2. Bayes Sequential Decision Procedure and the Computational Problems

When decisions are made sequentially, the previous measurements and decisions can be used to improve the decision to be made at the present time. If the cost of taking a measurement is taken into account in minimizing the system's risk function, the sequential decision procedure will be necessarily stopped somewhere since the reduction of the risk function due to further measurement would be less than the cost of taking such a measurement.

Consider that there are m pattern classes. The sequential procedure will terminate after not more than N measurements. For any sequential sampling plan† S whose element is S_j, $j = 0, 1, \ldots, N$, decision procedure d, and a priori

†A sequential sampling plan is a procedure for taking the measurements sequentially. The number of measurements is determined by the sequential decision rule.

probabilities P_i, 1, 2, . . . , m, the expected risk can be written as

$$R(P,S,d) = \sum_{j=0}^{N} \sum_{x \in S_j} \sum_{i=1}^{m} [C_j(x) + L(\omega_i,\ d(j,x))]\ P_i p(x/\omega_i) \tag{9.1}$$

where $C_j(x)$ is the cost of taking measurements $x = (x_1, x_2, \ldots, x_j)$, $d(j,x)$ is the decision rule based on the measurements $x_1, \ldots, x_j$, and $L(\omega_i, d_k)$ is the loss incurred when the ith pattern class is true and the kth pattern class is chosen. We assume in this chapter that the cost of taking a measurement is a constant denoted by C. The Bayes sequential decision procedure, which minimizes $R(P, D, d)$ for a given a priori probability $P = \{P_i\}$, is to make the decision sequentially such that:

$$\begin{aligned} R_0(P) &= \psi_0(P) = \min_j \sum_i L(\omega_i, d_j)P_i \\ R_1(P) &= \min\ [\psi_1(P),\ \ C + E\,(R_0(P^*))] \\ &\text{- -} \\ R_N(P) &= \min\ [\psi_N(P),\ \ C + E\,(R_{n-1}(P^*))] \\ R_{N+1}(P) &= \psi_{N+1}(P) \leqslant C \end{aligned} \tag{9.2}$$

where $R_j(P)$, j = 1, 2, . . . , N is the minimum risk after taking j measurements, $R_0(P)$ is the risk of choosing a pattern class without taking any measurement, and $E\ [R_j(P^*)]$ is the average (expected) risk if the $(j + 1)$th measurement is taken after taking j measurements. Here the average is with respect to all possible outcomes of the $(j + 1)$th measurement, with the a posteriori probability† P^* given by

$$P(\omega_i/x_1, \ldots, x_{j+1}) = \frac{P_i p(x_1, x_2, \ldots, x_{j+1})}{\sum_i P_i p(x_1, x_2, \ldots, x_{j+1})} \tag{9.3}$$

for the ith pattern class, i = 1, 2, . . . , m. Hence $C + E\ [R_j(P^*)]$ is the expected risk to continue taking a measurement while making no decision based on the j measurements already available. Also in equation (9.2), $\psi_j(P)$ is the same as $\psi_0(P)$ except that P_i is replaced by the a posteriori probability based on the j measurements. To insure termination of the sequential procedure by the Nth measurement, we have set $\psi_{N+1}\ (P) \leqslant C$, which is the criterion for selecting N and C. To determine the decision and stopping boundaries, we can work "backward" by rewriting equation (9.2) as

†The a posteriori probability can be computed recursively in the case of independent and identically distributed measurements.

$$R_j(P) = \min\,[\psi_j(P),\;\; C + E\,(R_{j+1}(P^*))] \tag{9.4}$$

since $R_j(P)$ and $R_{j+1}(P)$ have the same forms. So we can start with computing $R_N(P)$, then $R_{N-1}(P), \ldots,$ and finally $R_1(P)$. Two excellent examples of using equations (9.2) and (9.4) for $m = 2$ and independent and identically distributed measurements were given by Wald (reference 1, section 4.14) for the binary measurements with binomial distributions and Goode[4] for the Gaussian distributed measurements.

It would be much clearer from the computational viewpoint if the Bayes sequential procedure is restated as follows:[5]

Let $R(x_1, x_2, \ldots, x_n)$ = the minimum average risk of the entire sequential decision procedure having taken the measurements $(x_1, x_2, \ldots, x_n)$,

$\psi(x_1, x_2, \ldots, x_n, d_i)$ = the average risk of choosing the ith class after taking n measurements. (The cost of measurements is not included.)

If we take an additional measurement, the expected risk is

$$C + \int R(x_1, x_2, \ldots, x_n, x_{n+1})\; d\,p(x_{n+1} \mid x_1, \ldots, x_n) \tag{9.4a}$$

Then the Bayes sequential decision procedure is governed by the equation

$$R(x_1, x_2, \ldots, x_n) = \min \begin{cases} \text{continue:} \\ C + \displaystyle\int R(x_1, x_2, \ldots, x_{n+1}) \\ \qquad\qquad \cdot\, dp\,(x_{n+1} \mid x_1, \ldots, x_n) \\ \text{stop:} \\ \min\limits_i \psi(x_1, x_2, \ldots, x_n, d_i) \end{cases} \tag{9.5}$$

This procedure is the same as the dynamic programming process,[5] or the deferred decision theory.[4] It is noted from equation (9.5) that all previous measurements must be stored. Each measurement is assumed to take discrete values. Suppose the sequence of measurements $x_1, \ldots, x_{N-1}$ is known, the average risk when an additional measurement is taken can be obtained from the specified risk function. Then, by using dynamic programming the procedure can be performed backward to the first measurement. The stopping region for the initial measurement can then be determined. Sequential recognition can be performed according to such predetermined stopping and continuing regions, which are stored in the computer, and the recognition procedure will terminate after taking not more than N measurements. If the dimension of each measurement is high, the amount of computation and storage becomes excessive as n becomes large—even for the modern general purpose digital computer. For example, of three classes, $m = 3$, with features each being quantized into 20 levels, there are $\frac{m(m-1)}{2} \sum_{n=1}^{8} (20)^n$ possible ways to reach a terminal decision. The sequential procedure, however, is truly optimal except for small quantization errors. Bellman[5] suggested the use of sufficient statistics and numerical approximations to considerably reduce the required amount of computation and storage. This is called the dimensionality reduction in dynamic programming. Various strategies and algorithms for dimensionality reduction have been examined by Cardillo, Chien, and Fu[6-10] for both pattern classification and feature selection and ordering with independent or Markov-dependent measurements. Dynamic programming has proved to be a powerful tool in sequential pattern recognition. The following simple but nontrivial example[11] illustrates the use of equation (9.5).

Example Consider two pattern classes: handprinted English characters A and B. Eight features are taken for each sample as described by Marill and Green.† Successive measurements are assumed to be independent. For each measurement x_i, a threshold is computed and each x_i is classified as type A with assigned number 0, or type B with a number 1, where type A corresponds to pattern class 1 (character A) and type B to class 2 (character B). Thus each measurement is transformed to 0 or 1 and there are $2 + 2^2 + \cdots + 2^8 = 510$ possible ways to reach the terminal decision that either class 1 or class 2 is true. Successive measurements, after the transformation, are then independent and identically distributed. Let the probability of the occurrence of event type A by p, which is unknown, and the a priori distribution of p be uniform over the interval $[0, 1]$. Let m and n be the number of occurrences of type A and type B events. The functional equation (9.5) can be written as

$$R(m,n) = \min\, [C + p(m,n)R(m+1,n) + (1 - p(m,n))R(m,n+1);\ \psi(m,n)] \tag{9.6}$$

where $p(m, n)$ = probability of the occurrence of event type A when events of type A and type B have occurred m and n times respectively. As soon as $m + n = N = 8$, we stop the sequential procedure. Starting with the known values for $R(m, n)$, $m + n = N$, we can compute $R(m, n)$, $m + n < N$ sequentially. The boundary conditions are $R(m, n) = \psi(m, n)$, $m + n \geqslant N$. When $m + n = N$, choose class 1 if $m \geqslant n$, choose class 2 otherwise. $R(m, n)$ can be computed

†*IRE Trans. on Electronic Computers*, EC-9, no. 4, 1960. See also reference 18.

TABLE 9.1
RISK FUNCTIONS

Number of 1's (occurrences of type B)

Number of 0's (occurrences of type A)		0	1	2	3	4	5	6	7	8
	0	0.2500 0.244	0.0625 0.0194	0.0156 0.0069	0.0039 0.0039	0.0010 0.0010	0.0002 0.0002	0.0001 0.0001	0.000 0.000	0.000 0.000
	1	0.0625 0.0194	0.0723 0.0293	0.0421 0.0243	0.0319 0.01684	0.01584 0.01584	0.0115 0.0115	0.0062 0.0062	0.001 0.001	
	2	0.0156 0.0069	0.0421 0.0243	0.032 0.023	0.021 0.018	0.0127 0.0127	0.0073 0.0073	0.002 0.002		
	3	0.0039 0.0039	0.0319 0.01684	0.0210 0.018	0.014 0.0134	0.0084 0.0084	0.003 0.003			
	4	0.001 0.001	0.01684 0.01684	0.0127 0.0127	0.0084 0.0084	0.004 0.004				
	5	0.0002 0.0002	0.0115 0.0115	0.00733 0.00733	0.003 0.003					
	6	0.001 0.001	0.0062 0.0062	0.002 0.002						
	7	0.000 0.000	0.001 0.001							
	8	0.000 0.000								

starting from $R(m, n)$, $m + n = N - 1$. Computation of $p(m, n)$ corresponds to finding the Bayes estimate of the probability p of the occurrence of the event of type A. The probability of m occurrences of event type A in a sequence of $m + n$ measurements is $\binom{m+n}{n} p^m(1-p)^n$. The Bayes estimate of p is

$$p(m, n) = \frac{\int_0^1 p^{m+1}(1-p)^n dp}{\int_0^1 p^m (1-p)^n dp} = \frac{\Gamma(m+2)\Gamma(n+1)\Gamma(m+n+2)}{\Gamma(m+n+3)\Gamma(m+1)\Gamma(n+1)}$$

$$= \frac{m+1}{n+n+2} \tag{9.7}$$

Let the cost of each measurement be $C = 0.005$. In table 9.1 the risk functions for all possible occurrences of events are listed with the numbers in the upper halves of the cells indicating the risk of making a terminal decision, i.e., choosing a pattern class, and the numbers in the lower halves of the cells indicating the risk of continuing to take measurements.

3. Sequential Probability Ratio Test (SPRT) and Generalized Sequential Probability Ratio Test (GSPRT)

Sequential testing is a forward procedure which requires much less computation than the backward procedure discussed in the preceding section. For two pattern classes, Wald's sequential probability ratio test[2] (SPRT) can be used, which computes the likelihood ratio

$$L(x) = L(x_1, x_2, \ldots, x_k) = \frac{p(x_1, x_2, \ldots, x_k/\omega_1)}{p(x_1, x_2, \ldots, x_k/\omega_2)} \tag{9.8}$$

after taking k measurements. Two thresholds (stopping bounds) A and B, $0 < B < A < \infty$ are predetermined from the two types of errors

$$\alpha = Pr\,(\text{choose } \omega_2/\omega_1), \quad \beta = Pr\,(\text{choose } \omega_1/\omega_2)$$

according to the following approximate relationship,

$$A = \frac{1-\beta}{\alpha}, \quad B = \frac{\beta}{1-\alpha} \tag{9.9}$$

The decision rule is: choose class 1 if $L(x) > A$, class 2 if $L(x) < B$, and request an additional measurement if $B \leqslant L(x) \leqslant A$. Assume that the successive measurements be independent and identically distributed. Let $z_i = \log (p(x_i/\omega_1)/p(x_i/\omega_2))$ for a single measurement x_i, then $E(z_i) = E(z)$ for all i. The average numbers of measurements are given by

$$E_1(n) = \frac{\beta \log B + (1 - \beta) \log A}{E_1(z)}$$

and

$$E_2(n) = \frac{(1 - \alpha) \log B + \alpha \log A}{E_2(z)}$$

where $E_i(n)$, $i = 1, 2$ denotes the expected value of n when the ith class is true.

For more than two pattern classes, the generalized sequential probability ratio test[12] (GSPRT) can be used. After taking k measurements, the generalized sequential probability ratio for the ith pattern class is computed as

$$U_k(x/\omega_i) = \frac{p(x_1, x_2, \ldots, x_k/\omega_i)}{\left[\prod_{q=1}^{m} p(x_1, x_2, \ldots, x_k/\omega_q)\right]^{1/m}}, \quad i = 1, 2, \ldots, m \tag{9.10}$$

where the denominator is the geometric mean of the likelihood functions (probability densities) of all classes.† Then $U_k(x/\omega_i)$ is compared with the threshold (stopping bound) of the ith class, $A(\omega_i)$, and reject the ith class if $U_k(x/\omega_i) < A(\omega_i)$. If the inequality is not satisfied for any i, request an additional measurement. If the ith class is rejected, the total number of classes is reduced by one and a new sequential probability ratio is formed. After each measurement, the decision of whether to continue taking measurements or to reject certain pattern classes is based on the complete information thus far obtained; no information is lost even after rejection of certain pattern classes. The pattern classes are rejected until only one is left, which is accepted as the recognized class. The rejection criterion, though somewhat conservative, will lead to a high percentage of correct recognition because only the pattern classes which are most unlikely to be true are rejected. As the number of pattern classes is reduced, the pattern class which is most likely to be true becomes more evident. Let e_{iq} be the probability of choosing the ith class if the qth class is true. The error probabilities can be specified to compute the stopping bounds defined as

$$A(\omega_i) = \frac{1 - e_{ii}}{\left[\prod_{q=1}^{m} (1 - e_{iq})\right]^{1/m}}, \quad 1 = 1, 2, \ldots, m \tag{9.11}$$

†Other ways of forming the generalized likelihood ratio are possible but equation (9.10) appears to be the best choice.[12]

The optimality of SPRT has been proved by Wald and Wolfowitz[13] and Lehmann[14] who showed that the SPRT has the minimum expected number of measurements among all sequential tests with the same α and β. The optimality of the generalized sequential probability ratio test is not obvious except for the case of two pattern classes in which the generalized sequential probability ratio test is equivalent to Wald's sequential probability ratio test. In fact, optimum sequential testing for multiple pattern classes has been an unsolved problem except for the special cases such as various pattern classes differing only by the translational parameters.

Many other sequential schemes are possible. For example, a sequential tree scheme splits all pattern classes into two groups and chooses the group which most likely contains the true pattern class. We then proceed with such group until only one pattern class is left, which is chosen as the true pattern class. This procedure requires less expected number of measurements at the expense of a larger probability of misrecognition.

As the number of measurements required for making a terminal decision is a random variable, truncation is often necessary because the available number of measurements is usually finite. Truncation is a fixed-sample test. For two classes, a threshold T, $B < T < A$, can be set and if $L(x_1, \ldots, x_N) \geqslant T$, choose class 1, otherwise choose class 2. Here N is the total number of measurements. If truncation occurs at twice or more than twice the expected number of measurements, the effect of truncation is negligible. We may fix the total number of measurements and adjust the stopping bounds in a predetermined manner such that the sequential test automatically terminates by reaching the last measurement. Let $A(k)$ and $B(k)$ be the stopping bounds which vary with the number of measurements. Then $A(k)$ and $B(k)$ must be monotonically nonincreasing and nondecreasing functions of k respectively, such that $A(N) = B(N) = T$. For example,

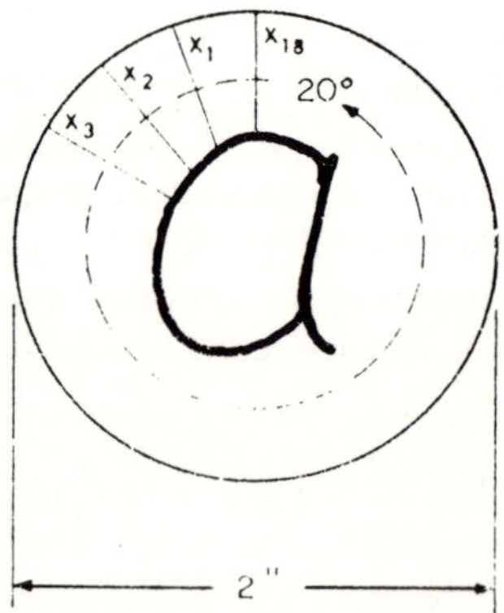

Fig. 9.2(a) A Typical Sample of Hand-Written Characters (for Recognition Experiment in Fig. 9.2(b))

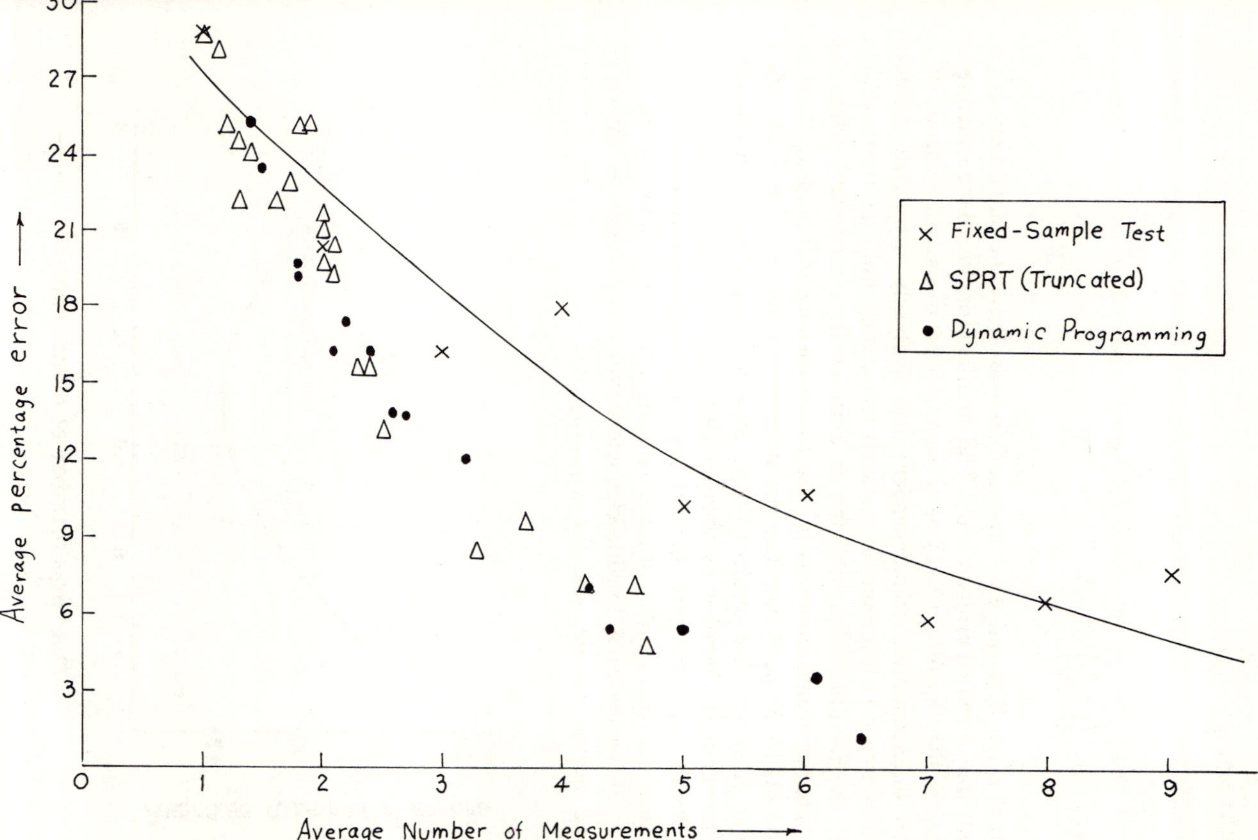

Fig. 9.2(b) A Comparison of Sequential and Fixed-Sample Recognition Procedures (Taken from K. S. Fu and G. P. Cardillo, "Optimal Finite Sequential Pattern Recognition," TR-EE67-9, Purdue University, 1967)

we can choose[15]

$$A(k) = A_0 \left(1 - \frac{k}{N}\right)^{r_1}$$

and

$$B(k) = B_0 \left(1 - \frac{k}{N}\right)^{r_2} \qquad (9.12)$$

where $0 < r_1, r_2 \leqslant 1$ and $A_0 = A(0)$ and $B_0 = B(0)$ are the initial bounds determined from specified errors α and β. The modified (or closed) sequential tests with bounds like equation (9.12) have been applied to pattern recognition.[16] Although the assumption of independent and identically distributed measurements of reference 15 is not met in character recognition problems, the feasibility of using the modified sequential test is quite evident, particularly when the average number of measurements is close to the total number of measurements. Theoretically, by properly adjusting the stopping bounds, this forward modified sequential procedure is equivalent to the backward sequential procedure (dynamic programming) described by equation (9.5).

If in Wald's sequential test, the average number of measurements is much smaller than the total number of measurements, available computer recognition results[17] of handwritten English characters with 18 features as shown in figure 9.2 clearly indicates that the sequential test and dynamic programming

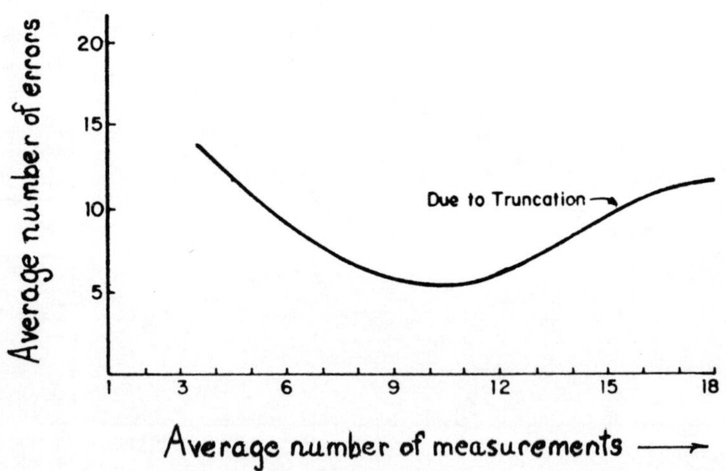

Fig. 9.3 ANE (Average Number of Errors) Versus ANM (Average Number of Measurements) In Sequention Recognition of Hand-Written Characters

are equally effective, as expected, and far better than the fixed-sample test. In a similar recognition experiment,[18] it is noted that the plot (figure 9.3) of the average number of errors versus the average number of measurements shows an optimum number of measurements, n_{opt} with $0 < n_{\text{opt}} \leqslant N(n_{\text{opt}} \simeq 10$ in this case) which will do the best job in recognition. This situation becomes more evident when the patterns are characterized by a large number of measurements (features). A comparison[11] between GSPRT and dynamic programming for the recognition of handwritten characters a, b, c, d is tabulated in table 9.2. The stopping bound is $A(\omega_i) = 0.9$ for all four classes in GSPRT. The characters are assumed to be multivariate Gaussian.

TABLE 9.2
Recognition of Handwritten Characters Using GSPRT and Dynamic Programming
(Features are unordered)

a. Using GSPRT

Out \ In	*a*	*b*	*c*	*d*
a	28	0	1	2
b	1	27	0	0
c	0	3	29	1
d	1	0	0	27

Stopping bound
$A(\omega_i) = 0.9$
$i = 1, 2, 3, 4$
$E_i(n)$ = average number of measurements for ith class
$E_a(n) = 10.40$
$E_b(n) = 9.32$
$E_c(n) = 15.30$
$E_d(n) = 11.65$

b. Using Dynamic Programming

Out \ In	*a*	*b*	*c*	*d*
a	26	0	3	0
b	0	28	1	1
c	3	1	26	1
d	1	1	0	28

$E_a(n) = 7.00$
$E_b(n) = 6.45$
$E_c(n) = 7.40$
$E_d(n) = 7.70$

4. Bayesian Sequential Analysis

The uncertainty of a pattern recognition system can often be described by a random variable, denoted as θ. If the a priori parameter density $p(\theta)$ of each class is known, then the sequential analysis discussed in the preceding section can be extended to the random parameter systems. Assume the classified learning samples, denoted as l_i, are available for each class. We shall prove that the sequential test will eventually terminate. The likelihood ratio can be written as

$$z_n = \frac{p(x, l_{11}, l_{12}, \ldots, l_{1n})}{p(x, l_{21}, l_{22}, \ldots, l_{2n})} = \frac{p(l_{12}, \ldots, l_{1n})p(x, l_{11} \mid l_{12}, \ldots, l_{1n})}{p(l_{22}, \ldots, l_{2n})p(x, l_{21} \mid l_{22}, \ldots, l_{2n})} \tag{9.13}$$

where l_{ij} denotes the jth learning sample of the ith class. The limiting behavior of z_n depends on $p(x, l_{11} \mid l_{12}, \ldots, l_{1n})$ and $p(x, l_{21} \mid l_{22}, \ldots, l_{2n})$. Now,

$$p(x, l_{11} \mid l_{12}, \ldots, l_{1n}) = \int p(x, l_{11} \mid \theta_1) p(\theta_1 \mid l_{12}, \ldots, l_{1n})\, d\theta_1 \tag{9.14}$$

and since $p(\theta_1 \mid l_{12}, \ldots, l_{1n})$ converges to a Dirac delta function under the conditions given by appendix B, $p(x, l_{11} \mid l_{12}, \ldots, l_{1n})$ converges to the integral of $p(x, l_{11} \mid \theta_1)$ with respect to the limit distribution. Thus $\lim_{n\to\infty} p(x, l_{11} \mid l_{12}, \ldots, l_{1n}) = p(x, l_{11} \mid \theta_{10})$ and $\lim_{n\to\infty} p(x, l_{21} \mid l_{22}, \ldots, l_{2n}) = p(x, l_{21} \mid \theta_{20})$ with probability one. Equation (9.13) can be written in the limit

$$\overline{Z} = \lim_{n\to\infty} Z_n = \overline{Z}Q$$

where

$$Q = \frac{p(x, l_{11} \mid l_{12}, \ldots, l_{1n})}{p(x, l_{21} \mid l_{22}, \ldots, l_{2n})}$$

Unless $p(x, l_{11} \mid \theta_{10}) = p(x, l_{21} \mid \theta_{20})$ with probability one (i.e., $Q = 1$ with probability 1), $\overline{Z}$ can only take the values 0 or ∞. Thus the convergence property of Bayesian sequential analysis can be stated as follows: If a sequential probability ratio based on the densities satisfying the condition of convergence, each having a unique true parameter value and probability $[p(x, l_{11} \mid \theta_{10}) = p(x, l_{21} \mid \theta_{20})] \neq 1$, then the SPRT and GSPRT based on likelihood ratios of this nature terminate with probability one. It is noted that the learning samples are assumed to be independent.

The rate of convergence is the same as the Bayesian learning system discussed before. The only difference is that the learning process here will terminate. To determine the expected number of learning samples required for the supervised learning procedure, we can consider the following sequential binary decision problem.[18,19,20] Let $L_1(\theta) = L(\theta, \omega_1)$ and $L_2(\theta) = L(\theta, \omega_2)$ be the losses associated with the decision to choose classes 1 and 2 respectively, given parameter θ. The decision boundaries are constructed so that they meet at the termination of the classified learning process. To simplify the analysis, we have assumed a single random parameter θ here. Define $Q(x^n, \theta)$, $x^n = (x_1, x_2, \ldots, x_n)$

as the probability that, for an x_n on the meeting point boundary, taking an additional learning sample results in choosing class 1. Then the risk at the meeting point is given by

$$Q(x^n, \theta) L_1(\theta) + [1 - Q(x^n, \theta)] L_2(\theta) \tag{9.15}$$

At the meeting point, one of the two decisions will be made. For instance, we may choose class 2; the resulting equation is the same whichever decision is made. Then x^n must satisfy

$$\int [Q(x^n, \theta) L_1(\theta) + (1 - Q(x^n, \theta)) L_2(\theta) + C]\ p(\theta/x^n)\, d\theta = \int p(\theta/x^n) L_2(\theta)\, d\theta$$

or

$$\int Q(x^n, \theta)\ [L_2(\theta) - L_1(\theta)]\ p(\theta/x^n)\, d\theta = C \tag{9.16}$$

where C is the cost of a learning sample. In the sequential learning case, $L_2(\theta) - L_1(\theta)$ can be replaced by the loss function denoted as $r(\theta, \hat{\theta}_n)$ between the random parameter θ and its conditional expected value $\hat{\theta}_n = E(\theta/x^n)$. We then have

$$\int_{\Omega} Q(x^n, \theta) r(\theta, \hat{\theta}_n)\ p(\theta/x^n)\, d\theta = C \tag{9.17}$$

where the left-hand side may be considered as the reduction of the conditional expected risk after taking n learning samples and the integration is over the parameter space Ω. By properly selecting the loss function $r(\theta, \hat{\theta}_n)$, and for reproducing parameter density $p(\theta)$, a closed-form solution of n is possible[19] from equation (9.17). For example, consider a one-dimensional normally distributed learning sample x with mean θ and unit variance. The mean θ is also normally distributed with initial variance σ_0^2. Let $r(\theta, \hat{\theta}_n) = |\theta - \hat{\theta}_n|$. Equation (9.17) then becomes

$$\frac{\sigma_N^2}{\sqrt{2\pi}\ \sqrt{1 + \sigma_N^2}} = C \tag{9.18}$$

where N is the required number of samples and

$$\sigma_N^2 = \frac{\sigma_0^2}{1 + N\sigma_0^2} \tag{9.19}$$

Thus

$$N \simeq \frac{1}{\sqrt{2\pi}\,C} - \frac{1}{\sigma_0^2} > 0 \tag{9.20}$$

As soon as the supervised learning process is terminated, the recognition system may switch to the unsupervised learning mode.[20]

5. Feature-Ordering and Selection Problems

In previous sections, the features are not ordered, i.e., they are in their original order. As the features are processed sequentially, there may be an advantage in processing features according to their order of importance. Here "importance" implies "informative" and "representative" properties of a feature or feature set. On the other hand, sequential decision procedures may be used to order and select features for pattern classification. Normally the order of importance of features can be predetermined by evaluating the features with the distance measures described in chapter 4. By processing the ordered features sequentially, experimental results have indicated the improvement in performance (recognition accuracy or average number of measurements) over the use of unordered features. Theoretically this has not been proved. By using conditional information measures (divergence and conditional entropy) to select and process the best feature at each stage of the sequential procedure, Chernoff[21] and DeGroot[22] have shown that the best performance among all sequential procedures is available. This is called the information feedback or "on-line" recognition system and will be discussed in the next chapter.

We shall be concerned in this section with features ordered in a predetermined manner. Once the features are ordered, we can compose a feature set using features high in the order list. This method of feature selection is quite efficient, though suboptimal. The optimum seeking of feature set is to examine all possible combinations of feature sets and test all of them. The optimum method obviously is impractical when the number of features is much larger than the dimension of the desired feature set (or better called feature subset).

As alternatives to the problem of finding the optimum feature set, we may use sequential forward and sequential backward selection procedures.† Starting with the best single feature, the sequential forward selection procedure establishes sequentially the best N-dimensional feature set by adding an additional feature to the best $(N-1)$-dimensional feature set. While the sequential backward selection procedure composes sequentially, starting with the given complete

†To select N out of M features, $M > N$, the optimum seeking method must examine $\binom{M}{N}$ possibilities while the sequential procedure examines only $M + (M-1) + \cdots + (M-N+1) = NM - N(N-1)/2$ possibilities.

feature set, the best N-dimensional feature set is composed by discarding a feature from the best $(N + 1)$-dimensional feature set. It is noted that the merit of the individual feature does not necessarily determine the capability of a feature set for multivariate statistical analysis. This is attributed to the correlations among measurements. Hence these correlations must be taken into consideration in determining the effectiveness of an N-dimensional feature set. It is still necessary to evaluate all possible subsets in sequential procedure but the number of possible subsets is greatly reduced. Depending on the measure of feature effectiveness, we consider the following four feature selection methods.

Method 1. Maximin divergence method discussed in section 4 of chapter 4.

Method 2. Minimax linear discriminant method.[23,24] When patterns are multivariate normal with unequal covariance matrices among all classes, Anderson and Bahadur[23] suggested minimizing the maximum probability of overall misclassification. In this way we obtain a family of linear discriminant functions of the form

$$f_{ij}(x) = b'_{ij}x - c_{ij} \tag{9.21}$$

between the ith and jth classes, where b_{ij} is a constant vector[24] and c_{ij} is a constant. The condition that minimizes the maximum error is[24]

$$d_{ij} = \frac{b'_{ij}\,(M_i - M_j)}{(b'_{ij}\,V_i\,b_{ij})^{1/2} + (b'_{ij}\,V_j\,b_{ij})^{1/2}} \tag{9.22}$$

where d_{ij} is called the separability measure between the ith and jth classes, M_i, M_j and V_i, V_j are mean vectors and covariance matrices respectively. For equal covariance matrices $V_i = V_j = V$, $b_{im} = V^{-1}\,(M_i - M_j)$ and $d_{ij} = \frac{1}{2}\sqrt{J_{ij}}$ where J_{ij} is the divergence between the two classes. The feature selection method is to maximize the average of all pairwise separability measures.

The three parametric feature selection methods--sequential forward selection, divergence, and minimax linear discriminant--have been applied to crop classification problems.[24,25] The data used were multispectral measurements taken from airborne scanning radiometers. The measurements (features) consist of 12 electrical signals, each one of which is proportional to the radiant energy from the scene in a different wavelength band. The 12 wavelength bands cover the range from 0.4 to 1.0 microns in the visible and near infrared portions of the spectrum. By simultaneously sampling the output of 12 bands, one obtains a 12-dimensional feature vector which characterizes the spectral information available about a given resolution element on the ground. The data from histogram studies[24] can be fairly reasonably remodeled by multivariate normal distributions with unequal covariance matrices. The maximum likelihood decision rule (MLDR) is used for classification, and the appropriate statistical parameters are estimated from an adequate number of training samples (approximately 400

TABLE 9.3
Optimal Feature Set (Method 2)

No. of Features	*Best Feature Set*	*Percent Correct Recognition*	d_t
1	x_9	62.4	17.9
2	x_1, x_9	89.4	29.7
3	x_1, x_{10}, x_{11}	95.0	33.8
4	x_1, x_6, x_{10}, x_{11}	95.1	35.1
5	$x_1, x_6, x_9, x_{10}, x_{11}$	95.6	36.2
6	$x_1, x_6, x_9, x_{10}, x_{11}, x_{12}$	95.8	36.8

NOTE: $d_t = \sum_{i,j} d_{ij}$

SOURCE: Fu, K. S., P. J. Min and T. J. Li. "Feature Selection in Pattern Recognition." *IEEE Trans. on Systems Science and Cybernetics*, vol. SSC-6, No. 1 (January 1970), 33–39.

samples from each class). Five major crops are considered in the experiment: soybeans, corn, oats, wheat, and red clover. Best feature sets are selected by using the three methods stated above and then tested by computing the percentage of misclassification with 7,530 test samples (approximately 1,500 samples per class) classified by the MLDR.

The optimal feature set selected by using method 2 is listed in table 9.3 along with the recognition result. A comparison of the three methods is shown in figure 9.4 for a typical experiment. The optimum feature sets were selected from all possible combinations. A typical example of the recognition results is tabulated in matrix form in table 9.4. It is noted from the experimental results that it is possible for smaller size feature subsets to be almost as effective as the complete feature set.

TABLE 9.4
Recognition Matrix of the Experiment Using Feature Set $\{x_1, x_6, x_{10}, x_{11}\}$

Class	*No. of Samples*	*Percent Correct Recognition*	*No. of Samples Classified Into*				
			Soybeans	*Corn*	*Oats*	*Wheat*	*Clover*
Soybeans	1,535	96.0	1,473	44	18	0	0
Corn	1,476	94.0	77	1,397	2	0	0
Oats	1,483	90.0	7	4	1,334	21	117
Wheat	1,538	97.8	2	0	32	1,504	0
Clover	1,498	96.9	5	24	18	0	1,451
Total	7,530	95.0	1,564	1,469	1,404	1,525	1,568

SOURCE: Fu, K. S., P. J. Min and T. J. Li. "Feature Selection in Pattern Recognition." *IEEE Trans. on Systems Science and Cybernetics*, vol. SSC-6, No. 1 (January 1970), 33–39.

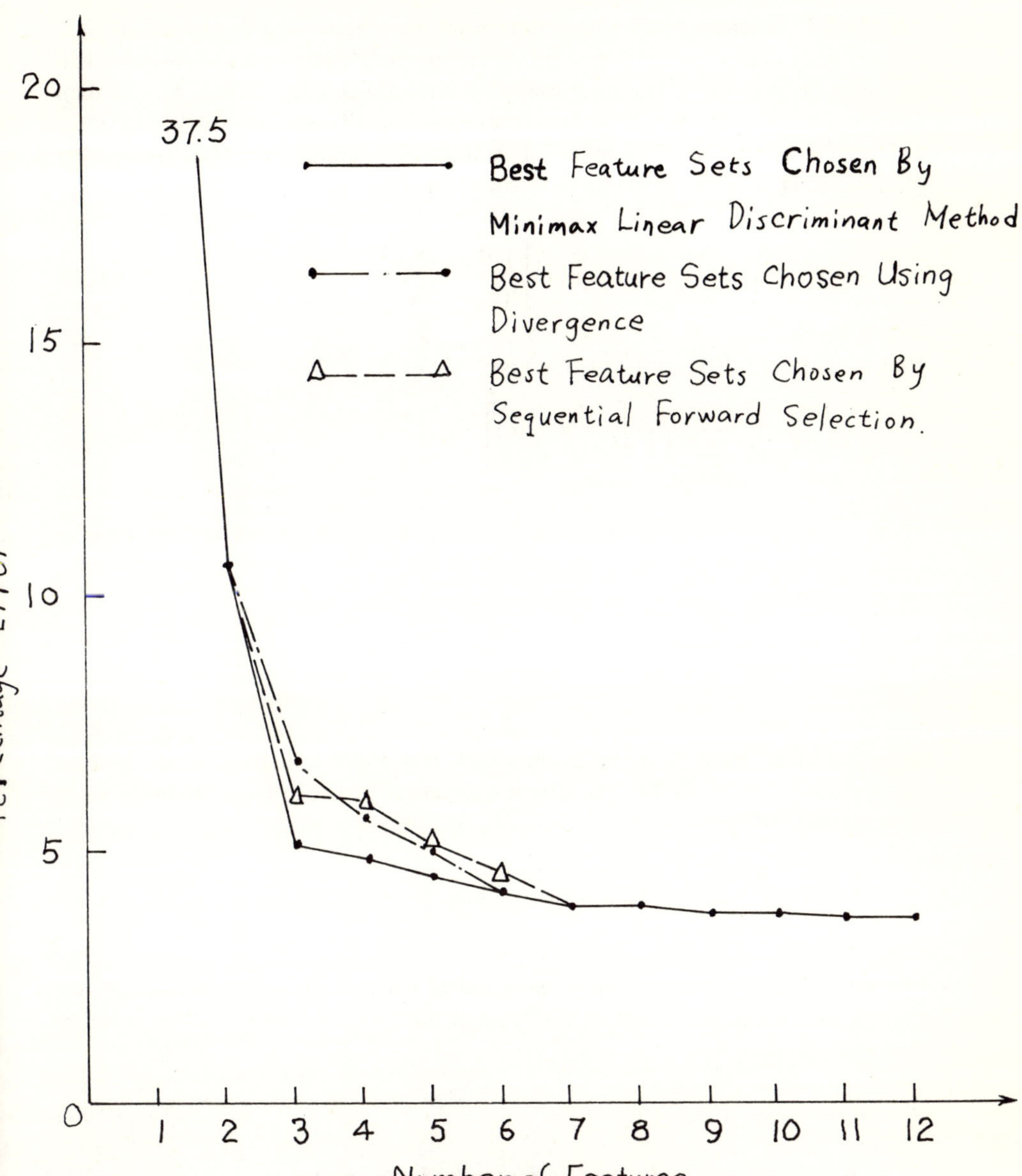

Fig. 9.4 A Typical Experiment (Taken from K. S. Fu, P. J. Min, and T. J. Li, "Feature Selection in Pattern Recognition," *IEEE Transactions on Systems Science and Cybernetics*, SSC-6, No. 1, pp. 33–39, January 1970)

Method 3. Nonparametric estimation of error probability. The probability density of each class can be estimated by using the Parzen method described in section 6 of chapter 7. The probability of error for a given feature set can then be estimated directly. Let X be the vector sample with components $(x_1, x_2, \ldots, x_N)$ and n be the total number of samples for estimation. Also assume the window (weighting) function be uniform defined by

$$K(y) = \prod_{j=1}^{N} U_j(y); \qquad U_j(y) = \begin{cases} \frac{1}{2} & \text{if } |y| < 1 \\ 0 & \geqslant \end{cases} \tag{9.23}$$

Then equation (7.30) can be written as

$$\hat{p}(X) = \frac{1}{nh^N} \sum_{i=1}^{n} \prod_{j=1}^{N} \left[U_j\left(\frac{x_j - x_{ij}}{h}\right)\right] \tag{9.24}$$

where x_{ij} refers to the jth component of the ith sample. Furthermore, each x_j can be uniformly quantized into S_j discrete values. Then the measurement space has altogether

$$S = \prod_{j=1}^{N} S_j \tag{9.25}$$

discrete values. Then X in equation (9.24) is a discrete random vector and we can replace $\hat{p}(x)$ by $\hat{P}(X)$. The direct estimation of the error probability from using the MLDR is

$$\hat{P}_n(\epsilon) = \sum_{i=1}^{S} \left\{ \sum_{j=1}^{m} P(X_i/\omega_j)P(\omega_j) - \max_j \, [P(X_i/\omega_j)P(\omega_j)] \right\} \tag{9.26}$$

where $P(X_i/\omega_j)$ is the conditional probability for class ω_j estimated from equation (9.24) by using the training samples of the jth class. Feature set α_k is better than feature set α_j if

$$\hat{P}_n(\epsilon/\alpha_k) < \hat{P}_n(\epsilon/\alpha_j) \tag{9.27}$$

The nonparametric feature selection method was applied to the crop classification problem. From each class 423 samples are used for the estimation of the density function. The results of the experiment are shown in table 9.5. For 3-feature subsets, the feature subsets $\{x_1, x_6, x_{12}\}$ and $\{x_1, x_9, x_{10}\}$ are equally effective. The results also show that all classes are separable for many 4-feature subsets (41 sets). The recognition results of method 2 are also included in table 9.5.

TABLE 9.5
Comparison of Methods 3 and 2

	Method 3		*Method 2*	
No. of Features	*Best Feature Set*	*Percent Correct Recognition*	*Best Feature Set*	*Percent Correct Recognition*
1	x_9	66.2	x_9	62.4
2	x_1, x_9	94.9	x_1, x_9	89.4
3	x_1, x_{10}, x_{11}	99.9	x_1, x_{10}, x_{11}	95.0
	x_1, x_9, x_{12}	99.9		
4	41-feature set	100	x_1, x_6, x_{10}, x_{11}	95.1

SOURCE: Fu, K. S., P. J. Min and T. J. Li. "Feature Selection in Pattern Recognition." *IEEE Trans. on Systems Science and Cybernetics*, vol. 1 SSC-6, No. 1 (January 1970), 33–39.

Method 4. Feature-space transformation. This is based on the generalization of the Karhunen-Loeve (K-L) expansion method (section 4 and problem 5 of chapter 3) to multiple pattern classes. The features are ordered according to the eigenvalues. A feature set of desired dimension can be composed from feature coordinates with the largest eigenvalues. This method was also applied to the crop classification problem and the experimental results are shown in table 9.6 along with the results of method 2. The transform method of feature selection is less effective but the difference in performance from method 2 for the 4-feature subset is only 1.3 percent. The computation time required, on the other hand, is much shorter for the transformation technique. The nonparametric method which makes no assumption of density function appears more effective but in general requires more computation time than methods 2 and 4.

TABLE 9.6
Comparison of Methods 4 and 2

Method 4		*Method 2*		
No. of Dimensions	*Percent Correct Recognition*	*No. of Features*	*Best Feature Set*	*Percent Correct Recognition*
1	48.2	1	x_9	62.4
2	75.6	2	x_1, x_9	89.4
3	92.8	3	x_1, x_{10}, x_{11}	95.0
4	93.8	4	x_1, x_6, x_{10}, x_{11}	95.1
5	94.2	5	$x_1, x_6, x_9, x_{10}, x_{11}$	95.6

SOURCE: Fu, K. S., P. J. Min and T. J. Li. "Feature Selection in Pattern Recognition." *IEEE Trans. on Systems Science and Cybernetics*, vol. 1 SSC-6, No. 1 (January 1970), 33–39.

It is remarked that the best feature sets selected by methods 2, 3, and 4 are the same in the problem discussed above. This, of course, is not necessarily true in general. The decision rule is the MLDR in each case.

6. Nonparametric Sequential Ranking Procedure

When no assumption is made as to the form of the underlying distributions of all pattern classes, we might look to the nonparametric methods for classifying the patterns. Recently Parent[26] examined two methods of assigning ranks in a sequential manner to measurements $x_1, x_2, \ldots, x_n$. Only one method will be presented here.

Define the sequential rank of x_n relative to $x_1, x_2, \ldots, x_n$ as S_n if x_n is the S_nth smallest in the sample vector $(x_1, x_2, \ldots, x_n)$. Thus the sequential rank of x_1 is always 1, the sequential rank of x_2 is 1 or 2 according as $x_2 < x_1$ or $x_1 < x_2$, and the sequential rank of x_3 is 1, 2, or 3 according as x_3 is the smallest, next largest, or largest of the sample vector (x_1, x_2, x_3), etc. In the sequel, the sequential rank of x_i will be denoted by S_i, and the sequential rank vector for the sample vector $(x_1, x_2, \ldots, x_n)$ will be denoted by $S(n) = (S_1, S_2, \ldots, S_n)$. It can be shown that there is a unique relation between the ordered measurements and the sequential rank vector. Thus the distribution for the sequential rank vectors is also completely specified by

$$P(x_{i(1)} < x_{i(2)} \leqslant \cdots \leqslant x_{i(n)}) = \int_{-\infty < x_{i(1)} \leqslant \cdots \leqslant x_{i(n)} < \infty} \cdots \int \cdot \prod_{j=1}^{n} dF_{i(j)}\,(x_{i(j)}) \tag{9.28}$$

where $F_{i(j)}\,(x_{i(j)})$ indicates the distribution function and the $x_{i(j)}$'s are assumed to be independent in this calculation.

For the special case when the distribution functions $F_i(x_i)$ are taken to be Lehmann alternatives introduced in his paper,[27] we let

$$F_i(x_i) = F^{r_i}\,(x_i) \quad \text{where} \quad r_i > 0$$

Then $dF(x_i) = r_i F^{r_i - 1}\,(x_i)\,dF(x_i)$ and equation (9.28) becomes

$$\begin{aligned} P(x_1 \leqslant x_2 \leqslant \cdots \leqslant x_n) &= \int_{-\infty < x_1 \leqslant x_2 \leqslant \cdots \leqslant x_n < \infty} \cdots \int \prod_{i=1}^{n} dF_i(x_i) \\ &= \prod_{i=1}^{n} r_i \int_{-\infty}^{\infty} F^{r_0 - 1}\,(x_n)\,dF(x_n) \end{aligned}$$

$$\cdot \left\{ \int_{-\infty}^{x_n} F^{r_{n-1}-1}(x_{n-1})\, dF(x_{n-1}) \right.$$

$$\left. \cdot \left[\cdots \int_{-\infty}^{x_2} F^{r_1-1}(x_1)\, dF(x_1) \right] \right\}$$

which with the fact that $F(-\infty) = 0, F(\infty) = 1$ leads to

$$P(x_1 \leqslant x_2 \leqslant \cdots \leqslant x_n) = \frac{\prod_{i=1}^{n} r_i}{\prod_{i-1}^{n} \left(\sum_{j=1}^{i} r_j \right)} \tag{9.29}$$

By relabeling the x_i's, the probability of any order of the x_i's can be found using equation (9.29), giving all values needed in equation (9.28) to specify the distribution of the sequential rank vectors.

To perform a sequential test, assume two sets of measurements $x = (x_1, x_2, \ldots, x_n)$ and $y = (y_1, y_2, \ldots, y_n)$ are available, each sampled from some probability distribution. The problem is to test the hypothesis that the two distributions are the same, against the alternative that they are different, using as few measurements as possible. This is called the sequential two-sample problem.

Let the successive measurements, $x_1, i = 1, 2, \ldots, n$ and $y_j, j = 1, 2, \ldots, n$ be independent and identically distributed random variables, and assume that we wish to test the hypothesis $H_0 : G = F(x)$ against the alternative $H_1 : G = f(F(x))$ where $F(x)$ is the distribution function of the x_i's and $f(F(x))$ is the distribution function of the y_i's. In order to use the sequential probability ratio test based on the sequential ranks, we assume that the measurements are taken alternatively as $x_1, y_1, x_2, y_2, \ldots, x_n, y_n$. Let $S(k) = (S_1, S_2, \ldots, S_k)$ be the sequential rank vector based on the first k combined measurements, and let $\Lambda(k) = P_1(S(k))/P_0(S(k))$ be the sequential probability ratio at the kth measurement, where P_1 refers to the alternative and P_0 refers to the hypothesis.

Under the hypothesis, $P(S(k) = S) = 1/k!$ for a certain outcome vector S of $S(k)$, and therefore we have $P_0(S(K)) = 1/k!$. Under the alternative, we can compute $P(S(k) = S)$ by noting that each outcome S corresponds, in a one-to-one manner, to a particular ordering of the combined measurements of the x_i's and y_j's. Let the combined measurements at the kth stage be denoted by a sample vector $U(k) = (U_1, U_2, \ldots, U_k)$ where $U_1 = x_1, U_2 = y_1$, etc. We obtain $P(S(k) = S)$ for all possible values of S by computing

$$P(U_1 \leqslant U_2 \leqslant \cdots \leqslant U_k)$$

where U_i is an x or a y according to the outcome in the successive measurements.

In fact we have

$$P(U_1 \leqslant U_2 \leqslant \cdots \leqslant U_k) = \int_{-\infty < t_1 \leqslant t_2 \leqslant \cdots \leqslant t_k < \infty} \cdots \int \prod_{i=1}^{k} dG(t_i) \quad (9.30)$$

where $G(t_i) = F(t_i)$ when $U_1 = x_i$ and $G(t_i) = f(F(t_i))$ when $U_i = y_i$. Again, in the case of Lehmann alternatives we have

$$H_0 : G = F(x) \text{ and}$$

$$H_1 : G = f(F(x)) = F^r(x), \quad r > 0$$

Using equations (9.29) and (9.30), we get for k even

$$P_1(S(k)) = P_1(S_1, S_2, \ldots, S_k) = \frac{r^{k/2}}{\prod_{i=1}^{k} \left(\sum_{j=1}^{i} A_j \right)} \quad (9.31)$$

where

$$A_j = \begin{cases} 1 & \text{if } U_j = x_j \\ r & \text{if } U_j = y_j \end{cases} \quad (9.31a)$$

and the sequential probability ratio at the kth measurement reduces to

$$\Lambda(k) = \frac{P_1(S(k))}{P_0(S(k))} = \frac{k!\, r^{k/2}}{\prod_{i=1}^{k} \left(\sum_{j=1}^{i} A_j \right)}, \quad \text{for } k \text{ even} \quad (9.32)$$

$$= \frac{k!\, r^{(k-1)/2}}{\prod_{i=1}^{k} \left(\sum_{j=1}^{i} A_j \right)}, \quad \text{for } k \text{ odd} \quad (9.33)$$

As the $(k + 1)$th measurement is taken, we pass from $\Lambda(k)$ to $\Lambda(k + 1)$. Using the sequential rank for the $(k + 1)$th measurement, we can rewrite equations (9.32) and (9.33) as

$$\Lambda(k + 1) = \frac{(k + 1)!\, r^{k/2}}{\prod_{i=1}^{S_{k+1}-1} \left(\sum_{j=1}^{i} A_j \right) \prod_{i=S_{k+1}-1}^{k} \left(1 + \sum_{j=1}^{i} A_j \right)}, \quad \text{for } k \text{ even} \quad (9.34)$$

$$\Lambda(k+1) = \frac{(k+1)!\, r^{(k+1)/2}}{\prod_{i=1}^{S_{k+1}-1} \left(\sum_{j=1}^{i} A_j\right) \prod_{i=S_{k+1}-1}^{k} \left(r + \sum_{j=1}^{i} A_j\right)}, \quad \text{for } k \text{ odd} \qquad (9.35)$$

where S_{k+1} is the sequential rank of the $(k + 1)$th measurement. The sequential probability ratio is compared with two stopping boundaries; the crossing of one of the boundaries will result in a terminal decision as described in section 3. Note that in the process of forming the probability ratio from one stage to another, one needs to know only the sequential rank S_{k+1} of the $(k + 1)$th measurement and the vector $A(k) = (A_1, A_2, \ldots, A_k)$ defined in equation (9.31a). If S_{k+1} is determined to be Z, then the $(k + 1)$th measurement comes between the $(Z - 1)$th and Zth smallest measurement of the preceding measurements. Thus we have a new vector $A(k + 1) = (A_1, A_2, \ldots, A_{Z-1}, A^*, A_Z, \ldots, A_k)$ with $k + 1$ elements, where $A^* = 1$ if $(k + 1)$th measurement is an x and $A^* = r$ if it is a y. The sequential probability ratio $(k + 1)$ is then obtained through equation (9.34) or (9.35) using $S(k + 1)$ and $A(k + 1)$. The test procedure can be summarized in the following steps:

Step 1: Obtain the sequential rank for the measurement taken.
Step 2: Form vector $A(k + 1)$ through $A(k)$.
Step 3: Compute the sequential probability ratio $\Lambda(k + 1)$ by equation (9.34) or (9.35) and compare it with stopping boundaries.

The above procedure does not require the reranking of all previous measurements to compute the sequential probability ratios. In fact, once the sequential rank of measurement [and consequently the vector $A(k)$] is determined, it remains unaltered in later computations.

The nonparametric sequential procedure described above applies to two-class problems. The procedure can be extended to more than two classes as follows. Let $F(x/\omega_i)$, $i = 1, 2, \ldots, m$, be the probability distribution (unknown) for m pattern classes, and let the set of successive measurements from class ω_i be denoted by $\{x^i\} = \{x_1^i, x_2^i, \ldots, x_n^i\}$, $i = 1, 2, \ldots, m$. To determine the pattern class to which a pattern vector $y = \{y_1, y_2, \ldots, y_n\}$ belongs, let hypothesis H_0 be $F(x/\omega_i)$, $i = 1, 2, \ldots, m$, and the alternative hypothesis H_1 be $F^{r_i}(x/\omega_i)$, $r_i > 0, i = 1, 2, \ldots, m$. Consider that

$$U_1(k) = [U_{11}, U_{12}, \ldots, U_{1k}] = [x_1^1, y_1, x_2^1, y_2, \ldots, x_n^1, y_n]$$
$$U_2(k) = [U_{21}, U_{22}, \ldots, U_{2k}] = [x_1^2, y_1, x_2^2, y_2, \ldots, x_n^2, y_n]$$
$$\vdots$$
$$U_m(k) = [U_{m1}, U_{m2}, \ldots, U_{mk}] = [x_1^m, y_1, x_2^m, y_2, \ldots, x_n^m, y_n]$$

where $k = 1, 2, \ldots, 2n$. The corresponding sequential rank vectors are

$$S_1(k) = [S_{11}, S_{12}, \ldots, S_{1k}]$$
$$S_2(k) = [S_{21}, S_{22}, \ldots, S_{2k}]$$
$$\vdots$$
$$S_m(k) = [S_{m1}, S_{m2}, \ldots, S_{mk}]$$

Following equation 9.32, the sequential probability ratio is

$$\Lambda_i(k) = \frac{P_1(S_i(k))}{P_0(S_i(k))} = \frac{k!\, r_i^{k/2}}{\prod_{q=1}^{k}\left(\sum_{j=1}^{q} A_{ij}\right)}, \quad \text{for } k \text{ even} \tag{9.36}$$

$$= \frac{k!\, r_i^{(k-1)/2}}{\prod_{q=1}^{k}\left(\sum_{j=1}^{q} A_{ij}\right)}, \quad \text{for } k \text{ odd} \tag{9.36}$$

where $i = 1, 2, \ldots, m$, and

$$A_{ij} = \begin{cases} 1 & \text{if } U_{ij} \text{ is an } x \text{ from } x^i \\ r_i & \text{if } U_{ij} \text{ is a } y \end{cases} \tag{9.37}$$

Adopting the rejection criterion, the pattern class ω_i is dropped from consideration at the kth measurement if

$$\Lambda_i(k) \geqslant A(\omega_i), \quad i = 1, 2, \ldots, m \tag{9.38}$$

where $A(\omega_i)$ may be set equal to $(1 - \beta_i)/\alpha_i$ where α_i and β_i are the specified errors of the ith class. The process of forming $\Lambda_i(k)$ continues until there is only one sequential probability ratio left not satisfying the inequality (9.38); its associated hypothesis is then accepted as the true pattern class to which y belongs.

The nonparametric sequential ranking procedure was applied to character recognition problems by Fu and Chien.[28] Applications of this and other sequential procedures to medical diagnosis are described in the next section.

7. Applications to Medical Diagnosis

Because the cost of medical diagnosis can be extremely high, both in dollars and in risk and discomfort to the patient, the use of sequential procedures for diagnosis is suggested. Measurements (medical tests) are taken in sequence, and the classification (diagnostic) procedure will terminate as quickly as possible, subject to the constraint of specified error probability or confidence level. Also, conventional statistical classification techniques usually require a substantial amount of data to establish the statistical characteristics, e.g., probability density functions or distribution functions, for the measurements associated with the different types of diseases under study. Insufficient data, especially for rare diseases, deny us an accurate estimation of the required statistical characteristics. This leads to the need for nonparametric classification schemes, which do not require the parametric knowledge of the statistical characteristics.

Specific results† of some real-data medical diagnoses are presented for the problems of separating primary liver cancer from primary cancer of the pancreas, and for the separation of those from normal cases. The measurements (features) used are blood chemistry and hematology values, urinalysis, x-ray and liver scan results, and ECG and EEG analysis. Classifications for the training data were determined according to the patient's most recent diagnosis, either by biopsy at surgery or pathology at autopsy. The records examined for use in this study included 34 cases of cancer of the pancreas, 21 of primary cancer of the liver, and 63 normal patients. A maximum set of 62 features as listed in table 9.7 was used, although no case had information available for all of the features. For example, many of the specialized tests (arteriograms, cholecystograms, brain scans, etc.) were reported in only a few cases, and the experiments had to be constructed so as to avoid undue weight to those measurements' diagnostic significance.

Experiment 1. Nonparametric sequential probability ratio test. A series of five two-class tests using the nonparametric procedure described in the preceding section was performed. It was found that the errors α, β have to be properly specified to achieve minimum error. The minimum number of measurements for the minimum error was also determined. Table 9.8 indicates the minimum α and β's obtained, and their corresponding numbers of required measurements. In the series of two three-class tests, the lower stopping bound was made small, ranging from 0.0005 to 0.005, to insure that a hypothesis would not be accepted too early in the sequential process. It was found that the minimum probability of misclassification was 0.2, and was reached after ten measurements with $r = 0.2$. The minimum number of measurements required was three, yielding an error probability of 0.35. In all cases, features were taken in the order indicated in table 9.7.

Experiment 2. Nonparametric sequential partition procedure. This procedure developed by Henrichon and Fu[30,31] seeks to partition the measurement (or feature) space into successively finer regions for classification purposes. The partitions are established during an off-line training period (i.e., when the classifica-

†These results were kindly provided by Dr. K. S. Fu of Purdue University. See also reference 29.

TABLE 9.7
Features Used for the EPA and Nonparametric SPRT

Feature No.	*Name*	*Feature No.*	*Name*
	Admitting Information	34	Bilirubin: Total
1	Sex	35	Direct
2	Race	36	White cell count
3	Age	37	Hemoglobin
4	Marital status	38	Hematocrit
5	Religion	39	Neutrophiles
6	Pulse	40	Eosinophiles
7	Blood pressure: Systolic	41	Basophiles
8	Diastolic	42	Lymphocytes
9	Respirations	43	Monocytes
10	Temperature		*Urinalysis*
11	Abdominal pain		
12	Weight loss	44	Specific gravity
13	Jaundice	45	Casts
14	Diabetes	46	WBC/hpf
15	Drink	47	RBC/hpf
16	Smoke		*X-Rays*
17	Anorexia	48	Chest
18	Nausea	49	Abdomen
19	Vomiting	50	Skull
20	Back pain		
21	Abdominal swelling		*Special Tests*
22	Diarrhea	51	ECG
23	Weakness	52	EEG
	Blood Biochemistry and Hematology	53	Liver scan
		54	Lung scan
24	Sodium	55	Brain scan
25	Potassium	56	Thyroid scan
26	Chlorides	57	UGI
27	CO_2	58	LGI
28	Fasting glucose	59	Arteriogram
29	Blood urea, nitrogen (BUN)	60	Cholecystogram
30	Glutamic oxaloacetic transaminase (SGOT)	61	Proctoscope
		62	Barium enema
31	Alkaline phosphatase		
32	Bromsulphalein retention (BSP)		
33	Amylase		

NOTE: Quantitative values were used for features 24 through 47; all others indicated simply the presence or absence or the normality or abnormality of the measurement.

SOURCE: Fu, K. S. and M. H. Lowe. "Automatic Medical Diagnosis Using Nonparametric Sequential Classification Procedure." XXIst AGARD Symposium on Artificial Intelligence, Rome, Italy, May 24–28, 1971.

TABLE 9.8
Results of Two-Class Nonparametric SPRT

(a) Number of measurements required (k) to achieve minimum error ($\alpha = \beta$) at termination of the procedure				(b) Error ($\alpha = \beta$) of a decision made after taking the minimum number of measurements to terminate the procedure			
Test	$\alpha = \beta$	k	r	*Test*	k	$\alpha = \beta$	r
1	0.18	41	0.6	1	2	0.38	0.2
2	0.18	41	0.6	2	2	0.38	0.2
3	0.16	56	0.6	3	2	0.38	0.2
4	0.28	3	14.0	4	2	0.38	10.0
5	0.19	41	0.6	5	2	0.38	0.2

SOURCE: Fu, K. S. and M. H. Lowe. "Automatic Medical Diagnosis Using Nonparametric Sequential Classification Procedure." XXIst AGARD Symposium on Artificial Intelligence, Rome, Italy, May 24–28, 1971.

tion of each sample is known a priori) by the empirical processing algorithm (EPA). Theoretically this algorithm is based on the theory of coverages (e.g., see Wilks[32]) in nonparametric statistics. Without getting into detail of this algorithm, we present the results of the experiment in table 9.9 for comparison purposes. The EPA may be constructed with a simple network of multithreshold elements which would offer negligible delay in processing and require no memory. Furthermore, the EPA processing time is independent of the number of classes. The nonparametric SPRT provides a direct measure of the probability of incorrect diagnosis and the range of SPRT error, about 0.2 to 0.4, is comparable to that of physicians with regard to the two diseases studied here.

Experiment 3. Dynamic sequential pattern recognition.[33,34] This method is based on some improved strategy in dynamic programming. For a small training set, a typical set of experimental results is shown in table 9.10. The medical data are the same as those described above, and the features used are also listed in table 9.10.

TABLE 9.9
Testing Results of Empirical Processing Algorithm

Test No.	*Feature Nos. and Order in Which Used*	*Class i*	*No. of Samples*	*No. Misclassified*
1	30	1	10	2
		2	7	3
2	34, 39	1	10	4
		2	7	3
		3	28	9

SOURCE: Fu, K. S. and M. H. Lowe. "Automatic Medical Diagnosis Using Nonparametric Sequential Classification Procedure." XXIst AGARD Symposium on Artificial Intelligence, Rome, Italy, May 24–28, 1971.

TABLE 9.10
Typical Experimental Result of Dynamic Sequential Pattern Recognition

Sample No.	*True Class*	*Classified to Class*	*Feature Ordering*†
1	1	1	92
2	1	1	982
3	1	1	942
4	1	1	942
5	2	2	942
6	2	2	942
7	2	2	942
8	2	2	942

NOTE: The training set contains 80 samples; 40 samples from class 2 (normal patients) and 40 samples from class 1 (sick patients). For class 1, 20 samples are taken from liver cancer and 20 samples are taken from pancreas cancer. There are nine features and their measured quantities are: 1. potassium, 2. chlorides, 3. fasting glucose, 4. SGOT, 5. alkaline phosphatase, 6. bilirubin (total), 7. WBC, 8. HTC, 9. monocytes.

†The ordering 92, for example, indicates that first feature 9 is taken. Based on the outcome of feature 9, the method decides to take feature 4. After feature 4 is taken, the procedure stops.

SOURCE: "Medical Diagnosis Using Dynamic Sequential Pattern Recognition." *Proc. Fifth Hawaii International Conference on System Sciences*, January 1972.

8. Remarks

With the present high-speed digital computer, it has been argued that the saving of the number of measurements in the sequential decision approach is not a practical advantage. This is true only in some problems where a fixed-sample procedure provides satisfactory results and where all measurements are available when the classification is performed. In many problems, such as in medical diagnosis of rare diseases, the measurements are very costly and are provided sequentially; the classification usually starts before all measurements are available. It would then be necessary to use the sequential decision approach. Furthermore, the fixed-sample procedure does not necessarily use the measurements efficiently in practical recognition problems. The sequential decision procedure with features (measurements) properly ordered represents a truly optimal procedure. With a possibly slight increase in the amount of computation and memory, especially in updating the stopping and continuing regions, the sequential system processes the best available feature measurements with a minimum of redundancy. In high-dimensional measurements, the sequential system can operate at a lower dimension so that the amount of computation can in fact be reduced. Computer results presented in this chapter have shown low error rates and a saving in the average number of measurements. The saving normally is one-third to one-half the total number of measurements.

Theoretically most sequential analysis assumes that the successive measurements are independent and identically distributed. This assumption, however, is not true in most recognition problems. Better performance can be achieved if correlation or dependence among feature measurements or learning samples is properly taken into account. Although the problem of dependent and non-identically distributed measurements does not yet have a general solution, the solution for Markov-dependent measurements is a natural extension of conventional sequential analysis.[35,36,37]

Application of sequential decision theory to pattern recognition was first proposed by Fu[38] and the improvement available from feature-ordering was examined by Chen,[11] Chien,[39] and Cardillo.[9,17] Nelson and Levy[40] also used dynamic programming to select features sequentially. Instead of minimizing the average risk, they used the Fisher return function as a performance measure. The main problem with sequential pattern recognition, from the engineering standpoint, is still the computation problem for the backward procedure. In the forward sequential procedure, the selection of thresholds usually requires some trial and error. Complete results on the crop classification problem described in section 5 have been reported by Fu.[41] Detailed results on character recognition are available in chapters 2–5 of reference 10.

PROBLEMS (Chapter IX)

1. In using the SPRT for a sequential classification system suppose that x_1, $x_2, \ldots$ are independent feature measurements with $p(x/\omega_i)$, $i = 1, 2$, $j = 1, 2, \ldots$ a univariate Gaussian density function with mean μ_i and variance σ^2. Show that the SPRT becomes that if

$$\sum_{i=1}^{n} x_i \geqslant \frac{\sigma^2}{\mu_1 - \mu_2} \log A + \frac{n}{2} (\mu_1 + \mu_2), \text{ then choose class 1,}$$

$$\sum_{i=1}^{n} x_i \leqslant \frac{\sigma^2}{\mu_1 - \mu_2} \log B + \frac{n}{2} (\mu_1 + \mu_2), \text{ then choose class 2}$$

and if

$$\frac{\sigma^2}{\mu_1 - \mu_2} \log B + \frac{n}{2} (\mu_1 + \mu_2) < \sum_{i=1}^{n} x_i < \frac{\sigma^2}{\mu_1 - \mu_2} \log A + \frac{n}{2} (\mu_1 + \mu_2)$$

then an additional measurement x_{n+1} will be taken.

2. Consider two pattern classes with character samples as shown in Fig. 9.2(a). Assume that the feature measurements satisfy the first order Markov dependence.
   (a) Write the likelihood ratio $L(x)$.
   (b) Obtain an approximate expression of the average number of measurements. Make any necessary assumption on probability distributions.

3. The probability of misrecognition usually cannot be determined exactly in sequential pattern recognition if the number of feature measurements is small. It is of interest to examine the asymptotic behavior of the probability of misrecognition, P_e, and the average number of measurements, $E(n)$. Wald[2] has shown that as $A \to \infty$ and $B \to 0$,

$$P_e \simeq \frac{P_1}{A} + P_2 B.$$

$$E(n) \simeq \frac{P_1}{I_1} \log A + \frac{P_2}{I_2} \log B$$

where P_i, $i = 1, 2$ is the *a priori* probability with $P_1 + P_2 = 1$, and $I_i = \mu_i'(0)$, $\mu_i(t) = \log \phi_i(t)$ and

$$\phi_i(t) = E_i\,[e^{zt}] = \int_{-\infty}^{\infty} \left[\frac{p(x/\omega_1)}{p(x/\omega_2)}\right]^t p(x/\omega_i)\,dx$$

For fixed $E(n)$, show that P_e can be minimized with the result

$$P_e = K' e^{-IE(n)}$$

where K' is a constant depending on P_i but independent of n and

$$\frac{1}{I} = \frac{P_1}{I_1} + \frac{P_2}{I_2}.$$

Refs. E. M. Hofstetter, "Asymptotic behavior of optimum fixed-length and sequential dichotomies," MIT RLE QPR April 15, 1959 and E. M. Hofstetter, and "Large-sample sequential decision theory," MIT RLE TR 359, Dec. 1959.

Note: For large-sample case, Chernoff[21] expressed $E_i(n)$ in terms of directed divergence.

REFERENCES

1. Wald, A. *Statistical Decision Functions.* Wiley, New York, 1950.
2. Wald, A. *Sequential Analysis.* Wiley, New York, 1947.
3. Blackwell, D. and M. A. Girshick. *Theory of Games and Statistical Decisions.* Wiley, New York, 1954.
4. Goode, H. H. "Deferred Decision Theory. In *Recent Developments in In-*

formation and Decision Process, edited by R. E. Machol and P. Gray, 71–91. Macmillan, New York, 1962.

5. Bellman, R., R. Kalaba, and D. Middleton. "Dynamic Programming, Sequential Estimation and Sequential Detection Processes." In *Proc. National Academy of Science*, 47 (1961), 338–341.
6. Fu, K. S., Y. T. Chien, and G. P. Cardillo. "A Dynamic Programming Approach to Sequential Pattern Recognition." *IEEE Trans. on Electronic Computers*, 16 (1967), 790–803.
7. Fu, K. S. and G. P. Cardillo. "An Optimum Finite Sequential Procedure for Feature Selection and Pattern Classification." *IEEE Trans. on Automatic Control*, 12 (1967), 588–591.
8. Chien, Y. T. and K. S. Fu. "An Optimal Pattern Classification System Using Dynamic Programming." *International Journal of Mathematical Biosciences*, 1 (1967), 439–461.
9. Cardillo, G. P. and K. S. Fu. "A Dynamic Programming Procedure for Sequential Pattern Classification and Feature Selection." *International Journal of Mathematical Biosciences*, 1 (1967), 463–491.
10. Fu, K. S. *Sequential Methods in Pattern Recognition and Machine Learning.* Academic Press, New York, 1968.
11. Chen, C. H. "A Study of Pattern Recognition Systems with Sequential Learning Procedure." Ph.D. dissertation, Purdue Univ., January 1965.
12. Reed, F. C. "A Sequential Multidecision Procedure." In *Proc. Symposium on Decision Theory and Applications to Electronic Equipment Development.* USAF Development Center, Rome, New York, April 1960.
13. Wald, A. and J. Wolfowitz. "Optimum Character of Sequential Probability Ratio Tests." *Ann. Math. Stat.*, 19 (1948), 326–329.
14. Lehmann, E. L. *Testing Statistical Hypotheses.* Wiley, New York, 1959, Chapter 3.
15. Bussgang, J. J. and M. B. Marcus. "Truncated Sequential Hypothesis Tests." *IEEE Trans. on Information Theory*, IT-13 (July 1967). Also as RAND Corp. Memo RM-4268-ARPA, November 1964.
16. Chien, Y. T. and K. S. Fu. "A Modified Sequential Recognition Machine Using Time-Varying Stopping Boundaries." *IEEE Trans. on Information Theory*, IT-12 (April 1966), 206–214.
17. Cardillo, G. P. "Optimum Finite Sequential Pattern Recognition." Ph.D. dissertation, Purdue Univ., August 1967.
18. Chen, C. H. "A Note on Sequential Decision Approach to Pattern Recognition and Machine Learning." *Information and Control*, 9 (1966), 549–562.
19. Wetherill, G. B. "Bayesian Sequential Analysis." *Biometrika*, 48 (1961), 281–292.
20. Chen, C. H. "A Theory of Bayesian Learning Systems." *IEEE Trans. on Systems Science and Cybernetics*, SSC-5 (January 1969), 30–37.
21. Chernoff, H., "Sequential Design of Experiments." *Ann. Math. Stat.*, 30 (1959), 755–770.
22. DeGroot, M. H. "Uncertainty, Information and Sequential Experiments." *Ann. Math. Stat.*, vol. 33 (1962), 404–419.

23. Anderson, T. W. and R. R. Bahadur. "Classification into Two Multivariate Normal Distributions with Different Covariance Matrices." *Ann. Math. Stat.* 33 (1962), 420–431.
24. Fu, K. S. and P. J. Min. "On Feature Selection in Multiclass Pattern Recognition." Purdue Univ. Technical Report TR-EE 68–17, July 1968.
25. Fu, K. S., P. J. Min, and T. J. Li. "Feature Selection in Pattern Recognition." *IEEE Trans. on Systems Science and Cybernetics*, SSC-6 (January 1970), 33–39.
26. Parent, E. A., Jr. "Sequential Ranking Procedures." Dept. of Statistics Technical Report 80, Stanford Univ., April 1965.
27. Lehmann, E. L. "The Power of Rank Tests." *Ann. Math. Stat.*, 24 (1953), 23–43.
28. Fu, K. S. and Y. T. Chien. "Sequential Recognition Using a Nonparametric Ranking Procedure." *IEEE Trans. on Information Theory*, vol. IT-13, No. 3 (July 1967), 484–492.
29. Fu, K. S. and M. H. Loew. "Automatic Medical Diagnosis Using Nonparametric Sequential Classification Procedures." *Proc. Twenty-first AGARD Symposium on Artificial Intelligence.* Rome, Italy, May 24–28, 1971.
30. Fu, K. S. and E. G. Henrichon, Jr. "On Nonparametric Methods for Pattern Recognition." Purdue Univ. TR-EE 68–19, August 1968.
31. Henrichon, E. G., Jr. and K. S. Fu. "A Nonparametric Partitioning Procedure for Pattern Classification." *IEEE Trans. on Computers*, vol. C-18, No. 7 (July 1969), 614–624.
32. Wilks, S. S. *Mathematical Statistics*. Wiley, New York, 1952.
33. Persoon, E. "Dynamic Sequential Pattern Recognition Applied in Medical Diagnosis." Purdue Univ. TR-EE 71–24, July 1971.
34. Fu, K. S. and E. Persoon. "Medical Diagnosis Using Dynamic Sequential Pattern Recognition." In *Fifth Hawaii International Conference on System Sciences.* January 1972.
35. Bhat, B. R. "Bayes Solution of Sequential Decision Problem for Markov Dependent Observations." *Ann. Math. Stat.*, vol. 35 (1964), 1656–1662.
36. Phataford, R. M. "Large Sample Sequential Analysis of Markovian Observations." *J. Indian Stat. Ass.* (1963) –1, pp. 615–637.
37. Newbold, P. M. and Y. C. Ho. "Detection of Changes in the Characteristics of a Gauss-Markov Process." *IEEE Trans. on Aerospace and Electronic Systems*, AES-4 (September 1968), 707–718.
38. Fu, K. S. "A Sequential Decision Model for Optimum Recognition." In *Biological Prototypes and Synthetic Systems*, vol. 1. Plenum, New York, 1962.
39. Chien, Y. T. and K. S. Fu. "Selection and Ordering of Feature Observations in a Pattern Recognition System." *Information and Control*, 12 (May 1968).
40. Nelson, G. D. and D. M. Levy. "A Dynamic Programming Approach to the Selection of Pattern Features." *IEEE Trans. on Systems Science and Cybernetics*, SSC-4 (July 1968).
41. Fu, K. S. "On the Application of Pattern Recognition Techniques to Remote Sensing Problems." Purdue Univ. TR-EE 71–13, June 1971.

Bibliography

1. Benenson, Z. M. and E. M. Khazen. "Sequential Analysis in Problems of Recognition of Many Hypotheses." *Engineering Cybernetics* (English translation), 4 (July–August 1966), 12–26.
2. Berk, R. H. "Asymptotic Properties of Sequential Probability Ratio Test." Ph.D. dissertation, Department of Statistics, Harvard University, 1964.
3. Bussgang, J. J. and M. B. Marcus. "Sufficiency and Information Rate of Multi-stage Statistical Tests." Memorandum RM-4405-ARPA, The RAND Corp., Santa Monica, Calif., February 1965.
4. Bussgang, J. J. and D. Middleton. "Optimum Sequential Detection of Signals in Noise." *IRE Trans. on Information Theory*, vol. IT-1 (Dec. 1955), 5–18.
5. Hong, J. P. "A Multiclass Sequential Hypothesis Test With Applications in Pattern Recognition." Technical Memorandum 33-482, Jet Propulsion Laboratory, Pasadena, Calif., June 1971.
6. Hong, J. P. "An Invariant Feature Extractor and a Statistical Sequential Classifier." In *IEEE Symposium on Feature Extraction and Selection in Pattern Recognition.* Argonne, Ill., October 1970.
7. Hussain, A. B. S. and K. S. Fu, et. al. "On the Correctness of Some Sequential Classification Schemes in Pattern Recognition." *IEEE Trans. on Computers* (corresp.), vol. C-21, No. 3 (March 1972), 318–320.
8. Ifram, A. F. "On the Asymptotic Behavior of Densities with Applications to Sequential Analysis." *Ann. Math. Stat.*, vol. 36 (April 1965), 615–637.
9. Kulikowski, C. A. "Pattern Recognition Approach to Medical Diagnosis." *IEEE Trans. on Systems Science and Cybernetics*, SSC-6 (July 1970).
10. Lindley, D. V. "Dynamic Programming and Decision Theory." *Applied Statistics*, 10 (1961), 39–51.
11. Murden, P. and M. Symons. "A Recognition System Using Probabilistic Decisions Based on Extracted Features." Technical Report, E.M.I. Electronics Limited, Hayes, Middlesex, England, 1970.
12. Nelson, G. D. and D. M. Levy. "Selection of Pattern Features by Mathematical Programming Algorithms." *IEEE Trans. on Systems Science and Cybernetics*, vol. SSC-6, No. 1 (January 1970), 20–25.
13. Newman, R. and B. Reisine. "Practical Applications of Sequential Pattern Recognition Techniques." In *Proc. Seventh Space Congress.* Cocoa Beach, Fla., April 1970.
14. Selin, I. "The Sequential Estimation and Detection of Signals in Normal Noise." Memorandum, RM-2994-PR, The RAND Corp., Santa Monica, Calif., June 1962.
15. Slagle, J. R. and R. C. T. Lee. "Application of Game Tree Searching Techniques to Sequential Pattern Recognition." *Comm. of ACM*, 14 (1971), 103–110.
16. Som, A. and A. K. Nath. "Sequential Pattern Classifier Using Least–Mean–Square Error Criterion." *IEEE on Systems, Man, and Cybernetics* (corresp.), vol. SMC-2, No. 2 (July 1972), 439–443.

17. Wee, W. G. "Application of a Pattern Recognition System to Electrophysiological Measurements." Third Asilomar Conference on Circuits and Systems, Pacific Grove, Calif., December 1969.
18. Wetherill, G. B. *Sequential Methods in Statistics*. Methuen, London and Wiley, New York, 1966.
19. Wong, E. and J. A. Steppe. "Invariant Recognition of Geometric Shapes." In *Methodologies of Pattern Recognition*, edited by S. Watanabe. Academic Press, New York, 1969.

CHAPTER X

Recognition Systems with Finite Memory and Feedback

1. Introduction

As the optimum recognition systems require using all the previous measurements as well as the current ones, it is often necessary to reduce the data to save the memory requirement and simplify the computations involved. It has been frequently observed that the data may be reduced by a sufficient statistic without loss of information. Let $x_1, x_2, \ldots, x_n$ be the independent and identically distributed random measurements. The sample mean $\bar{x}_n = (1/n) \sum_{i=1}^{n} x_i$ is known as the sufficient statistic for testing the mean of a Gaussian distribution. However, while it is generally true that the mapping corresponding to a sufficient statistic is many-to-one, and is in this sense data reducing, it is generally not true that the cardinality of the required memory is reduced. For example, in the case of the univariate Gaussian, the mapping from the n vector measurements $(x_1, x_2, \ldots, x_n)$ to a single vector measurement $\bar{x}_n$ leaves the memory requirements uncountably infinite. Thus the sufficient statistic has not really reduced the memory requirement. The memory allowed by any practical recognition machine, e.g., the conditional probability computer, is finite. Learning (or estimating) and recognition with a finite memory system will be considered in sections 2 and 3.

Memory is usually required, though not essential, for a recognition system with feedback. Feedback takes several different forms. The sequential decision theory approach described in chapter 9 is considered as a decision feedback. The on-line feature ordering is an example of information feedback. A simple rejection option in the recognition process can also be considered as a decision feedback. Recognition systems with the rejection option and information feedback will be examined in sections 4 and 5.

Historically, the finite memory learning and recognition problem originates from the two-armed bandit problem[1,2] or the sequential design of experiment problem. Information feedback in the recognition systems may be treated as a sequential design of experiment problem. Sequential decision theory[3,4] in its fullest sense includes all the problems stated above, as well as the sequential recognition procedures described in chapter 9. Thus the two seemingly uncorrelated topics, recognition system with a finite memory and recognition with feedback, actually have a similar mathematical origin.

2. Learning with Finite Memory

Consider testing the hypothesis H_0: $p(x) = p_0(x)$ vs. H_1: $p(x) = p_1(x)$. For a given decision procedure which assigns each possible measurement $(x_1, x_2, \ldots, x_n)$, $n = 0, 1, 2, \ldots$, to H_0 or H_1, we may define $\alpha_n = P_r$ [decide H_1/H_0] and $\beta_n = P_r$ [decide H_0/H_1]. Thus α_n and β_n are the probabilities of error of each kind, based on the first n measurements, for the given decision procedure. It is well known that the standard likelihood ratio decision procedure results in $\alpha_n \to 0$ and $\beta_n \to 0$ exponentially in n, with rates which depend on the information distance (e.g., divergence) between $p_0(x)$ and $p_1(x)$. To apply this procedure at the time n requires a memory capacity sufficient to store the measurements $x_1, x_2, \ldots, x_n$. Thus, even in the simplest case, the memory must grow indefinitely with time. Any truncation of memory to the last k measurements, for example, as in the most familiar definition of finite memory,[2] will preclude the convergence of α_n and β_n to 0, except in the singular case.

Consider testing the mean μ of a Gaussian distribution with the known variance σ^2. We wish to decide whether $\mu = 1$ or $\mu = -1$ from $\bar{x}_n$ which can be written as

$$\bar{x}_n = \frac{n-1}{n}\bar{x}_{n-1} + \frac{1}{n}x_n \tag{10.1}$$

The decision procedure that decides $\mu = \pm 1$ accordingly as $\bar{x}_n \gtrless 0$ would result in $\alpha_n, \beta_n \to 0$. Suppose now that $\bar{x}_n$ may be recalled only to some arbitrary decimal place accuracy. Let $[\bar{x}_n]$ denote the rounded version of $\bar{x}_n$. Rounding at each stage results in the algorithm

$$[\bar{x}_n] = \left[\frac{n-1}{n}[\bar{x}_{n-1}] + \frac{1}{n}x_n\right] \tag{10.2}$$

Unfortunately, $[\bar{x}_n]$ does not converge to the true mean,[5] and thus α_n and β_n converge to the nonzero limits. The rounding method to save memory obviously does not work.

The solution to this problem has recently been considered by Cover[6] and Hellman[7,8,9] and others. In particular, they are concerned with the algorithm

$$\begin{aligned} T_n &= f(T_{n-1}, x_{n-1}) \\ d_n &= d(T_n) \end{aligned} \tag{10.3}$$

where the memory (or statistic) T_n takes one of m values in the set $\{1, 2, \ldots, m\}$, d_n is the nth decision, and f is a function (perhaps randomized), independent of n and the data. The algorithm is said to have a *finite memory* of size m if T_n is m-valued for $n = 1, 2, \ldots$. The goal is to minimize the expected asymptotic proportion of errors

$$P(e) = E\left\{\lim_{n\to\infty} \frac{1}{n}\sum_{i=1}^{n} e_i\right\} \tag{10.4}$$

where $e_i = 1$ or 0 accordingly as $d_i \neq H_t$ or $d_i = H_t$, where H_t denotes the true hypothesis. In the case in which f described an aperiodic ergodic process on $\{1, 2, \ldots, m\}$, it may be seen that

$$P(e) = \lim_{n\to\infty} P_r[d_n \neq H_t] \tag{10.5}$$

From the elementary decision theoretic considerations, it is clear that no randomization of d is required for optimal procedures. However, a truly optimal algorithm does not in general exist. Let P_e^* be the greatest lower bound on $P(e)$, i.e.,

$$P_e^* = \min_{(f,d)} P(e) \tag{10.6}$$

Then an ϵ-optimal class of algorithms does exist, i.e., for any $\epsilon > 0$ there is an (f, d) in this class for which $P(e) \leqslant P_e^* + \epsilon$. In the case of discrete distribution, this requires artificial randomization.

The pair (f, d) describes a finite-state machine (automaton) with inputs x_n, outputs $d_n = d(T_n)$, and state space $S = \{1, 2, \ldots, m\}$. The state of the machine at the time n is T_n. Under hypothesis H_t, $t = 0$ or 1, the sequence T_n, together with some specified initial states, forms a Markov chain over the state space S. The action of f is prescribed by a stochastic transition matrix.

Let $l(x) = p_i(x)/p_0(x)$, $\alpha = P_r$ [decide H_1/H_0], and $\beta = P_r$ [decide H_0/H_1], and $\overline{l}$, and $\underline{l}$ be the upper and lower bounds respectively of $l(x)$. Cover and Hellman[8] showed that every algorithm with the time-invariant m-state memory, as described by equation (10.3), must satisfy the inequality

$$(\alpha + t)(\beta + t) \geqslant t(1 + t) \tag{10.7}$$

where $t = (\gamma^{m-1} - 1)^{-1}$ and $\gamma = \underline{l}/\overline{l}$. When the equality is achieved, the algorithm is truly optimal.

By using different methods, the time-varying learning with the finite memory algorithm

$$\begin{aligned} &T_n = f(T_{n-1}, x_n, n), \quad T_n \in \{1, 2, \ldots, m\} \\ &d_n = d(T_n) \quad d\colon \{1, 2, \ldots, m\} \to \{H_0, H_1\} \end{aligned} \tag{10.8}$$

has been shown by Cover[10] to yield $P_e^* = 0$ for a memory of size $m = 4$. Thus there exist learning rules for a time-varying finite memory which yield asymptotically zero probability of error. In the time-invariant memory problem, however, such rules exist only in special cases.

3. Recognition Algorithms with Finite Statistics

In this section, several hypothesis testing (recognition) algorithms with a finite memory will be presented. The number of pattern classes is assumed as two. We start with two general results.[5]

ALGORITHM 1. When the likelihood ratio $l(x_n) = p_1(x_n)/p_0(x_n)$ is unbounded, there are sequences of thresholds $\{\bar{l}_n\}$, $\{\underline{l}_n\}$ such that the algorithm

$$T_n = \begin{cases} 1, & l(x_n) > \bar{l}_n \\ -1, & l(x_n) < \underline{l}_n \\ T_{n-1}, & \text{otherwise} \end{cases} \tag{10.9}$$

results in $T_n \to 1$ wp1 (with probability one) under H_1 and $T_n \to -1$ wp1 under H_0. Thus $\alpha_n \to 0$ and $\beta_n \to 0$ with a 2-state memory under either hypothesis. With probability one, only a finite number of mistakes will be made by $\{T_n\}$.

ALGORITHM 2. Consider the basic problem of testing the hypothesis that a coin with bias $p = P_r[x_i = 1]$ has bias $p \geqslant p_0$ vs. $p < p_0$. Note that the general two hypothesis testing problem with the random variables $x_1, x_2, \ldots$ independent and identically distributed may be put in this framework under the correspondence

$$x_i = \begin{cases} 1, & l(x_i) \geqslant 1 \\ 0, & l(x_i) < 0 \end{cases}$$

and $p_0 = \frac{1}{2}(P_r[x_i = 1/H_1] + P_r[x_i = 1/H_0])$.

The likelihood ratio is assumed as bounded. There exists an algorithm with a 4-state memory for which the hypothesis $p \geqslant p_0$ vs. $p < p_0$ is resolved with limiting probability of error zero under either hypothesis.

The following alogrithms are examples of the results stated above.

ALGORITHM 3. For testing the mean μ of a Gaussian distribution with unit variance as stated in the preceding section, the problem may be solved with only a 2-state memory $T_n \epsilon (-1, 1)$. The algorithm is

$$T_n = \begin{cases} 1, & x_n > \sqrt{2 \log n} \\ -1, & x_n < -\sqrt{2 \log n} \\ T_{n-1}, & \text{otherwise} \end{cases} \tag{10.10}$$

T_0 arbitrary $\epsilon(-1, 1)$

and $T_n \to 1$ or -1 accordingly as $\mu > 0$ or $\mu < 0$.

ALGORITHM 4. Let $x_1, x_2, \ldots$ be independent and identically distributed Gaussian random variables with mean zero and the unknown variance σ^2. Let

$$Y_i = \begin{cases} 1, & x_i^2 \geqslant c^2 \\ 0, & x_i^2 < c^2 \end{cases}$$

where c is a constant. Note that $P_r[Y_i = 1/\sigma^2] = 2\Phi(c/\sigma)$ where

$$\Phi(x) = \int_x^\infty \frac{1}{\sqrt{2\pi}} e^{-(y^2/2)}\, dy.$$

Let $p_0 = 2\Phi(c/\sigma)$. Then the 4-state test described in algorithm 2 will test $\sigma^2 \geqslant c^2$ versus $\sigma^2 < c^2$, with limiting probability of error zero. Let $p = P_r[Y_i = 1]$, we are testing the hypothesis $p \geqslant p_0$ vs. $p < p_0$. Note: The memory consists of the pair (T, Q) where T and Q both take values, say, in $(0, 1)$.

ALGORITHM 5. In the univariate case, let

$$Y_i = \begin{cases} 1, & x_i \geqslant c \\ 0, & x_i < c \end{cases}$$

The test in this section resolves $F(c) \gtrless p_0$, where F is the unknown cumulative distribution function of x. If $p_0 = 1/2$, we have a nonparametric finite-memory test of whether or not the median is greater than c.

4. Recognition Systems with Rejection Option

The error rate (probability of misrecognition) and the reject rate are commonly used to describe the performance of a recognition system. An error or misrecognition occurs when a pattern from one class is identified as that of a different class. A reject occurs when the recognition system withholds its recognition decision, and the pattern is rejected for exceptional handling, such as rescan or manual inspection. Because of uncertainties and noise inherent in any pattern recognition task, errors are generally unavoidable. The option to reject is introduced to safeguard against excessive misrecognition. However, when the rejection option is exercised, some would-be correct recognitions are also converted into rejects. Thus the problem of best error-reject tradeoff must be considered.

Chow[11] has shown that the optimum recognition rule is to reject the pattern if the maximum of the a posteriori probabilities is less than some threshold.

Let the threshold be $t (0 \leqslant t \leqslant 1)$ and M be the number of pattern classes. The decision is to accept the pattern x for recognition and to identify it as of the kth class whenever

$$P_k p(x/\omega_k) \geqslant P_j p(x/\omega_j) \quad \text{for all } j = 1, 2, \ldots, M \tag{10.11}$$

and

$$P_k p(x/\omega_k) \geqslant (1 - t) \sum_{i=1}^{M} P_i p(x/\omega_i); \tag{10.12}$$

and the decision is to reject the pattern whenever†

$$\max_i \, [P_i p(x/\omega_i)] < (1 - t) \sum_{i=1}^{M} p_i p(x/\omega_i). \tag{10.13}$$

For the given t, let $E(t)$, $R(t)$, $C(t)$, and $A(t)$ be the error rate, rejection rate, the probability of correct recognition, and the acceptance rate respectively. Obviously, $C(t) = 1 - R(t) - E(t)$ and $A(t) = C(t) + E(t)$. Chow[12] has established some simple properties of the rejection threshold t. They are:

1. $E(t)$ is monotonic increasing with t; $R(t)$ is monotonic decreasing with t.
2. t is an upper bound of the error rate, i.e.,

$$E(t) \leqslant t \tag{10.14}$$

3. $E(t)$ and $R(t)$ are uniquely related through t, i.e., $E(t)$ is a Stieltjes integral of t with respect to $R(t)$ namely,

$$E = \int_{t=0}^{t} t dR(t) \tag{10.15}$$

If $R(t)$ is differentiable with respect to t, then the above Stieltjes integral reduces to the ordinary Riemann integral,

$$E = \int_{R}^{1} t dR \tag{10.16}$$

It is noted that the integral of equation (10.16) is not always meaningful when $R(t)$ is discontinuous. On the other hand, equation (10.15) always

†It is seen that $t > 1 - \frac{1}{M}$ yields a Bayes decision scheme with no rejects.

exists. Both equations (10.15) and (10.16) state that $E(t)$ can be derived from $R(t)$ and thus $R(t)$ alone suffices to completely characterize the optimum recognition performance.

4. It is a differential error-reject tradeoff ratio, i.e.,

$$\frac{dE}{dR} = -t \leqslant 0 \tag{10.17}$$

It is known[11] that the optimum decision rule given in equations (10.11) to (10.13) is also a minimum risk rule if no distinction in cost is made among the errors, among the rejects, and among the correct recognition. The rejection threshold is then related to the costs as follows:

$$t = \frac{W_r - W_c}{W_e - W_c} \tag{10.18}$$

where W_e, W_r, and W_c are the costs for making an error, reject, and correct recognition respectively. Usually $W_e > W_r > W_c$. The rejection threshold is simply the normalized cost for the rejection. We can take $W_c = 0$ and $W_c = 1$, and the minimum (Bayes) risk is

$$\text{risk}\,(t) = E(t) + tR(t) = \int_0^t R(t)\,dt \tag{10.19}$$

So far we have considered the Bayes decision rule with rejection. The rejection option has also been introduced to the nearest-neighbor decision rule.[13] This rule looks at the k nearest neighbors and rejects if less than k' of these are from the same class; if k' or more are from one class, a decision is made in favor of that class. Let there be two classes, E_B and R_B, the error and reject rates, under the Bayes rule. If k is odd and $k' = (k + 1)/2$, no rejects are made, and we obtain the k - *NN* rule described in section 4 of chapter 7. To insure a nonzero reject rate, k' must be greater than or equal to $(k/2) + 1$. Let $E_{k,k'}(t)$ be the error rate with this (k, k') nearest-neighbor rule. Define

$$C_{k,k'} = \max_t \frac{E_{k,k'}(t)}{E_B} \tag{10.20}$$

where t is adjusted such that $R_B = R_{k,k'}$ and $R_{k,k'}$ is the reject rate. Computer search can be performed[13] and the values of $C_{k,k'}$ are given in table 11. For $k = k'$,

$$C_{k,k} = 1 + \frac{k}{2} \tag{10.21}$$

TABLE 11
Values of $C_{k,k'}$ for $k \leqslant 10$

k'	$k = 2$	$k = 3$	$k = 4$	$k = 5$	$k = 6$	$k = 7$	$k = 8$	$k = 9$	$k = 10$
2	2.00	1.32							
3		2.50	1.32	1.22					
4			3.00	1.40	1.22	1.17			
5				3.50	1.53	1.26	1.17	1.15	
6					4.00	1.66	1.33	1.20	1.15
7						4.50	1.80	1.40	1.24
8							5.00	1.94	1.49
9								5.50	2.08
10									6.00

independent of the statistics of the problem.[13] Equation (10.21) is the upper bound of the nearest-neighbor rule with rejection. If eight *NN*s are examined and a decision made only if at least six of them are from the same class, table 11 shows that the resulting error rate is no greater than 1.33 times the Bayes error rate.

5. Recognition Systems with Information Feedback

In sequential recognition of a vector pattern, a feature may be selected by using the information from the features which have already been measured. In recognition of printed text, information (including the decisions made) on the characters which have been recognized may be used to decide on the character yet to be recognized. The information feedback implies an on-line process in either feature selection or contextual analysis. Off-line contextual analysis is discussed in chapter 11. We shall consider on-line feature ordering and selection in this section.

Suppose there are available r feature sets of dimension k each. Let C be the class of all feature sets which are measured sequentially in stages. At each stage, the selection of a feature set to be measured may depend on the outcome of all feature sets that have been chosen at earlier stages.[14] It is desired that a minimum number of feature sets be selected to reach a decision with a minimum error. An uncertainty function[15] with certain desirable properties can be used to select or order the feature sets. Let $X = (x_1, x_2, \ldots, x_k)$ be the feature set and $G(X)$ be an uncertainty function depending on the previous choices of feature sets. After having measured $n - 1$ feature sets, the a posteriori distribution among all possible feature sets is ξ_{n-1}. Then, clearly, the best choice of the nth feature set is an $X_n^* = (x_1, x_2, \ldots, x_k)_n^* \epsilon\, C$ such that

$$E[G(\xi_{n-1}(X_n^*))|\xi_{n-1}] = \min_{X \epsilon C} E[G(\xi_{n-1}(X))|\xi_{n-1}], \quad n = 1, 2, \ldots, r \tag{10.22}$$

in which it is assumed that all minima taken over the class C are actually attained at some $X \epsilon C$. Equation (10.22) essentially defines a backward or dynamic programming procedure[15] for selecting feature sets which are ordered according to the information gained a posteriori. This is the information feedback in feature selection.

To gain more insight into this information feedback system, consider the joint optimization[16] of receptor and categorizer in a statistical recognition machine. Define a risk function $R(X, Y, P)$ as the risk of incorrectly selecting the feature set $x \epsilon X$ on the basis of the observation $y \epsilon Y$. Let P be the set of a priori probabilities of all pattern classes. A statistical recognizer is truly optimal if $R(X, Y, P)$ is minimized with respect to all feature sets and all pattern classes. That is to say that the receptor and the categorizer must be jointly optimized so that there is no "mismatching" between the feature sets selected and the subsequent decision on the pattern class. The optimization can be performed in two steps. First, a feature set is selected by using available pattern data. This step is called the receptor optimization. Second, based on the observations (measurements) of the selected feature sets, a decision on the pattern class is made. This is called the categorizer optimization.

The risk function is given by

$$R(X, Y, P) = \sum_{x \epsilon X_u} \sum_{i=1}^{m} \int_Y [C(y) + L(\omega_i, d(x, y))] \, P_i p(y/\omega_i, x) \, dy \tag{10.23}$$

where the summation with respect to x is taken over all unobserved feature sets X_u, P_i is the a priori probability of the ith class, $C(y)$ is the cost of observation y, and $d(x, y)$ is the decision based on all available feature measurements. The minimization risk function can be written as

$$\min_{x, y} R(X, Y, P) = \min_{d(x^*(y))} \sum_{x \epsilon X_u} \min_x \sum_{i=1}^{m} \int_Y [C(y) + L(\omega_i, d(x, y))] \cdot P_i p(y/\omega_i, x) \, dy \tag{10.24}$$

where $x^*(y)$ is the best feature set which minimizes the risk function, i.e.,

$$R(x^*(y), Y, P) = \min_x \sum_{i=1}^{m} \int_Y [C(y) + L(\omega_i, d(x, y))] \cdot P(\omega_i/y, x) \, p(y) \, dy \tag{10.25}$$

where we have used the relationship that

$$p(y/x) = p(y) \tag{10.26}$$

which states that the observed feature sets are independent of the unobserved feature sets. But the unobserved feature sets are very much correlated with each pattern class. Equation (10.24) can be rewritten as

$$\min_{x,y} R(X,Y,P) = \min_{d(x^*(y))} \sum_{x \epsilon X_u} \int_Y \left\{ \min_x \sum_{i=1}^{m} [C(y) + L(\omega_i, d(x,y))] \cdot P(\omega_i/y, x) \right\} p(y)\, dy \qquad (10.27)$$

Hence, the joint optimization can be accomplished in two separate steps by first selecting the best feature set among all unobserved feature sets using all available previous observations and then by making the minimum risk decision. The result is due to the relationship given by equation (10.26). If the cost of taking an observation is a constant, feature selection criterion is independent of the cost of observation.

In the receptor optimization, the conditional uncertainty function, such as the conditional entropy[17] and the conditional risk function, can be used to select the feature set. The on-line feature selection and ordering system is shown by a block diagram in figure 10.1. Here a forward sequential procedure is used and the threshold $T_{n+1}(x_n^*)$ is computed at each stage. The threshold may be defined as the expected risk (including the cost of observation) when the best new feature set is supplied. If the risk incurred after observing the new feature set is smaller than $T_{n+1}(x_n^*)$, a terminal decision (classification) is made, otherwise continue the sequential process.

For the system described in figure 10.1, Nikolic[18,19] has used the equivocation to select the best feature sets in a character recognition experiment and shown that the on-line system has a smaller recognition error than the system without feedback. Cardillo[20] considered using dynamic programming in on-line feature selection. Recently Chien[21] has employed sequential design with memory as a strategy for on-line selection of the best feature subset possible as pattern samples are successively recognized by the classifier.

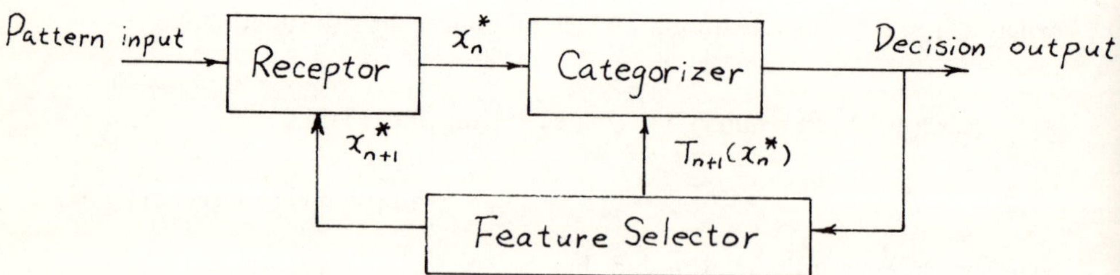

Fig. 10.1 On-Line Feature Selection and Ordering System

6. Remarks

That only a small number of memory states is required for some recognition algorithms with the finite memory is a surprising and very encouraging result. Additional applications of the theory of finite memory hypothesis testing to practical recognition problems are very much needed. Roberts[22,23] considered the dependence of sequential estimation and decision on finite memory size. Pattern recognition with a rejection option has been very important in practical applications such as the design of a character reader. The tradeoff between error and reject rate should always be considered in design of recognition systems. Recognition systems with information feedback is a problem much less explored. Computationally feasible algorithms remain to be developed and performance improvement over recognition systems without feedback must be determined theoretically.

PROBLEMS

1. Verify that the rejection threshold is an upper bound of error rate (equation 10.14). Discuss whether this bound is tight or not.
2. Consider two univariate Gaussian distributions with means μ_1 and μ_2, $\mu_1 > \mu_2$ and equal variance σ^2. Find $E(t)$ and $R(t)$ for given t and verify equation (10.16).
3. Consider two uniform distributions

$$p(x/\omega_1) = \begin{cases} 1, & 0 \leqslant x \leqslant 1 \\ 0, & \text{elsewhere} \end{cases}$$

$$p(x/\omega_2) = \begin{cases} \frac{1}{2}, & \frac{1}{2} \leqslant x \leqslant \frac{5}{2} \\ 0, & \text{elsewhere} \end{cases}$$

Sketch $E(t)$ and $R(t)$ and E versus R. Verify equation (10.15).

REFERENCES

1. Robbins, H. "Some Aspects of the Sequential Design of Experiments." *Bull. Amer. Math. Soc.*, 58 (1952), 527–535.
2. Robbins, H. "A Sequential Decision Problem with Finite Memory." In *Proc. National Academy of Science, U.S.A.*, 42 (1956), 920–923.
3. Wald, A. *Statistical Decision Functions.* Wiley, New York, 1950.
4. Blackwell, D. and M. A. Grischick. *Theory of Games and Statistical Decisions.* Wiley, New York, 1954.
5. Cover, T. M. "Hypothesis Testing with Finite Statistics." *Ann. Math. Stat.*, 40 (1969), 828–835.
6. Cover, T. M. "Learning in Pattern Recognition." In *Methodologies of Pattern Recognition,* edited by S. Watanabe. Academic Press, New York, 1969.

7. Hellman, M. E. and T. M. Cover. "The Two-Armed Bandit Problem with Time Invariant Finite Memory." *IEEE Trans. on Information Theory,* IT-16 (March 1970), 185–195.
8. Hellman, M. E. and T. M. Cover. "Learning with Finite Memory." *Ann. Math. Stat.,* 41 (1970), 765–782.
9. Hellman, M. E. and T. M. Cover. "On Memory Saved by Randomization." *Ann. Math. Stat.,* 42 (1971), 1075–1078.
10. Cover, T. M. "A Note on the Two-Armed Bandit Problem with Finite Memory." *Information and Control,* 12 (1968), 371–377.
11. Chow, C. K. "An Optimum Character Recognition System Using Decision Functions." *IRE Trans. on Electronic Computers,* EC-6 (December 1957), 247–254.
12. Chow, C. K. "On Optimum Recognition Error and Reject Tradeoff." *IEEE Trans. on Information Theory,* IT-16 (January 1970), 41–46.
13. Hellman, M. E. "The Nearest Neighbor Classification Rule with a Reject Option." *IEEE Trans. on Systems Science and Cybernetics,* SSC-6 (July 1970), 179–185.
14. Fu, K. S. and C. H. Chen. "A Sequential Decision Approach to Problems in Pattern Recognition and Learning." Preprints, *Third Symposium on Adaptive Processes.* Chicago, October 1964.
15. DeGroot, M. H. "Uncertainty, Information, and Sequential Experiments." *Ann. Math. Stat.,* 33 (1962), 404–419.
16. Chen, C. H. "Statistical Recognizer with On-line Feature Selection and Ordering." In *Seventh Annual Allerton Conference on Circuit and System Theory.* Monticello, Ill., October 1969.
17. Chen, C. H. "A Note on Sequential Decision Approach to Pattern Recognition and Machine Learning." *Information and Control,* 9 (1966), 549–569.
18. Fu, K. S. and Z. J. Nikolic. "A Study of Learning Systems Operating in Unknown Stationary Environments." Purdue Univ. TR-EE66-20, November 1966.
19. Nikolic, Z. J. and K. S. Fu. "On the Selection of Features in Statistical Pattern Recognition." In *Proc. of the Second Annual Princeton Conference on Information Sciences and Systems.* Princeton, N. J., March 1968.
20. Fu, K. S. and G. P. Cardillo. "Optimum Finite Sequential Pattern Recognition." Purdue Univ. TR-EE67-9, 1967.
21. Chien, Y. T. "A Sequential Decision Model for Selecting Feature Subsets in Pattern Recognition." *IEEE Trans. on Computers,* C-20 (March 1971), 282–290.
22. Roberts, R. A. and J. R. Tooley. "Estimation with Finite Memory." *IEEE Trans. on Information Theory,* IT-16 (November 1970), 685–691.
23. Mullis, C. T. and R. A. Roberts. "Memory Limitation and Multistage Decision Processes." *IEEE Trans. on Systems Science and Cybernetics,* SSC-4 (September 1968), 307–316.

Bibliography

1. Bongard, M. *Pattern Recognition.* Translated from Russian by T. Cheron. Edited by J. K. Hawkins. Spartan Books, New York, 1970. Chapter 7.

2. Chandrasekaran, B. "Finite-Memory Hypothesis Testing: A Critique." *IEEE Trans. on Information Theory,* IT-16 (July 1970), 494–496.
3. Chandrasekaran, B. "Reply to Finite Memory Hypothesis Testing: Comments on a Critique." *IEEE Trans. on Information Theory,* IT-7 (January 1971), 104–105.
4. Chow, C. K. "On 'Note on a Partition for Decision Feedback Strategy.'" *IEEE Trans. on Information Theory,* IT-17 (March 1971), 210–211.
5. Cover, T. M. and M. E. Hellman. "Finite-Memory Hypothesis Testing: Comments on a Critique." *IEEE Trans. on Information Theory,* IT-16 (July 1970), 496–497.
6. Flower, R. A. and M. E. Hellman, "Hypothesis Testing with Finite Memory in Finite Time," *IEEE Trans. on Information Theory* (corresp.) IT-18 (May 1972), 429–431.
7. Hellman, M. E. "The Effects of Randomization on Finite-Memory Decision Schemes." *IEEE Trans. on Information Theory,* vol. IT-18, No. 4 (July 1972), 499–502.
8. Nadler, M. "Error and Reject Rates in a Hierarchical Pattern Recognizer." *IEEE Trans. on Computers* (December 1971).
9. Sagalowicz, D. "Hypothesis Testing with Finite Memory." Ph.D. thesis, Stanford University, 1971.
10. Wagner, T. J. "Estimation of the Mean with Time-Varying Finite Memory." *IEEE Trans. on Information Theory* (corresp.), vol. IT-18, No. 4 (July 1972), 523–525.

CHAPTER XI

Contextual Analysis in Pattern Recognition

1. Introduction

When the pattern is described by a finite number of correlated measurements or features, knowledge of correlation among features will improve the performance as compared with the assumption that the features are statistically independent. In the same manner, knowledge of context dependence such as in character recognition will also improve the performance as compared with the common assumption that the successive patterns are statistically independent. There have been in the past two basic approaches in pattern recognition using contextual constraints. The first approach is the table look-up method based on the assumption that every word in the text is selected from a known finite table. A word of text is classified by comparing it with every table word having the same length and finding the best match. Gold[1] used such a table of legal Morse code symbols in his system for recognizing handsent Morse code, and Bledsoe and Browning[2] used a table of English words in their pioneering experiments in recognizing handprinted characters.

The second or the Markov approach is based on thc assumption that the true class of a character is related in a probabilistic manner to the true classes of a small number of surrounding characters. Its use leads to the estimation, from the sample text, of the probabilities of all possible pairs, triples, or in general n-triples of characters. The estimation of the first-order Markov dependence in an English literary text is obtained by counting the frequency of occurrence as shown in table 12 for illustrative purposes. The Markov method can be expected to correct locally improbable character strings, but it ignores global considerations. Harmon[3] used this method to detect errors in the recognition of cursive script. Edwards and Chambers[4] and Carlson[5] also employed this technique to correct errors encountered in conventional optical character recognition. An interesting mixture of the two approaches was used by McElwain and Evens[6] to correct garbled Morse code, and both methods were compared experimentally in a lucid paper by Vossler and Branston.[7]

Both of these approaches rest on the theoretical foundations of compound de-

TABLE 12
FREQUENCIES of English DIGRAMS
(Actual count, made on 10,000 letters of literary text)

	A	*B*	*C*	*D*	*E*	*F*	*G*	*H*	*I*	*J*	*K*	*L*	*M*	*N*	*O*	*P*	*Q*	*R*	*S*	*T*	*U*	*V*	*W*	*X*	*Y*	*Z*	*Total*
A	1	8	44	45	131	21	11	84	18			34	56	54	9	21		57	75	56	18	15	32	3	11		805
B	32			18	11	2	2	1	7			7	9	7	18	1		4	13	14	5				11		162
C	39		12	4	64	9	1	2	55			8	1	31	18			14	21	6	17		3	5	10		320
D	15			10	107	1	1	1	16			28	2	118	16			16	6	9	11		4		4		365
E		58	55	39	39	25	32	251	37	2	28	72	48	64	3	40		148	84	94	11	53	30	1	12	5	1,231
F	10		1	12	23	14	3	2	27			5		8	94			6	13	5	1		1		3		228
G	18			2	20	1	1		10			1		75	3			6	6	1	12				5		161
H			46	3	15	6	16	5					1	9	3	7		3	30	315	2		48		5		514
I	16	6	15	57	40	21	10	72			8	57	26	37	13	8		77	42	128	5	19	37	4	18	2	718
J		2		1	1	1						1		3				1									10
K	10		8		2				8			3		3	5			11	2								52
L	77	21	16	7	46	10	4	3	39			55		10	17	29		12	6	12	28		4		6	1	403
M	18	1		9	43	3	1	1	32			4	5	7	44			15	14	14	9		1		4		225
N	172			5	120	2	3	2	169		3	1	3	9	145			12	19	8	33		10		3		719
O	2	11	59	37	46	38	23	46	63	4	3	28	28	65	23	28		54	71	111	2	6	17	1	28		794
P	31		1	7	32	3	1	1	3			2	16	7	29	26		8	24	8	17		2	4	7		229
Q	1			1	14							2							2								20
R	101	6	7	10	154	4	21	8	21			2		5	113	42		18	6	30	49		1		5		603
S	67	5	1	32	145	8	7	3	106		2	12	6	51	37	3		39	41	32	42		3		17		659
T	124		38	39	80	42	13	22	88		1	19	6	110	53	14		63	121	53	45		6	1	21		959
U	12	25	16	8	7	11	8	2		4		8	13	12	96	7	20	6	30	22			1	1	1		310
V	24			4	16	1			14			2		4	13			5	2	4			1		3		93
W	7		1	9	41	4	2	7	1		3	5	2	15	36	1		10	27	16			2		14		203
X					17				1					1							1						20
Y	27	19		6	17	1	1	1			3	47	3	14	4	2		17	4	21	1						188
Z	1								4						2						1					1	9
Total	805	162	320	365	1,231	228	161	514	719	10	51	403	225	719	794	229	20	602	659	960	310	93	203	20	188	9	10,000

SOURCE: Prepared by O. Phelps Meaker.

NOTE: To learn the frequency of any digram, find its first letter at the top, find its second letter at the side, and observe the figure in the cell at which the column headed by the first letter crosses the row headed by the second. Frequency for EA, 131; for AE, zero.

cision theory described in chapter 7. Both Abend[8] and Raviv[9] point out the importance of considering the alternatives that can be supplied by a classifier. They derive the formal decision-theoretic solution for the optimum use of context and show how it can be simplified by the Markov dependence assumption. This assumption has made the optimum procedure computationally feasible, though it limits the ability to exploit global relations. The decision-theoretic solution with the Markov dependence assumption is presented in sections 2, 3, and 4.

A practical solution of the problem must take advantage of the special nature of the text. For example, the structure of the language must be analyzed and utilized to a much larger extent than the Markov dependence. Duda and Hart[10] point out the two serious drawbacks in the general formal solution based on compound decision theory:

(1) The solution requires explicit enumeration of all possible strings of characters of the given length and thus rapidly gets out of hand combinatorially. For example, a statement only ten characters long with, say, four alternatives for each character gives rise to over a million possibilities. Even if we enumerate only the strings with highest confidence, the number of possibilities is still quite large. Also, the problem of ordering the strings is far from trivial.

(2) The solution is unable to use the semantic information in a natural way.

The recently emerging linguistic approach to pattern recognition (e.g., see reference 11) may overcome some of the difficulties described above.

The decision-theoretic solution nevertheless has an important role in providing a unified approach to recognition systems with contextual analysis. Many experimental results have also demonstrated the performance improvement available from this approach.

2. Bayes Decision Making in Markov Chains

A typical printed text may be modeled as a Markov chain. In decision making, the a posteriori probability of each class can be evaluated and the class with the highest a posteriori probability is chosen as the true class. This is an optimum Bayes decision procedure[9] for a zero-one loss function. Let θ_n be the pattern class at time n and x_n be the measurement of the pattern vector at time n. Then the a posteriori probability that the kth class, $k = 1, 2, \ldots, m$, is true is

$$P(\theta_n = k/x_1, x_2, \ldots, x_n) = \frac{P(\theta_n = k, x_1, \ldots, x_n)}{P(x_1, \ldots, x_n)}$$

$$= \frac{\sum_{l=1}^{m} \cdots \sum_{j=1}^{m} \sum_{i=1}^{m} [p_i p_{ij} \ldots p_{lk} P(x_1, \ldots, x_n/\theta_1 = i, \theta_2 = j, \ldots, \theta_{n-1} = l, \theta_n = k)]}{\sum_{\gamma=1}^{m} \sum_{l=1}^{m} \cdots \sum_{j=1}^{m} \sum_{i=1}^{m} [p_i p_{ij} \ldots P_{er} P(x_1, \ldots, x_n/\theta_1 = i, \theta_2 = j, \ldots, \theta_{n=1} = l, \theta_n = \gamma)]} \quad (11.1)$$

where p_i is the initial probability, $P(\theta_i = i)$, and p_{ij} is the transition probability that at any time n, the Markov chain is in state j, given that at time $n - 1$, it was in state i. In many recognition problems, it is reasonable to assume that the distribution of a measurement vector depends on the identity of the pattern class alone and is independent of the identities of previous or future pattern classes. For this reason, it is assumed that $x_1, \ldots, x_n$ are conditionally independent, which implies that

$$P(x_1, \ldots, x_n/\theta_1 = i, \theta_2 = j, \ldots, \theta_{n-1} = l, \theta_n = k) = P(x_1/\theta_1 = i) \cdot P(x_2/\theta_2 = j) \ldots P(x_{n-1}/\theta_{n-1} = l) P(x_n/\theta_n = k) \quad (11.2)$$

We notice that equation (11.1) can be calculated iteratively as follows. Since

$$P(\theta_n = k/\theta_{n-1} = i) = P(\theta_n = k/\theta_{n-1} = i, x_1, \ldots, x_{n-1}) \quad (11.3)$$

we have

$$P(\theta_n = k/x_1, \ldots, x_{n-1}) = \sum_{i=1}^{m} P(\theta_{n-1} = i/x_1, \ldots, x_{n-1}) \cdot P(\theta_n = k/\theta_{n-1} = i) \quad (11.4)$$

Using the fact that

$$P(x_n/\theta_n = k) = P(x_n/\theta_n = k, x_1, \ldots, x_{n-1}) \quad (11.5)$$

and

$$P(\theta_n = k/x_1, \ldots, x_n) = \frac{P(\theta_n = k, x_n/x_1, \ldots, x_{n-1})}{P(x_n/x_1, \ldots, x_{n-1})} \quad (11.6)$$

we obtain

$$P(\theta_n = k/x_1, \ldots, x_{n-1}, x_n) = \frac{P(\theta_n = k/x_1, \ldots, x_{n-1})P(x_n/\theta_n = k)}{\sum_{j=1}^{m} P(\theta_n = j/x_1, \ldots, x_{n-1})P(x_n/\theta_n = j)} \tag{11.7}$$

The vector $P(\theta_n = k/x_1, \ldots, x_{n-1})$, $k = 1, \ldots, m$, expresses the information relevant to θ_n based only on all the past experience. The measurement x_n is taken and if it is assumed that $P(x_n/\theta_n = k)$ is available, the state of the decision process is obtained at time n using Bayes' theorem with the vector $P(\theta_n = k/x_1, \ldots, x_{n-1})$ as a vector of a priori probabilities. The state vector at time n is obtained in equation (11.7) and the decision on θ_n is based on the value of k which corresponds to the largest a posteriori probability.

The Markov chain model described above is a first-order approximation to the natural language. Equations (11.1) through (11.7) can be written for any higher-order approximation to the natural language. For a second-order approximation, for example, the transition probability

$$P_{ijk} = P(\theta_n = k/\theta_{n-1} = j, \theta_{n-2} = i) \tag{11.8}$$

must be used. The transition probabilities p_{ij}, p_{ijk}, etc. can be estimated from the samples.

In estimating $P(x_n/\theta_n = k)$, Raviv[9] assumed that all features are independent and then introduced in equation (11.7) a design factor F as a simple first-order correction to the independence assumption. Equation (11.7) is modified as

$$P(\theta_n = k/x_1, \ldots, x_{n-1}, x_n) = \frac{P(\theta_n = k/x_1, \ldots, x_{n-1}) \, [P(x_n/\theta_n = k)]^F}{\sum_{j=1}^{m} P(\theta_n = j/x_1, \ldots, x_{n-1}) \, [P(x_n/\theta_n = j)]^F} \tag{11.9}$$

Thus, setting $F = 1.0$ is equivalent to not using a design factor. If we let $F = 0$, we use contextual information only. As F becomes larger, more information from the measurement is used. For $0 < F < 1.0$, the optimum F can be determined from the best recognition results.

3. Compound Decision Theory for Contextual Analysis

If we let c denote the context and drop the subscript n, then the a posteriori probability of θ given by equation (11.1) can be written as

$$P(\theta/x, c) = \frac{P(x/\theta)P(\theta/c)}{P(x/c)} \tag{11.10}$$

where we have assumed, as before, that x is independent of c when θ is given, $P(x/\theta, c) = P(x/\theta)$. So the decision is based on the product

$$P(x/\theta)P(\theta/c) \tag{11.11}$$

where $P(x/\theta)$ can be estimated from the samples and the Markov development was made in the previous section to determine $P(\theta/c)$. A description of the language in terms of a Markov chain is possible if the neighboring characters are known. In practice the neighboring characters are not known, however. The context c is only available through observations on preceding characters. Our knowledge of preceding characters can be based on the decisions made on such characters. If the context were used in this way, errors would tend to "propagate." What is needed is the optimum (minimum risk) sequential compound decision procedure for dependent states of nature.

From equations (7.18), (7.19), and (7.20) we can write the kth component risk as

$$R(\theta^N, t_k) = \int \sum_{j=1}^{m'} L_{\theta_k j}\, t_k(j/x_k) p(x^k/\theta^k)\, dx^k = R(\theta^k, t_k) \tag{11.12}$$

and the kth component sequential Bayes risk as

$$\begin{aligned} \bar{R}(G, t_k) &= \sum_{\theta^N} R(\theta^k, t_k) G(\theta^N) = \sum_{\theta^k} R(\theta^k, t_k) G(\theta^k) \\ &= \int \sum_{j=1}^{m'} \sum_{\theta^k} L_{\theta_k j}\, p(x^k/\theta^k) G(\theta^k) t_k(j/x^k)\, dx^k \end{aligned} \tag{11.13}$$

where $G(\theta^k)$ is the a priori parameter distribution. Hence $t_k(j/x_k) = 1$ for that j which minimizes the quantity

$$\begin{aligned} Q &= \sum_{\theta^k} L_{\theta_k j}\, p(x^k/\theta^k) G(\theta^k) \\ &\sum_{\theta^k} L_{\theta_k j}\, p(x^k, \theta^k) = \sum_{\theta_k} L_{\theta_k j}\, p(x^k \theta_k) \end{aligned} \tag{11.14}$$

For $L_{\theta j}$ given, and the action j corresponding to the decision $\theta = j$, t_k chooses that value of θ_k which maximizes $p(x^k, \theta_k)$. This is equivalent to maximizing the a posteriori probability $G(\theta_k/x^k)$. That $p(\theta_k/x^k)$ or $p(x^k, \theta_k)$ can be calculated iteratively when θ^k forms a Markov chain was described in the preceding section. It is noted here that for a first-order Markov chain,

$$\begin{aligned} p(x^k, \theta_k) &= p(x^{k-1}, x_k, \theta_k) = p(x_k/\theta_k)\, p(x^{k-1}, \theta_k) \\ &= p(x_k/\theta_k) \sum_{\theta_{k-1}} p(x^{k-1}, \theta_{k-1}, \theta_k) \\ &= p(x_k/\theta_k) \sum_{\theta_{k-1}=1}^{m} G(\theta_k/\theta_{k-1})\, p(x^{k-1}, \theta_{k-1}) \end{aligned} \tag{11.15}$$

The kth decision $t_k(j/x^k)$ depends on x_k and a function of θ_{k-1} which had already been calculated in order to make the previous decision. It does not depend on the (unknown) value of θ_{k-1} nor on the decision about it.

For the zero-one loss function, $L_{ij} = 1 - \delta_{ij}$ (action j corresponds to deciding that $\theta_k = j$) the kth component Bayes risk becomes the probability of error,

$$e_k = \text{Prob}\ [d_k \neq \theta_k] = \bar{R}\,(G, t_k) = 1 - \sum_{j=1}^{m'} \int_{\Gamma_k(j)} p(x^k, j)\, dx^k \tag{11.16}$$

The error probability is minimized by choosing $d_x(x^k)$ equal to the value of θ_k that maximizes $p(x^k, j)$ given by equation (11.15), that is

$$\Gamma_k(j) = \{x_k : p(x^k, j) \geqslant p(x^k, \theta_k) \text{ for all } \theta_k\} \tag{11.17}$$

Since $p(x_k, \theta_k/x^{k-1}) = p(x^k, \theta_k)/p(x^{k-1})$, this rule is equivalent to choosing $d_k(x^k)$ equal to the value of θ_k that maximizes

$$p(x_k, \theta_k/x^{k-1}) = p(x_k/\theta_k)\, G\,(\theta_k/x^{k-1}) \tag{11.18}$$

An alternate (suboptimum) rule would be to choose $d_k^*\,(x_k)$ as equal to the values of θ_k that maximizes

$$p(x_k, \theta_k/d_{k-1}^*\,(x_{k-1})) = p(x_k/\theta_k)\, G\,(\theta_k/d_{k-1}^*) \tag{11.19}$$

Letting e_k and e_k^* represent the error probabilities for d_k and d_k^* respectively, we have $e_k \leqslant e_k^*$. Let e_1 represent the error probability for the simple rule $t(j/x_k)$, which does not take context into account but merely chooses $d_1(x_k)$ equal to the value of θ_k that maximizes

$$p(x_k, \theta_k) = p(x_k/\theta_k)\, G\,(\theta_k) \tag{11.20}$$

We note that $d_1^*\,(x_1) = d_1\,(x_1)$ and hence $e_1 = e_1^*$.

A general sequential decision rule is denoted as $t_k(j/\theta^N, x^N)$ which considers not only x^N but also θ^N. The corresponding error probability is the minimum error probability denoted as e_c. It can be shown[8] that $\{e_k\}$ is a monotonically nonincreasing sequence bounded below by e_c and hence has a limit $e_\infty = e$, i.e.,

$$e_1 \geqslant e_2 \geqslant \cdots \geqslant e_k \geqslant e_{k+1} \cdots \geqslant e \geqslant e_c \tag{11.21}$$

Furthermore, e_k is also upper bounded by e_k^*. When the distributions of all classes are not well separated, the decision-directed rule d_k^* performs poorly and $e_k^* > e_1$. If the distributions are well separated, d_k^* is almost as good as the optimal sequential rule and $e_k^* < e_1$.

4. Error Bounds for Contextual Recognition Procedures

In the preceding section, the error probability of sequential compound decision procedure was briefly discussed. The error probability is very difficult if not impossible to evaluate exactly, mainly because the decision regions usually cannot be determined analytically. Upper bounds, however, may often be derived. Consider a simple first-order Markov chain with two pattern classes. Then an optimal Bayes decision procedure and the corresponding average probability of error are

$$d_k(x_{k-1}, x_k) = \begin{cases} \text{Class } 1, & \sum_{i=1}^{2} p_i p_{i1}\, p_i(x_{k-1})\, p_1(x_k) \geqslant \sum_{i=1}^{2} p_i p_{i2}\, p_i(x_{k-1})\, p_2(x_k) \\ \text{Class } 2, & \text{otherwise} \end{cases} \tag{11.22}$$

and

$$P_e = \int_{W_2}\int \sum_{i=1}^{2} p_i p_{i1}\, p_i(x_{k-1}) p_1(x_k)\, dx_{k-1} dx_k + \int_{W_1}\int \sum_{i=1}^{2} p_i p_{i2}\, p_i(x_{k-1}) P_2(x_k)\, dx_{k-1} dx_k \tag{11.23}$$

where

$$p_i(x_k) = p(x_k/\theta_k = i), i = 1, 2, k = 1, 2, \ldots, N \tag{11.24}$$

and

$$W_j = \{(y_{k-1}, y_k): d_k(x_{k-1}, x_k) = j\}, j = 1, 2 \tag{11.25}$$

are the decision regions.

Suppose that for any $k = 1, 2, \ldots, N$, $p_i(x_k)$, $i = 1, 2$, of equation (11.24) satisfies the condition

$$\int_{\text{all } y_k} | p_1(x_k) - p_2(x_k) | \, dx_k \geqslant 2\delta \geqslant 0 \tag{11.26}$$

and let $\epsilon_i = p_{i1} - p_{i2}$, $i = 1, 2$. Then it can be shown that[12]

$$P_e \leqslant \begin{cases} \Delta - \dfrac{\delta^2}{4} \max (p_1 | \epsilon_1 |, \; p_2 | \epsilon_2 |, \; \prod_{i=1}^{2} p_i \epsilon_i < 0 & (11.27) \\ \Delta - \dfrac{\delta}{4} (p_1 | \epsilon_1 | + p_2 | \epsilon_2 |), \text{ otherwise} & (11.28) \end{cases}$$

where P_e is defined in equation (11.23) and $\Delta = \frac{1}{2} - \frac{\delta}{4}$. The quantities $| \epsilon_i |$, $i = 1, 2$, may be viewed as measures of interdependence between the consecutive characters in the context. Reduction in error probability by the use of context if the consecutive characters depend on each other is evident in the second terms of equations (11.27) and (11.28). Such reduction may not be very significant, however, because the second terms are the product of δ and $| \epsilon_i |$.

For the sequential compound decision procedure with a first-order Markov chain as described in the preceding section, the upper bound of the error probability has also been derived.[13] The decision regions Γ_1 and Γ_2 are defined by equation (11.17). The average error probability is

$$P_e = \int_{\Gamma_2} p_1 p_1(x^k) \, dx^k + \int_{\Gamma_1} p_2 p_2(x^k) \, dx^k \tag{11.29}$$

The upper bound, for $\epsilon_1 \epsilon_2 \geqslant 0$, is

$$P_e \leqslant \frac{1}{2} - \frac{\delta}{4} - \frac{\delta}{4} \sum_{i=1}^{2} p_i | \epsilon_i | \tag{11.30}$$

while if $\epsilon_1 \epsilon_2 < 0$ and $n \geqslant 2$. Also,

$$P_e \leqslant \frac{1}{2} - \frac{\delta}{4} - \frac{\delta}{4} \sum_{\gamma=1}^{n-2} \left(\frac{\rho}{2}\right)^{\gamma} - \frac{\delta}{2} \rho \left(\frac{\rho}{2}\right)^{n-2} \max (p_1, p_2) \tag{11.31}$$

where Σ disappears if $n = 2$.

$$\rho = \tau - || \epsilon_1 | - | \epsilon_2 ||/2 \tag{11.32}$$

and τ is any nonnegative number satisfying

$$\int_{\text{all } x^k} || \epsilon_1 | p_1(x^k) - | \epsilon_2 | p_2(x^k) | \, dx^k \geqslant 2\tau \tag{11.33}$$

It is noted that equation (11.3) is the same as (11.28), while (11.31) is a more complicated expression. The additional improvement in performance by using the sequential compound decision procedure, however, can be seen from equation (11.31).

5. A Practical Context Algorithm for Image Interpretation

As an application of the compound decision theory we consider a practical algorithm[14] using the neighbor dependence rule.[15] Consider an image divided by n cells. Each cell can be classified as one of m categories. Then we have a compound decision problem described in chapter 7. Let $x^n = (x_1, x_2, \ldots, x_n)$ be n vector samples corresponding to n cells. Then the decision rule which minimizes the compound Bayes risk chooses the action a_k for each individual cell k, which minimizes the expression (see equation 7.20)

$$\sum_{\theta_k=1}^{m} L(\theta_k, a_k) p(x^n/\theta_k) G(\theta_k) \tag{11.34}$$

where θ_i is the state of nature. Direct calculation of equation (11.34) is impossible in most practical situations. For instance, in the simulation experiment of reference 14, $n = 289$, $m = 22$. It is necessary to make simplifying assumptions so that equation (11.34) can be computed. First the neighbor dependence assumes that each cell k depends only on its four adjacent cells (figure 11.1). If cells b and c are nonadjacent,

$$p(x_b/\theta_c, \text{any other } x \text{ or } \theta) = p(x_b/\text{any other } x \text{ or } \theta) \tag{11.35}$$

The next assumption is the same as the fundamental assumption made in section 2, i.e.,

$$\begin{cases} p(x_k/\theta_k, \text{any other } \theta \text{ or } x) = p(x_k/\theta_k) \\ p(x_b/x_c, \text{any other } \theta \text{ or } x) = p(x_b/\text{any other } \theta \text{ or } x), \\ \qquad \text{if cells } b \text{ and } c \text{ are nonadjacent.} \end{cases} \tag{11.36}$$

From figure 11.1,

$$\begin{aligned} p(x^n/\theta_k) &= p(x_{NA}, x_{AD}, x_k/\theta_k) \\ &= p(x_{NA}/x_{AD}, x_k, \theta_k) p(x_{AD}, x_k/\theta_k) \end{aligned} \tag{11.37}$$

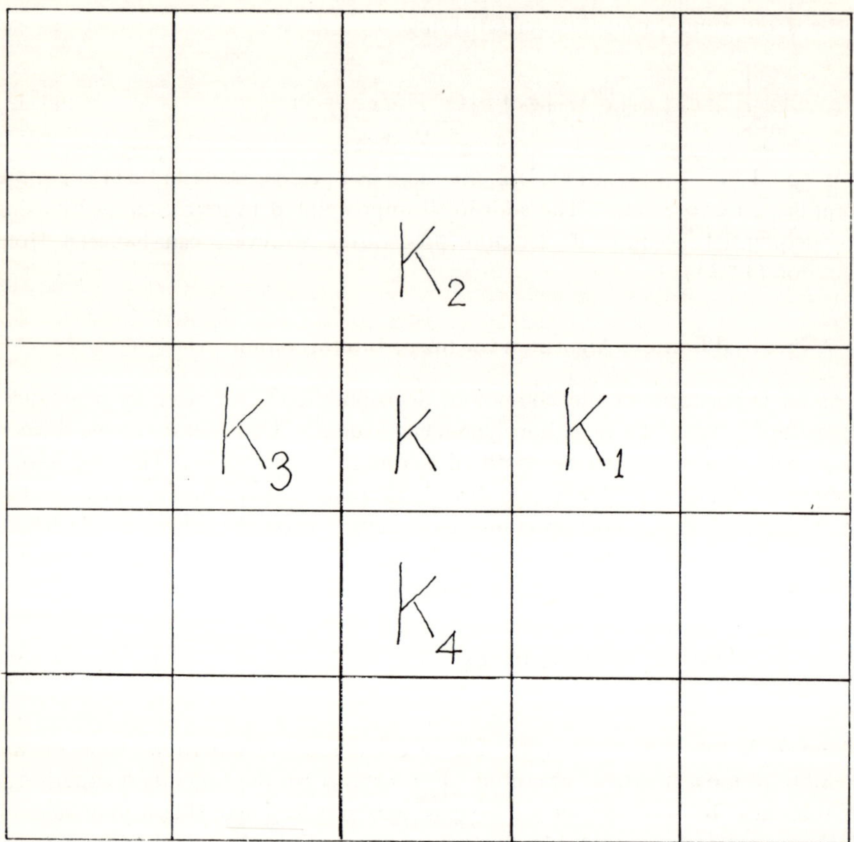

Fig. 11.1 Labelling of Neighbors of Cell K

where $x_{AD} = (x_{k1}, x_{k2}, x_{k3}, x_{k4})$ is a collection of vector samples from the four cells adjacent to k, and x_{NA} is a collection of vector samples not adjacent to k. From equations (11.35) and (11.36) we have

$$p(x^n/\theta_k) = p(x_{NA}/x_{AD})p(x_{AD}, x_k/\theta_k) \tag{11.38}$$

The term $p(x_{NA}/x_{AD})$ is independent of θ_k, so minimization of equation (11.34) is to choose action a for the cell k to minimize

$$\sum_{\theta_k=1}^{m} L(\theta_k, a)p(x_{AD}, x_k/\theta_k)G(\theta_k) \tag{11.39}$$

Using equation (11.36) again, we have

$$\begin{aligned} p(x_{AD}, x_k/\theta_k) &= p(x_k/x_{AD}, \theta_k)p(x_{AD}/\theta_k) \\ &= p(x_k/\theta_k)p(x_{AD}/\theta_k) \end{aligned} \tag{11.40}$$

but

$$\begin{aligned} p(x_{AD}/\theta_k) &= p(x_{k1}, x_{k2}, x_{k3}, x_{k4}/\theta_k) \\ &= p(x_{k1}/x_{k2}, x_{k3}, x_{k4}, \theta_k)p(x_{k2}/x_{k3}, x_{k4}, \theta_k) \\ &\qquad \cdot p(x_{k3}/x_{k4}, \theta_k)p(x_{k4}/\theta_k) \\ &= \prod_{i=1}^{4} p(x_{ki}/\theta_k) \end{aligned} \tag{11.41}$$

Next expanding each $p(x_i/\theta_k)$ in terms of θ_i and using equation (11.36), we have

$$\begin{aligned} p(x_i/\theta_k) &= \sum_{\theta_i} p(x_i, \theta_i/\theta_k) \\ &= \sum_{\theta_i} p(x_i/\theta_i, \theta_k)p(\theta_i/\theta_k) \\ &= \sum_{\theta_i} p(x_i/\theta_i)p(\theta_i/\theta_k) \end{aligned} \tag{11.42}$$

Now combining equations (11.40), (11.41), and (11.42) gives

$$p(x_{AD}, x_k/\theta_k) = p(x_k/\theta_k) \prod_{i=1}^{4} \sum_{\theta_{ki}} p(x_{ki}/\theta_{ki})p(\theta_{ik}/\theta_k)$$

so that the decision rule now is to choose the action a to minimize

$$\sum_{\theta_i=1}^{m} L(\theta_k, a)p(x_k/\theta_k)G(\theta_k) \prod_{i=1}^{4} \sum_{\theta_{ki}} p(x_{ki}/\theta_{ki})p(\theta_{ki}/\theta_k)$$

This is the context algorithm in its final form. Notice that the part of the expression outside of the product sign is identical to the simple decision rule without considering other cells at all. The product term represents the contextual information for cell k. The four multipliers in the product term represent the contextual contributions from the four adjacent neighbor cells.

6. Remarks

In the recognition of handprinted FORTRAN programs, Duda and Hart[10] examine a context-direct analyzer. The input to the analyzer is a list of possible alternative classifications for each character. Each alternative is associated with a confidence measure (a number) also input to the analyzer. The analyzer then makes appropriate choices from among the alternatives. Substantial reduction in error rate was reported. By using the curve-following feature to extract information from handprinting, Donaldson and Toussaint[16] also showed experimentally the significant improvement in recognition accuracy by using the contextual information. Use of contextual analysis in speech recognition was considered by Alter.[17]

PROBLEMS

1. Consider the normal distributions which are independent

$$p_i(x_k) = \frac{1}{\sqrt{2\pi}} e^{-(x_k - m_i)^2/2} \qquad i = 1, 2$$

Determine the probability of error of the Bayes rule and compare the result with the upper bound of error probability given in equation 13 of reference 12.

2. Consider the same normal distributions in problem 1 but assume that they are first-order Markov dependent. Determine the upper bound of the error probability and compare the result with equations (11.27) and (11.28). The decision rule is given by equation (11.22).

REFERENCES

1. Gold, B. "Machine Recognition of Hand-Sent Morse Code." *IRE Trans. on Information Theory*, IT-5 (March 1959), 17–24.
2. Bledsoe, W. W. and J. Browning. "Pattern Recognition and Reading by Machine." In *Proc. EJCC*, pp. 225–232. December 1959. Also in *Pattern Recognition*, edited by L. Uhr, pp. 301–316. Wiley, New York, 1966.
3. Harmon, L. D. "Automatic Reading of Cursive Script." In *Optical Character Recognition*, edited by George L. Fischer, Jr. et al, pp. 151–152. Spartan Books, New York, 1962.
4. Edwards, A. W. and R. L. Chambers. "Can a priori Probabilities Help in Character Recognition." *Journal of ACM*, 11 (1964), 465–470.
5. Carlson, G. "Techniques for Replacing Characters that are Garbled on Input." In *AFIPS Conference Proc.*, vol. 28, pp. 189–192. Spring Joint Computer Conference, 1966.
6. McElwain, C. K. and M. B. Evens. "The Degarbler: A Program for Correcting Machine-read Morse Code." *Information and Control*, 5 (1962), 368–384.
7. Vossler, C. M. and N. M. Branston. "The Use of Context for Correcting Garbled English Text." In *Proc. ACM Nineteenth National Conference.* Paper D2 4-1, D2 4-13, 1964.
8. Abend, K. "Compound Decision Procedures for Unknown Distribution and for Dependent States of Nature." In *Pattern Recognition*, edited by L. Kanal. Thompson, Washington, D.C., 1968.

9. Raviv, J. "Decision Making in Markov Chains Applied to the Problem of Pattern Recognition." *IEEE Trans. on Information Theory*, IT-13 (October 1967), 536–551.
10. Duda, R. O. and P. E. Hart. "Experiments in the Recognition of Hand-printed Text. Part II: Context Analysis." In *1968 Fall Joint Computer Conference, AFIPS Conference Proc.*, vol. 33, pt. 2, pp. 1139–1149. Thompson, Washington, D. C., 1968.
11. Fu, K. S. "Stochastic Automata, Stochastic Languages, and Pattern Recognition." *IEEE Ninth Symposium on Adaptive Processes*, Austin, Tex., December 1970.
12. Chu, J. T. "Error Bounds for a Contextual Recognition Procedure." *IEEE Trans. on Computers*, C-20 (October 1971), 1203–1207.
13. Chu, J. T. "Sequential Contextual Recognition of Markovian Patterns." Submitted for publication.
14. Welch, J. R. and K. G. Salter. "A Context Algorithm for Pattern Recognition and Image Interpretation." *IEEE Trans. on Systems, Man, and Cybernetics*, SMC-1 (January 1971), 24–30.
15. Chow, C. K. "A Recognition Method Using Neighbor Dependence." *IRE Trans. on Electronic Computers*, EC-11 (October 1962), 683–690.
16. Donaldson, R. W. and G. T. Toussaint. "Use of Contextual Constraints in Recognition of Contour-Traced Handprinted Characters." *IEEE Trans. on Computers*, vol. C-19, No. 11 (November 1970), 1096–1099.
17. Alter, R. "Use of Contextual Constraints in Automatic Speech Recognition." *IEEE Trans. on Audio*, AU-16 (March 1968), 6–11.

Bibliography

1. Christensen, C. S. "An Investigation of the Use of Context in Character Recognition Using Graph Searching." Ph.D. dissertation, Cornell University, Ithaca, N. Y., Technical Report AFOSR 68-2470, November 1968.
2. Raviv, J. "Decision Making in Incompletely Known Stochastic Systems." *International Journal of Engineering Science*, vol. 3 (July 1965), 119–140.
3. Riseman, E. M. and R. W. Erich. "Contextual Word Recognition Using Binary Diagrams." *IEEE Transactions on Computers*, vol. C-20, No. 4 (April 1971), 397–403.
4. Tappert, C. C. "A Preliminary Investigation of Adaptive Control in the Interaction Between Segmentation and Segment Classification in Automatic Recognition of Continuous Speech." *IEEE Transactions on Systems, Man, and Cybernetics*, vol. SMC-2 (January 1972), 66–72.

CHAPTER XII

Pattern Recognition and Communication Theory

1. Introduction

Many techniques developed for statistical pattern recognition have found applications in communication theory and systems. The supervised Bayesian learning system described in chapter 5, for example, provides essentially an adaptive correlation receiver with signals corresponding to m pattern classes. The conventional maximum likelihood decision method for detecting Gaussian signals from Gaussian noise is a one-shot operation. The adaptive or learning receiver mentioned above, however, is a sequential operation. If the signal statistics are known exactly but the channel characteristics are unknown, then the channel may be considered as a random variable which is estimated sequentially from the receiver inputs. The Bayesian approach of the unsupervised learning, also described in chapter 5, can similarly be applied to problems of adaptive signal detection (with amplitude and/or phase of the signal being unknown) and channel estimation, when it is unknown whether the received data contain information of certain signals. The immediate extensions of the above work are the nonparametric methods to the problems encountered in adaptive communication systems. Feature selection discussed in chapter 4 is also closely related to the selection of the best signal sets in communication theory (e.g., see Grettenberg[1] and Kailath[2]).

2. Adaptive Correlator Likelihood Computer

We first consider the likelihood function $L(X)$ when the mean vector (signal) M and the covariance matrix K of the noise are known. Then the likelihood calculation consists of linear and quadratic data processing on the measurement X. Assume the covariance matrix K is nonsingular. Then K^{-1} is positive definite and can be written as $K^{-1} = (K^{-1/2})^T K^{-1/2}$, where "$T$" denotes transpose. The likelihood function is

$$L(X) = X^T K^{-1} M - \tfrac{1}{2} X^T K^{-1} X$$
$$= (K^{-1/2} X)^T (K^{-1/2} M) - \tfrac{1}{2} (K^{-1/2} X)^T (K^{-1/2} X) \tag{12.1}$$

The matrix operation $K^{-1/2}$ on the measurement X or on the known mean vector M can be interpreted as a linear bleaching filter which serves to whiten the variations about the mean. The linear term of equation (12.1) can be interpreted as a correlation of the whitened input measurement with the whitened mean vector; the quadratic term of equation (12.1) can be interpreted as an energy measurement on the whitened input. Equation (12.1) can be implemented as a likelihood computer, as shown in figure 12.1a, with matched filter, correlation, and energy detection systems.

The Bayesian learning system expressed by equations (5.6) and (5.7) can be also implemented as a likelihood computer by replacing in equation (12.1) M by μ and K by $K + \Phi$. The result is an adaptive correlator shown in figure 12.1b. If the covariance matrix K is unknown, then learning the inverse covariance matrix K^{-1} can be interpreted as an inverse filter realization of the adaptive system, expressed by equation (P.1) in the problems following chapter 5.

Now we consider a special case that the received waveform X may or may not contain the unknown pattern, and which always contains noise. The unknown pattern Z is assumed to occur at random, with a probability p of occurring at any time. We define a binary variable θ_n such that $\theta_n = 1$ indicates the presence of the pattern at time n, and $\theta_n = 0$ indicates its absence. We assume the noise vector N_n is additive, so that the input at time n may be expressed as $X_n = \theta_n Z + N_n$. Then the optimum decision rule is to decide

$$\hat{\theta}_n = 1 \quad \text{if} \quad P(\theta_n = 1 \mid X^n, \theta^{n-1}) > \tfrac{1}{2}$$
$$\text{or} \quad \hat{\theta}_n = 0 \quad \text{if} \quad P(\theta_n = 1 \mid X^n, \theta^{n-1}) \leqslant \tfrac{1}{2} \tag{12.2}$$

where $P(\theta_n = 1 \mid X^n, \theta^{n-1})$ is the a posteriori probability that the input contains a pattern. Computation of $P(\theta_n = 1 \mid X^n, \theta^{n-1})$ has been considered by Scudder.[3,4] We can show that the decision rule is the same as computing the quadratic form Q_n and compare it with a threshold δ_n. Here $Q_n = X_n{}^T K^{-1} X_n - (X_n - \mu_n)^T (K + \Phi_n)^{-1} (X_n - \mu_n)$ where

$$\mu_n = \mu_{n-1} + \Phi_n K^{-1} (X_n - \mu_{n-1}) \, \theta_n \tag{12.3}$$
$$\Phi_n = [\Phi_{n-1}^{-1} + \theta_n K^{-1}]^{-1}$$

and

$$\delta_n = \log \frac{(1-p)^2}{p^2} + \log \frac{|K + \Phi_n|}{|K|}$$

Decide $\hat{\theta}_n = 1$ if $Q_n > \delta_n$ and $\hat{\theta}_n = 0$ otherwise.

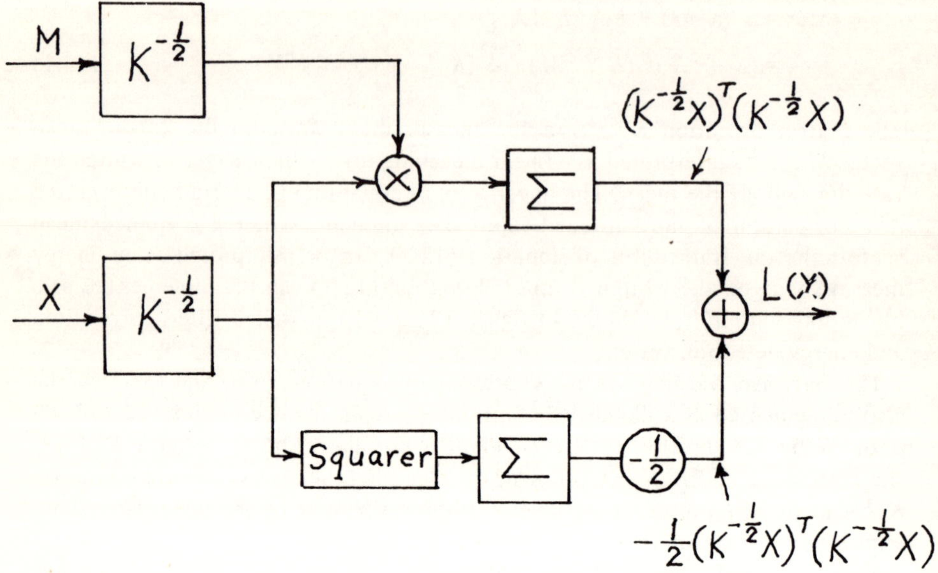

Fig. 12.1(a) Likelihood Computer for the Known Mean Vector and Covariance Matrix

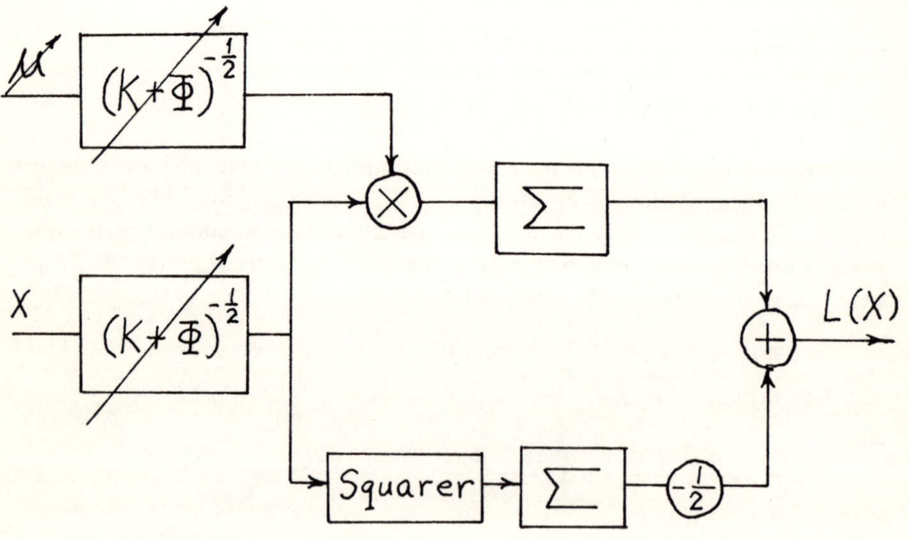

Fig. 12.1(b) Adaptive Correlator Likelihood Computer

Assume that both the additive noise and the mean vector have been "prewhitened" so that the covariance of the noise is $K = \sigma_N^2 I$ and the covariance of the pattern Φ_0 is a diagonal matrix. Then we can write more explicitly

$$\mu_n = \left(I + \frac{1}{N}\sigma_N^2 \Phi_0^{-1}\right)^{-1} \frac{1}{N}\sum_{i=1}^{n} \theta_i X_i + \left(I + \frac{N\Phi_0}{\sigma_N^2}\right)^{-1} \mu_0$$

$$\Phi_n = \frac{1}{N}\sigma_N^2 \left(I + \frac{\sigma_N^2 \Phi_0^{-1}}{N}\right)^{-1} \tag{12.4}$$

Here μ_0 and Φ_0 are the initial mean vector and covariance matrix for the pattern Z and N is the number of times the pattern has appeared in the learning sequence. The parameters are updated only if the pattern is present.

3. Decision-Directed Receivers

The conventional decision-directed approach is to take some reference, obtain a correlation with a successive measurement and, upon decision, update the reference (or references) by a linear average of the most recently classified measurement with the previous reference for that class. Once the reference is established the correlation receiver has the same structure as shown in figure 12.1a or figure 12.1b. We again consider the special case described by the preceding section, assuming now that the external supervision is not available. We will denote quantities used in the decision-directed receiver with a "^". Then we have

$$Q_n = X_n{}^T K^{-1} X_n - (X_n - \hat{\mu}_n)^T (K + \hat{\Phi}_n)^{-1} (X_n - \hat{\mu}_n) \tag{12.5}$$

where

$$\hat{\mu}_n = \hat{\mu}_{n-1} + \hat{\theta}_n K^{-1} \hat{\Phi}_n (X_n - \hat{\mu}_{n-1})$$

$$\hat{\Phi}_n = [\Phi_{n-1}^{-1} + \hat{\theta}_n K^{-1}]^{-1}$$

and

$$\hat{\delta}_n = \log \frac{(1-p)^2}{p^2} + \log \frac{|K + \hat{\Phi}_n|}{|K|}$$

The decision rule is to decide $\hat{\theta}_n = 1$ if $\hat{Q}_n > \hat{\delta}_n$ and $\hat{\theta}_n = 0$ otherwise. As the receiver will make errors, the decision-directed receiver will not behave as well as the adaptive correlator described in the preceding section, in general. The receiver may make two types of errors, either calling $\hat{\theta}_i = 0$ where $\theta_i = 1$ or calling $\hat{\theta}_i = 1$ where $\theta_i = 0$. The first type is a "miss" and slows down the rate at which the receiver will converge, but does not affect the estimator $\hat{\mu}_n$. The second type is a "false alarm" and is more serious, since it averages a measurement into $\hat{\mu}_n$ when the pattern is not present.

If $\hat{N} = \sum_{i=1}^{n-1} \hat{\theta}_n$ approaches ∞ as $n \to \infty$, then for large n, $\hat{\mu}_n \cong \frac{1}{\hat{N}} \sum_{i=1}^{n-1} \hat{\theta}_i X_i$ and since the covariances of the components of X_i are bounded, as $\hat{N} \to \infty$ the covariances of $\hat{\mu}_n \to 0$. This implies that $\hat{\mu}_n \to E[\hat{\mu}_n]$ which approaches a finite vector which we will call μ. In general, $\mu \neq Z$ so $\hat{\mu}_n$ is a biased estimator of Z and the decision-directed receiver will not approach a matched filter. The foregoing argument, however, has shown heuristically that the decision-directed receiver will converge. Experimental results have shown that the convergence is at least consistent (i.e., if it were started with a large $\hat{N}$ and a fairly accurate $\hat{\mu}_n$ then it would stay that way). This condition was termed "good initial knowledge" in chapter 5.

If both the signal waveform and the noise statistics are unknown, then we have a complete mixture of measurements belonging to both classes. Assuming a linear operation (correlation only) on the data, an optimum method of extracting the parameters which describe the noise and the discrete signal waveform is to minimize the measurement time (or the number of measurements) while jointly minimizing the variance of the decision-directed estimator and maximizing a measure of the estimator convergence rate. This method provides a more efficient weighting of past data in establishing the reference as compared with the uniform weighting in the conventional decision-directed scheme described above. The feasibility of the method, however, is questionable in view of the complexities that we must go through to obtain the optimum weighting, even for the linear operation on the measurement data.

4. Learning Receivers for the Random Channel

In the preceding two sections, we have assumed that the signals are random when the channel is known. A learning feature was introduced to estimate the signal waveform. On the other hand, if the signals are known while the channel is random, the optimum receiver for one short operation can be considered as an estimator-correlator.[5,6] Consider the discrete channel model as shown in figure 12.2a. $S^{(k)}(t)$ is the kth transmitted signal. Matrix A is the channel. $Z^{(k)} = AS^{(k)}(t)$. $X(t) = Z^{(k)}(t) + n(t)$. The optimum receiver for known A is shown in figure 12.2b. If Z and thus A for a given $S^{(k)}$ is Gaussian, and the additive noise n is also Gaussian, the received signal, in matrix form,

$$X = AS^{(k)} + n = Z^{(k)} + n \tag{12.6}$$

is Gaussian of the dimension $2WT$ where W and T are the bandwidth and duration respectively of the signal. We shall assume that channel A is such that $Z^{(k)}$ is

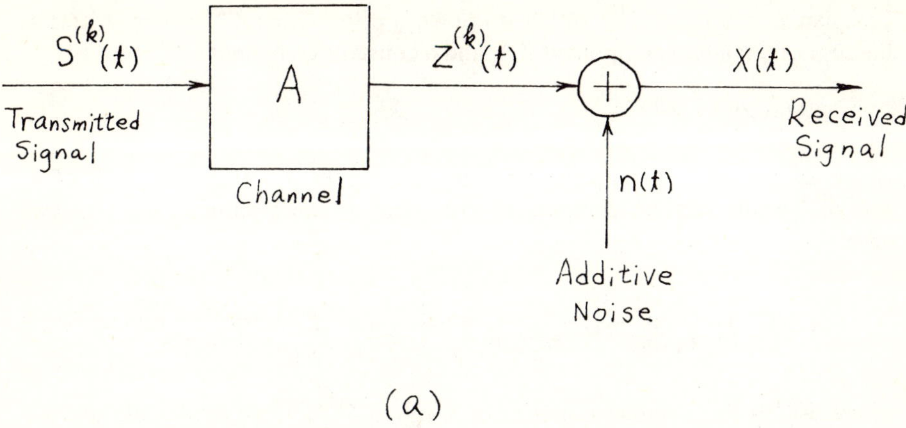

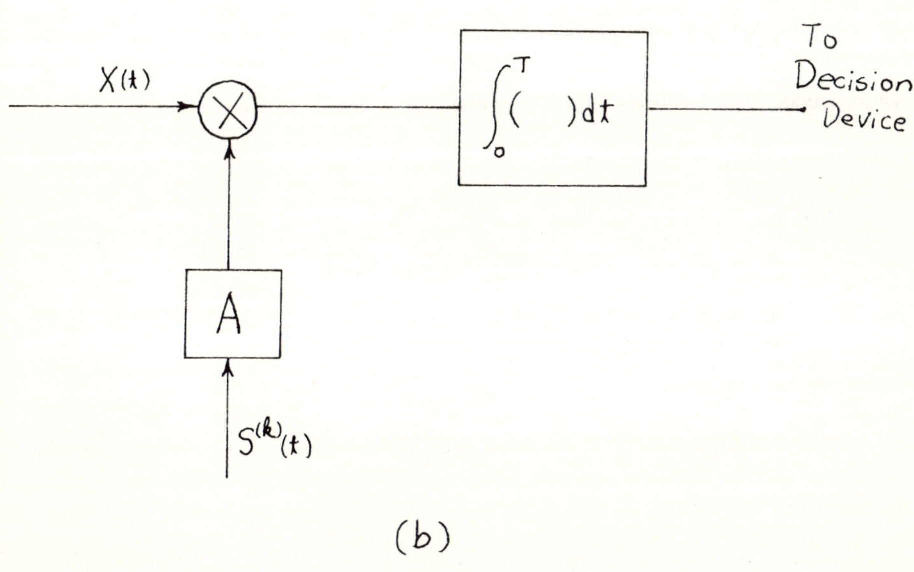

Fig. 12.2 Channel Model (a), and Optimum Receiver for Known Channel Matrix A (b)

Gaussian with a mean $\overline{Z}^{(k)}$ which is known a priori. Then $Z^{(k)}$ can be written as the sum of a random component $Z_r^{(k)}$ and a constant component $\overline{Z}^{(k)}$:

$$Z^{(k)} = Z_r^{(k)} + \overline{Z}^{(k)}$$

where $\overline{Z}^{(k)} = \overline{A}S^{(k)}$ is the specular component with $\overline{A}$ being the mean of A, and $Z_r^{(k)}$ is the random component with mean 0 and covariance Φ_Z. Thus we have

$$p(X/S^{(k)}) = \frac{1}{(\sqrt{2\pi})^{2TW}} \frac{1}{|\Phi_X^{(k)}|^{1/2}} \exp\left[-\frac{1}{2}(X - \overline{Z}^{(k)})\,[\Phi_X^{(k)}]^{-1}\,(X - \overline{Z}^{(k)})\right]$$

where $\Phi_X^{(k)}$ is the covariance matrix of X (given $S^{(k)}$). If we assume the additive noise to be statistically independent of the channel, then

$$\Phi_X^{(k)} = \Phi_Z^{(k)} + \Phi_n \tag{12.7}$$

Essentially, the optimum receiver is required to compute the quadratic form,

$$\Lambda'^{(k)} = X^T[\Phi_X^{(k)}]^{-1}X$$

where we set $\overline{Z}^{(k)} = 0$ for simplicity in analysis.

Since

$$\begin{aligned}[\Phi_X^{(k)}]^{-1} &= [\Phi_n]^{-1} - ([\Phi_n]^{-1} - [\Phi_Z^{(k)} + \Phi_n]^{-1})\\ &= [\Phi_n]^{-1} - [\Phi_n]^{-1}\,[\Phi_Z^{(k)}]\,[\Phi_n + \Phi_Z^{(k)}]^{-1}\\ &= [\Phi_n]^{-1} - [\Phi_n]^{-1}H^{(k)}\end{aligned}$$

where we have defined

$$H^{(k)} = \Phi_Z^{(k)}[\Phi_n + \Phi_Z^{(k)}]^{-1} = I - \Phi_n[\Phi_X^{(k)}]^{-1} \tag{12.8}$$

we can write

$$\Lambda'^{(k)} = X^T[\Phi_n]^{-1}X - X^T[\Phi_n]^{-1}H^{(k)}X \tag{12.9}$$

Since the first term on the right-hand side of equation (12.9) is independent of $S^{(k)}$, we need only to consider the second term

$$\Lambda^{(k)} = X^T[\Phi_n]^{-1}H^{(k)}X \tag{12.10}$$

If the additive noise is white Gaussian, with a noise power of one watt per hertz, $\Phi_n = I$, the identity matrix, then

$$\Lambda^{(k)} = X^T H^{(k)} X = X^T (H^{(k)} X)$$

To compute this we can use the receiver structure that is shown in figure 12.3a; that is, we pass X through the filter H, then multiply the output of H by X and

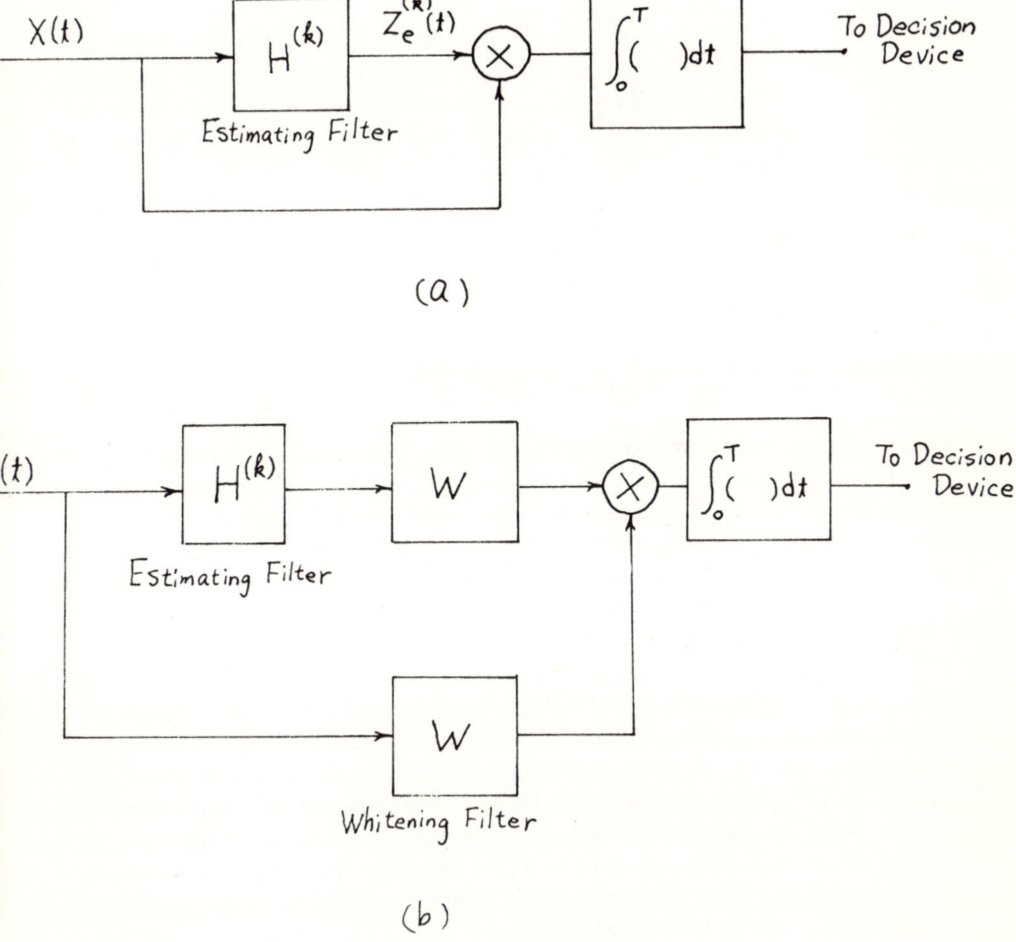

Fig. 12.3 Estimator–Correlator Receiver Structure for White Gaussian Noise (a), and Colored Gaussian Noise (b)

integrate for a time T. The output of the integrator at time T is directly related to $p(X/S^{(k)})$; the multiplier and integrator combination is just a crosscorrelator. $H^{(k)}$ may be considered as a filter that operates on X to give an estimate, $Z_e^{(k)}$, say, of Z. This estimate is a minimum average mean square error (or Wiener) estimate (it is also a Bayesian estimate), which is equivalent to a maximum likelihood estimate for our situation, where we have Gaussian statistics. The filters H are, in general, unrealizable. When we have white Gaussian noise, however, the $H^{(k)}$ are symmetric, and therefore we can write

$$\Lambda^{(k)} = X^T H'^{(k)} X$$

where $H'^{(k)}$ is a realizable filter. $H'^{(k)}$ is obtained from $H^{(k)}$ by omitting all terms above the main diagonal and doubling all terms below the main diagonal (see reference 5 for a delay-line channel interpretation). If the noise is not white, then we can express Φ_n^{-1} as the product of a triangular matrix W, and its transpose,

$$\Phi_n^{-1} = W^T W \tag{12.11}$$

where W is a matrix with all zeros above the main diagonal. Using equation (12.11) we can write

$$\Lambda^{(k)} = X^T W^T W H^{(k)} X = (XW)^T (WH^{(k)} X)$$

Here W may be considered as a whitening filter. The optimum receiver is again the crosscorrelation of Z and $Z_e^{(k)}$ (see figure 12.3b). The one-shot operation of the optimum receiver for a random channel can be easily extended to the sequential operation if the classification of the received data is known (the supervised learning case). All $Z^{(k)}$'s may be viewed as random signals considered in section 2 and the sequential operation is also a recursive estimation of the $Z^{(k)}$. The knowledge of classification of signals will remove the ambiguity about the $Z^{(k)}$'s. As the number of learning measurements approaches infinity, $\Phi_Z^{(k)} \to 0$ for all k. The estimating filter H defined by equation (12.8) will be updated if the learning measurement consists of the kth signal. Furthermore, the specular components will also be updated according to equation (12.3) of section 2. Although all $Z^{(k)}$'s are different, each learning measurement has been perturbed by the same random channel which is assumed to be time-invariant. In the supervised case, each time an estimate $Z_e^{(k)}$ is obtained, an estimate of A can also be computed. We have not been able, however, to obtain an estimate of channel A itself directly in the unsupervised case.

When the correct classification regarding signals is not available, we may treat the problem in the same way as the unsupervised learning of chapter 5 by considering $Z^{(k)}$ as the random signal (variable) of the kth pattern class. We may also implement a decision-directed receiver to simulate a supervised learning receiver.

For the binary antipodal signals, $Z^{(1)}(j) = -Z^{(2)}(j)$ for all j, and $\Phi_Z^{(1)}(0) = \Phi_Z^{(2)}(0)$. If we proceed with the supervised case by computing $H^{(k)}$ according to equation (12.8) with the updated $\Phi_Z^{(k)}$, then the covariance matrix, denoted as $\hat{\Phi}_Z^{(k)}$, becomes

$$\hat{\Phi}_Z^{(1)}(1) = \tfrac{1}{2}E[(Z - \overline{Z}(1))^T (Z - \overline{Z}(1))] + \tfrac{1}{2}E[(Z + \overline{Z}(1))^T (Z + \overline{Z}(1))]$$
$$= \Phi_Z^{(1)}(1) + 4\overline{Z}(1)^T \overline{Z}(1)$$

where $\Phi_Z^{(1)}(1) = E[(Z - \overline{Z}(1))^T (Z - \overline{Z}(1))]$ and $\Phi_Z^{(1)}(1)$ is related to $\Phi_Z^{(1)}(0)$ according to equation (12.3). Hence, due to the lack of precise information on which signal is transmitted, there is a bias $4\overline{Z}(1)^T\overline{Z}(1)$ in the covariance of the estimator if we retain the supervised receiver. Similarly, $\hat{\Phi}_Z^{(2)}(1) = \Phi_Z^{(2)}(1) + 4\overline{Z}^T\overline{Z}$. We can remove such bias and consider the resulting Φ_Z as the correct covariance matrix for each signal. The result is an unsupervised learning receiver very close to the supervised learning receiver. The specular components $\overline{Z}^{(1)}$, $\overline{Z}^{(2)}$ can be updated as follows: Compute the average of the two estimates, $\hat{\overline{Z}}^{(1)}$ and $\hat{\overline{Z}}^{(2)}$, $\frac{1}{2}(\hat{\overline{Z}}^{(1)} + \hat{\overline{Z}}^{(2)})$, update $\overline{Z}^{(1)}$ if such average is greater than zero and update $\overline{Z}^{(2)}$ otherwise. The true value of the average is zero. The procedure here again relies on the decision-directed method to decompose the mixture.

5. Optimum Unsupervised Learning Receivers: Known Parameter Statistics

We have examined the learning receivers for the antipodal signaling system. The decision-directed receiver is not optimum though it is simple to implement. In this section, an optimum solution[7] is presented assuming that the a priori parameter statistics are known. Furthermore, we assume intersymbol interference exists for an adjacent symbol duration T. This is shown in figure 12.4 where we define the symbol $S(t)$ = *the part of the received pulse between 0 and*

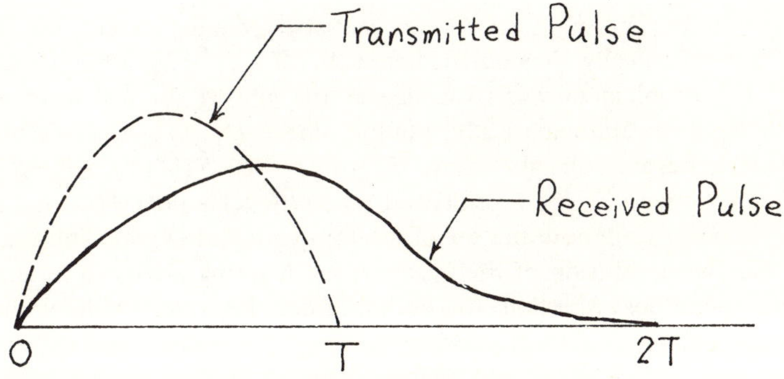

Fig. 12.4 Transmitted and Received Binary Symbols (Pulses)

T, R(t) = the part of the received pulse between T and 2T. The encoder sends to the transmitter a sequence of binary digits, $B_1, B_2, \ldots, B_n$, which are independent. Each B_k is equally likely to be "+1" or "−1." Assume time synchronization between transmitter and receiver, thus $X(t)$ can be sampled and processed in special purpose digital computers. The received input $X(t)$ is a bandlimited process of one-side bandwidth WHz. Hence it is completely specified by $L = 2WT$ samples taken $\frac{1}{2W}$ seconds apart. Let a vector X_k denote these $2WT$ samples, then $X_k^T = [X_{k1}, X_{k2}, \ldots, X_{kL}]$, where X_{ki} is the ith sample in the kth baud.†

The receiver input is $X(t) = Y(t) + n(t)$, where $Y(t)$ is the signal portion of the received input and $n(t)$ is the additive noise. Expressing all time functions as vector quantities, we have

$$X_k = Y_k + N_k, \quad k = 1, 2, \ldots, n \tag{12.12}$$

where N_k is normally distributed with mean zero and covariance matrix $\sigma_n^2 I$. Each vector is of dimension L. The components of the vectors $S^T = [S_1, S_2, \ldots, S_L]$, $R^T = [R_1, R_2, \ldots, R_L]$ always satisfy the following condition in practice:

$$\sum_{i=1}^{L} S_i > \sum_{i=1}^{L} R_i > 0 \tag{12.13}$$

The sequence of vectors, $Y_1, Y_2, \ldots, Y_n$ form a Markov chain with four possible states for each vector Y_k:

$$\begin{aligned}
Y_k &= R + S \quad &&\text{when} \quad B_{k-1} = 1, \quad &&B_k = 1\\
Y_k &= -R + S \quad &&\text{when} \quad B_{k-1} = -1, \quad &&B_k = 1\\
Y_k &= R - S \quad &&\text{when} \quad B_{k-1} = 1, \quad &&B_k = -1\\
Y_k &= -R - S \quad &&\text{when} \quad B_{k-1} = -1, \quad &&B_k = -1
\end{aligned}$$

The noise vectors $N_1, N_2, \ldots, N_n$ are statistically independent, but $Y_1, Y_2, \ldots, Y_n$ are statistically dependent; hence $X_1, X_2, \ldots, X_n$ are statistically dependent. The problem now is to decide at the end of the kth baud whether $B_k = 1$ or $B_k = -1$. Mathematically, the hypothesis H_1: $(Y_k = -R + S) \cup (Y_k = R + S)$ is tested against the alternative H_2: $(Y_k = -R - S) \cup (Y_k = R - S)$, where S and R are defined by the a priori statistics $p(S, R) = p(\theta)$. Here the random variable θ is used to denote the set of random variables (S, R). This is a special case of the Bayes solution of the unsupervised learning discussed in chapter 5. For the zero-one loss function, the optimum decision rule computes the likeli-

† Here a baud is one binary signal duration.

hood ratio

$$L_k(X) = \frac{\int_\Omega p(V_n, B_k = 1, \theta)\, d\theta}{\int_\Omega p(V_n, B_k = -1, \theta)\, d\theta} = \frac{\int_\Omega P(B_k = 1 \mid \theta, V_n)\, p(\theta \mid V_n)\, d\theta}{\int_\Omega P(B_k = -1 \mid \theta, V_n)\, p(\theta \mid V_n)\, d\theta}$$

and accept $H_1: B_k = 1$ if $L_k(X) \geqslant 1$ and accept $H_2: B_k = -1$ otherwise. Here Ω denotes the parameter space and $V_n = (X_1, X_2, \ldots, X_n)$ denotes the sequence of n vectors of X_i's. $P(B_k = -1/\theta, V_n) = 1 - P(B_k = 1/\theta, V_n)$. The main problem now is to compute $p(\theta/V_n)$ or $p(\theta/V_k)$. Using the Bayes rule

$$\begin{aligned} p(\theta/V_k) &= \frac{p(V_k, \theta)}{p(V_k)} = \frac{p(X_k, V_{k-1}, \theta)}{p(X_k, V_{k-1})} \\ &= \frac{p(X_k \mid \theta, V_{k-1})\, p(\theta \mid V_{k-1})}{p(X_k \mid V_{k-1})} \\ &= \frac{p(X_k \mid \theta, V_{k-1})\, p(\theta \mid V_{k-1})}{\int_\Omega p(X_k \mid \theta, V_{k-1})\, p(\theta \mid V_{k-1})\, d\theta} \end{aligned} \qquad (12.14)$$

Hence $p(\theta/V_k)$ can be computed iteratively from $p(\theta/V_{k-1})$ and $p(X_k/\theta, V_{k-1})$. Now

$$\begin{aligned} p(X_k/\theta, V_{k-1}) = {} & p(X_k \mid \theta, V_{k-1}, B_k = 1)\, P(B_k = 1 \mid \theta, V_{k-1}) \\ & + p(X_k \mid \theta, V_{k-1}, B_k = -1)\;\; P(B_k = -1 \mid \theta, V_{k-1}) \end{aligned} \qquad (12.15)$$

The event $B_k = 1$ is independent of the previous measurements V_{k-1} and the particular value of θ. Hence

$$P(B_k = 1/\theta, V_{k-1}) = P(B_k = 1) \qquad (12.16)$$

Similarly, $P(B_k = -1/\theta, V_{k-1}) = P(B_k = -1)$

Substituting equation (12.16) in (12.15), we have

$$\begin{aligned} p(X_k/\theta, V_{k-1}) = {} & p(X_k/\theta, V_{k-1}, B_k = 1)\, P(B_k = 1) \\ & + p(X_k/\theta, V_{k-1}, B_k = -1)\, P(B_k = -1) \end{aligned} \qquad (12.17)$$

where

$$p(X_k/\theta, V_{k-1}, B_{k-1} = 1, B_k = 1) = p(X_k \mid \theta, V_{k-1}, B_{k-1} = 1)\, P(B_{k-1} = 1 \mid \theta,$$

$$V_{k-1}, B_k = 1) + p(X_k | \theta, V_{k-1}, B_k = 1,$$
$$B_{k-1} = -1) \, P(B_{k-1} = -1 \,|\, \theta, V_{k-1}, B_k = 1) \quad (12.18)$$

Given $\theta, B_k = 1$ and $B_{k-1} = 1$, X_k is independent of V_{k-1}; therefore

$$p(X_k/\theta, V_{k-1}, B_k = 1, B_{k-1} = 1) = p(X_k/\theta, B_k = 1, B_{k-1} = 1) \quad (12.19)$$

Similarly,

$$p(X_k/\theta, V_{k-1}, B_k = 1, B_{k-1} = -1) = p(X_k/\theta, B_k = 1, B_{k-1} = -1).$$

When X_k is not given, the event B_{k-1} and the event $B_k = 1$ are independent, hence

$$P(B_{k-1} = 1/\theta, V_{k-1}, B_k = 1) = P(B_{k-1} = 1/\theta, V_{k-1})$$

Similarly,

$$P(B_{k-1} = -1/\theta, V_{k-1}, B_k = 1) = P(B_{k-1} = -1/\theta, V_{k-1}) \quad (12.20)$$

Substituting equations (12.19) and (12.20) in (12.17), we have

$$p(X_k/\theta, V_{k-1}, B_k = 1) = p(X_k | \theta, B_k = 1, B_{k-1} = 1) \, P(B_{k-1} = 1 \,|\, \theta, V_{k-1})$$
$$+ p(X_k | \theta, B_k = 1, B_{k-1} = -1) \, P(B_{k-1} = -1 \,|\, \theta, V_{k-1}) \quad (12.21)$$

Similarly,

$$p(X_k/\theta, V_{k-1}, B_k = -1) = p(X_k | \theta, B_k = -1, B_{k-1} = 1)$$
$$\cdot P(B_{k-1} = 1 \,|\, \theta, V_{k-1}) + p(X_k | \theta, B_k = -1,$$
$$B_{k-1} = -1) \, P(B_{k-1} = -1 \,|\, \theta, V_{k-1}) \quad (12.22)$$

Now substitute equations (12.21) and (12.22) in (12.16),

$$p(X_k/\theta, V_{k-1}) = P(B_k = 1) \, p(X_k | \theta, B_k = 1, B_{k-1} = 1) \, P(B_{k-1} = 1 | \theta, V_{k-1})$$
$$+ P(B_k = 1) \, p(X_k | \theta, B_k = 1, B_{k-1} = -1)$$
$$\cdot P(B_{k-1} = -1 | \theta, V_{k-1}) + P(B_k = -1) \, p(X_k | \theta,$$
$$B_k = -1, B_{k-1} = 1) \, P(B_{k-1} = 1 | \theta, V_{k-1})$$
$$+ P(B_k = -1) \, p(X_k | \theta, B_k = -1, B_{k-1} = -1)$$
$$\cdot P(B_{k-1} = -1 | \theta, V_{k-1}) \quad (12.23)$$

where $P(B_k = 1) = P(B_k = -1) = \frac{1}{2}$, and

$$p(X_k | \theta, B_k = 1, B_{k-1} = 1) = \eta[S + R, \sigma_n^2 I] = \frac{1}{(2\pi\sigma_n^2)^{L/2}} \cdot \exp\left\{-\frac{1}{2\sigma_n^2}[X_k - (S+R)]^T [X_k - (S+R)]\right\}$$

$$p(X_k | \theta, B_k = -1, B_{k-1} = -1) = \eta[S - R, \sigma_n^2 I]$$

$$p(X_k | \theta, B_k = -1, B_{k-1} = 1) = \eta[-S + R, \sigma_n^2 I]$$

$$p(X_k | \theta, B_k = -1, B_{k-1} = -1) = \eta[-S - R, \sigma_n^2 I] \qquad (12.23a)$$

where $\eta(M, K)$ denotes a Gaussian density with mean vector M and covariance matrix K. Hence $p(X_k/\theta, V_{k-1})$ can be computed iteratively if the two terms

$$P(B_{k-1} = 1/\theta, V_{k-1}) \quad \text{and} \quad P(B_{k-1} = -1/\theta, V_{k-1})$$

can be computed in an iterative manner for $k = 2, 3, \ldots, n$. Since $P(B_{k-1} = -1/\theta, V_{k-1}) = 1 - P(B_{k-1} = 1/\theta, V_{k-1})$, only $P(B_{k-1} = 1/\theta, V_{k-1})$ has to be computed iteratively.

$$\begin{aligned} P(B_{k-1} = 1/\theta, V_{k-1}) &= \frac{P(B_{k-1} = 1, V_{k-1} | \theta)}{p(V_{k-1} | \theta)} \\ &= \frac{p(V_{k-1} | \theta, B_{k-1} = 1) P(B_{k-1} = 1)}{p(V_{k-1} | \theta)} \\ &= \frac{P(B_{k-1} = 1)}{p(V_{k-1} | \theta)} p(X_{k-1}, V_{k-2} | \theta, B_{k-1} = 1) \qquad (12.24) \\ &= \frac{P(B_{k-1} = 1)}{p(V_{k-1} | \theta)} p(X_{k-1} | \theta, B_{k-1} = 1, V_{k-2}) \\ &\quad \cdot p(V_{k-2} | \theta, B_{k-1} = 1) \\ &= \frac{P(B_{k-1} = 1)}{p(X_{k-1} | \theta, V_{k-2}) p(V_{k-2} | \theta)} \\ &\quad \cdot p(X_{k-1} | \theta, V_{k-2}, B_{k-1} = 1) p(V_{k-2} | \theta) \\ &= P(B_{k-1} = 1) \frac{p(X_{k-1} | \theta, V_{k-2}, B_{k-1} = 1)}{p(X_{k-1} | \theta, V_{k-2})} \end{aligned}$$

The term $p(X_{k-1}/\theta, V_{k-2}, B_{k-1} = 1)$ can be expanded with equation (12.21). The term $p(X_{k-1}/\theta, V_{k-2})$ can be expanded with equation (12.23). Hence, $P(B_{k-1} = 1/\theta, V_{k-1})$ can be computed iteratively from $P(B_{k-2} = 1/\theta, V_{k-2})$.

$$P(B_{k-1}=1|\theta,V_{k-1})=\cfrac{1}{1+\cfrac{\left\{\begin{array}{l}P(B_{k-2}=1|\theta,V_{k-2})\,p(X_{k-1}|\theta,B_{k-1}=-1,\\ B_{k-2}=1)+[1-P(B_{k-2}=1|\theta,V_{k-2})]\\ \cdot p(X_{k-1}|\theta,B_{k-1}=-1,B_{k-2}=-1)\end{array}\right\}}{\left\{\begin{array}{l}P(B_{k-2}=1|\theta,V_{k-2})\,p(X_{k-1}|\theta,B_{k-1}=1,\\ B_{k-2}=1)+[1-P(B_{k-2}=1|\theta,V_{k-2})]\\ \cdot p(X_{k-1}|\theta,B_{k-1}=1,B_{k-2}=-1)\end{array}\right\}}} \tag{12.25}$$

when $k = 2$,

$$P(B_1=1/\theta,V_1)=\frac{P(B_1=1)\,p(X_1|\theta,B_1=1)}{P(B_1=1)\,p(X_1|\theta,B_1=1)+P(B_1=-1)\,p(X_1|\theta,B_1=-1)} \tag{12.26}$$

can be easily computed.

The conditional probability density $p(\theta/V_n)$ approaches the Direc delta function at the true parameter values and the unknown signals S and R are learned as n approaches infinity. If the decision regarding the kth binary digit can be delayed until the $n(n > k)$ measurements have been obtained, a better performance can be achieved. The procedure is the same as above except that the a posteriori probability $P(B_k = 1/\theta, V_n)$ must be computed. It can be shown that such computation is also iterative.

6. Optimum Unsupervised Learning Receivers: Unknown Parameter Statistics

When the a priori parameter statistics $p(\theta)$ are not available, the Bayes solution in the preceding section cannot be used. It is now necessary to obtain the proper sample moment estimates[7] of S and R. It can be easily shown that $E[X_{ki}] = E[X_{(k+1)j}] = 0$. Thus the first moment cannot be used for estimation purpose. We now examine all second moments.

$$\begin{aligned}\text{Cov. }[X_{ki}, X_{(k+1)j}] &= E[X_{ki}X_{(k+1)j}] - E[X_{ki}]\,E[X_{(k+1)j}]\\ &= E[X_{ki}X_{(k+1)j}]\end{aligned}$$

since $E[X_{ki}] = E[X_{(k+1)j}] = 0$

$$\begin{aligned}E[X_{ki}X_{(k+1)j}] &= E[(Y_{ki}+n_{ki})(Y_{(k+1)}+n_{(k+1)j})]\\ &= E[Y_{ki}\,Y_{(k+1)j}]\end{aligned} \tag{12.27}$$

since $E[n_{ki}] = E[n_{(k+1)j}] = 0$. The product $Y_{ki} Y_{(k+1)j}$ is a discrete random variable and

$$P[Y_{ki} Y_{(k+1)j} = (R_i + S_i)(R_i + S_j)] = P[B_{k-1} = 1]\, P[B_k = 1] \cdot P[B_{k+1} = 1] = \tfrac{1}{8} \qquad (12.28)$$

There are seven more equations similar to equation (12.28) and each is for a different combination of the three binary random variables, B_{k-1}, B_k, and B_{k+1}. From these eight equations we obtain $E[Y_{ki} Y_{(k+1)j}] = S_i R_j$. Then from equation (12.27) we have

$$E[X_{ki} X_{(k+1)j}] = S_i R_j \qquad (12.29)$$

Hence,

$$\text{Cov. } [X_{ki}, X_{(k+1)j}] = E[X_{ki} X_{(k+1)j}] = S_i R_j \qquad (12.30)$$

In similar steps, the other second moments are found as:

$$\text{Var. } [X_{ki}] = R_i^2 + S_i^2 + \sigma_n^2, \qquad \text{all } i$$

$$\text{Cov. } [X_{ki}, X_{kj}] = S_i S_j + R_i R_j, \quad i \neq j$$

Two covariance matrices can be constructed as follows:

$$\begin{bmatrix} \text{Var. } [X_{k1}] & \text{Cov. } [X_{k1}, X_{k2}] & \cdots & \text{Cov. } [X_{k1}, X_{kL}] \\ \text{Cov. } [X_{k2}, X_{k1}] & \text{Var. } [X_{k2}] & \cdots & \text{Cov. } [X_{k2}, X_{kL}] \\ \vdots & \vdots & & \\ \text{Cov. } [X_{kL}, X_{k1}] & \text{Cov. } [X_{kL}, X_{k2}] & \cdots & \text{Var. } [X_{kL}] \end{bmatrix}$$

$$= \begin{bmatrix} S_1^2 + R_1^2 + \sigma_n^2 & S_1 S_2 + R_1 R_2 & \cdots & S_1 S_L + R_1 R_L \\ S_1 S_2 + R_1 R_2 & R_2^2 + S_2^2 + \sigma_n^2 & \cdots & S_2 S_L + R_2 R_L \\ \vdots & \vdots & & \\ S_1 S_L + R_1 R_L & S_2 S_L + R_2 R_L & \cdots & R_L^2 + S_L^2 + \sigma_n^2 \end{bmatrix} \qquad (12.31)$$

$$\begin{bmatrix} \text{Cov.}\,[X_{k1}, X_{(k+1)1}] & \text{Cov.}\,[X_{k1}, X_{(k+1)2}] & \cdots & \text{Cov.}\,[X_{k1}, X_{(k+1)L}] \\ \text{Cov.}\,[X_{k2}, X_{(k+1)1}] & \text{Cov.}\,[X_{k2}, X_{(k+1)2}] & \cdots & \text{Cov.}\,[X_{k2}, X_{(k+1)L}] \\ \vdots & \vdots & & \\ \text{Cov.}\,[X_{kL}, X_{(k+1)L}] & \text{Cov.}\,[X_{kL}, X_{(k+1)2}] & \cdots & \text{Cov.}\,[X_{kL}, X_{(k+1)L}] \end{bmatrix}$$

$$= \begin{bmatrix} S_1R_1 & S_1R_2 & \cdots & S_1R_L \\ S_2R_1 & S_2R_2 & \cdots & S_2R_L \\ \vdots & \vdots & & \\ S_LR_1 & S_LR_2 & \cdots & S_LR_L \end{bmatrix} \qquad (12.32)$$

Note that S_i and R_i appear symmetrically in equation (12.31) and it is impossible to distinguish between the two using equation (12.31) only. S_i and R_i appear asymmetrically in equation (12.32), so it is possible to distinguish between the two with the aid of equation (12.32). This is to say that it is necessary to correlate every measurement with its immediately preceding and following measurements. If there is intersymbol interference among M measurements, then we have to correlate every measurement with $M - 1$ preceding and $M - 1$ following measurements.

Several different sample moment estimators can be used to obtain an estimate of S and R. For example, we may combine the ith diagonal elements of the two matrices to get

$$\begin{aligned} (S_i + R_i)^2 &= \text{Var.}\,[X_{ki}] + 2\,\text{Cov.}\,[X_{ki}, X_{(k+1)i}] - \sigma_n^2 \\ (S_i - R_i)^2 &= \text{Var.}\,[X_{ki}] - 2\,\text{Cov.}\,[X_{ki}, X_{(k+1)i}] - \sigma_n^2 \end{aligned} \qquad (12.33)$$

Then replace the quantities on the right-hand side of equation (12.21) by sample estimates (σ_n^2 is unchanged). The sample estimate of Var. $[X_{ki}]$ is

$$\frac{X_{1i}^2 + X_{2i}^2 + \cdots + X_{ni}^2}{n}$$

The sample estimate of Cov. $X_{ki}, X_{(k+1)i}$ is

$$\frac{X_{1i}X_{2i} + X_{2i}X_{3i} + \cdots + X_{(n-1)i}X_{ni}}{n - 1}$$

Denote the sample estimates by "^." Then

$$\widehat{(S_i + R_i)} = \sqrt{\widehat{(S_i + R_i)^2}} \tag{12.34}$$

where

$$\widehat{(S_i + R_i)^2} = \frac{X_{1i}^2 + X_{2i}^2 + \cdots + X_{ni}^2}{n} + 2\,\frac{X_{1i}^2 + X_{2i}^2 + \cdots + X_{(n-1)i}X_{ni}}{n-1} - \sigma_n^2 \tag{12.35}$$

Also

$$\widehat{(S_i - R_i)} = \pm \sqrt{\widehat{(S_i - R_i)^2}} \tag{12.36}$$

where

$$\widehat{(S_i - R_i)^2} = \frac{X_{1l}^2 + X_{2l}^2 + \cdots + X_{nl}^2}{n} - 2\,\frac{X_{1i}X_{2i} + X_{2i}X_{3i} + \cdots + X_{(n-1)i}X_{ni}}{n-1} - \sigma_n^2 \tag{12.37}$$

A plus sign will be used in equation (12.35) if $S_i > R_i$ and a minus sign if $S_i < R_i$. It can be shown that

$$E\left[\widehat{(S_i + R_i)^2}\right] = (S_i + R_i)^2 \quad \text{and} \quad E\left[\widehat{(S_i - R_i)^2}\right] = (S_i - R_i)^2$$

It can also be shown that $\widehat{(S_i + R_i)^2}$ and $\widehat{(S_i - R_i)^2}$ converge respectively to $(S_i + R_i)^2$ and $(S_i + R_i)^2$ in mean square error and with probability one. The proof is left as an exercise. $\hat{S}_i$ and $\hat{R}_i$ can thus be determined from equations (12.34) to (12.37).

Other moment estimators can be used if they possess the convergence properties. The rate of convergence of different estimators usually has to be determined from the experimental results.

7. Remarks

The discussion in previous sections has demonstrated the applicability of adaptive and learning techniques in statistical pattern recognition to problems in communication theory and systems. Although the adaptive concept was not new, work along this line has been reported in the literature for only 15 years. All reports have indicated the feasibility of adaptive and learning receivers in dealing with certain unknown environments or system parameters. In the area of adaptive communication systems, Price and Green[8] examined the "Rake" communication systems, which measured some properties of the channel while receiving the signals. Kailath[5,6] considered the problem of transmission through a randomly varying channel. Jakowatz, Shuey, and White,[9] Glaser,[10] and Hinich[11] have examined learning in detection systems in different forms. Abramson and Braverman[12] provided adaptive crosscorrelator interpretation of supervised Bayesian learning. Scudder[13] examined the decision-directed receiver. Fralick[14,15] has applied unsupervised Bayesian learning to communication over random channels as well as detection of unknown-frequency signals. Patrick[16] also considered the use of decision-directed estimation in two-signal cases. In a different approach, Kozin[17] employed the empirical-pseudo-Bayes estimator to estimate the desired message in a random-access, discrete-address communication system.

In the years to come, we anticipate that more pattern recognition techniques will be applied to communication systems problems in connection with computer data processing. For example, when the channel statistic is completely unknown, nonparametric methods can be used to process channel measurements. Development of new methods in statistical pattern recognition will continue to contribute to the improvement of communication systems design.

PROBLEMS

1. Consider two antipodal signals $+S(\theta)$ and $-S(\theta)$ depending on the random parameter θ. Assume that there is no intersymbol interference. Let $x_1, x_2, \ldots, x_n$ be n Gaussian distributed vector measurements. Show that

$$\log p(\theta/x_1, x_2, \ldots, x_n) = \log\,[Cp(\theta)] + \sum_{i=1}^{n} \left[\log\cosh\,(x_i^T\,\Phi_i^{-1}\,S(\theta)) - \frac{1}{2}S(\theta)^T\,\Phi_i^{-1}\,S(\theta)\right]$$

where Φ_i is the noise covariance matrix for the ith vector measurement and C is a constant.

2. Consider an additive Gaussian noise channel with unity noise power. Two signals (means) M_1 and M_2 are fixed but unknown. Let $\overline{X}$ and $\overline{Y}$ be the sample means corresponding to signals M_1 and M_2 respectively. If n measurements are taken, and $M_1 < M_2$, show that
   (a) the decision rule is to choose signal M_1 if $X < \dfrac{\overline{X} + \overline{Y}}{2} = \Delta$, with the converse decision if the inequality is reversed,
   (b) the asymptotic probability of error is

$$P_e(n) \simeq \frac{1}{\sqrt{2\pi}} \int_{-\infty}^{-\alpha\Delta_0} \exp - \frac{x^2}{2}\, dx$$

where

$$\alpha = [1 + (2n)^{-1}]^{-1/2} \quad \text{and} \quad \Delta_0 = \frac{M_2 - M_1}{2}.$$

Compare the above result with the case that M_1 and M_2 are known exactly.

3. Sketch the block diagrams for the receiver structures discussed in paragraphs 5 and 6.

REFERENCES

1. Grettenberg, T. L. "Signal Selection in Communication and Radar Systems." *IEEE Trans. on Information Theory,* IT-9 (October 1963), 265–275.
2. Kailath, T. "The Divergence and Bhattacharyya Distance Measures in Signal Selection." *IEEE Trans. on Communication Technology,* COM-15 (February 1967), 52–60.
3. Scudder, H. J. III. "Adaptive Communication Receivers." *IEEE Trans. on Information Theory,* IT-11 (April 1965), 167–174.
4. Scudder, H. J. III. "Probability of Error of Some Adaptive Pattern-Recognition Machines." *IEEE Trans. on Information Theory,* IT-11 (July 1965), 363–371.
5. Kailath, T. "Correlation Detection of Signals Perturbed by a Random Channel." *IRE Trans. on Information Theory,* IT-6 (June 1960), 361–366.
6. Kailath, T. "Adaptive Matched Filters." In *Symposium on Mathematical Optimization Techniques.* Santa Monica, Calif., Oct. 1960.
7. Hancock, J. C. and R. W. Chang. "Unsupervised Learning Receivers for Binary Channels with Intersymbol Interference." Purdue Univ. TR-EE 65-2, January 1965.
8. Price, R. and P. E. Green, Jr. "A Communication Technique for Multipath Channels." *Proc. of IRE,* 46 (1958), 555–570.
9. Jakowatz, C. V., R. L. Shuey, and G. M. White, "Adaptive Waveform Recognition." In *Proc. Fourth London Symposium on Information Theory,* edited by C. Cherry. Butterworths, Washington, D.C., 1961.
10. Glaser, E. "Signal Detection by Adaptive Filters." *IRE Trans. on Information Theory,* IT-7 (April 1961), 87–98.
11. Hinich, M. J. "A Model for a Self-Adapting Filter." *Information and Control,* 5 (1962), 185–194.
12. Abramson, N. and D. Braverman. "Learning to Recognize Patterns in a Random Environment." *IRE Trans. on Information Theory,* IT-8 (September 1962), 58–63.
13. Scudder, H. J. III. "Adaptive Communication Receivers." Electronics Research Laboratory Report 64-3, Univ. of Calif., Berkeley, April 1964.
14. Fralick, S. C. "Optimum Adaptive Receivers for Random Channel Communication." In *First IEEE Annual Communications Convention Conference Record.* Boulder, Colo., June 1965.
15. Fralick, S. C., G. L. Slenkovich, and D. L. Wilson. "An Adaptive Receiver for Signals of Unknown Frequency." *IEEE Trans. on Communication Technology,* COM-16 (October 1968).

16. Patrick, E. A., J. P. Costello, and F. C. Monds. "Decision-Directed Estimation of a Two-Class Decision Boundary." *IEEE Trans. on Computers,* C-19 (March 1970).
17. Kozin, C. H. P. "The Use of Prior Estimates in Successive Point Estimations of a Random Signal." Ph.D. dissertation, Purdue Univ., June 1964.

Bibliography

1. Abend, K., T. J. Harley, B. D. Fritchman, and C. Gumacos. "On Optimum Receivers for Channels Having Memory." *IEEE Trans. on Information Theory,* IT-14 (November 1968).
2. Baxa, Jr., E. G. and L. W. Nolte, "Adaptive Signal Detection with Finite Memory," *IEEE Trans. on Systems, Man, and Cybernetics,* SMC-2 (January 1972), 42–49.
3. Chang, R. W. and J. C. Hancock. "On Receiver Structures for Channels Having Memory." *IEEE Trans. on Information Theory.* IT-12 (October 1966), 463–468.
4. Chen, C. H. and K. S. Fu. "On an Adaptive Sequential Detection System." *First IEEE Annual Communications Convention Conference Record.* Boulder, Colo., June 1965.
5. Daly, R. F. "The Adaptive Binary-Detection Problem on the Real Line." Technical Report 2003-3, Stanford Electronics Labs, Stanford University, California, February 1962.
6. Goode, B. B. "Synthesis of a Nonlinear Bayes Detector for Gaussian Signal and Noise Field Using Wiener Filters." *IEEE Trans. on Information Theory*, IT-13, No. 1 (January 1967), 116–118.
7. Gregg, W. D. and J. C. Hancock. "An Optimum Decision-Directed Scheme for Gaussian Mixtures." *IEEE Trans. on Information Theory*, IT-14, No. 3 (May 1968), 451–461.
8. Hancock, J. C. and P. A. Wintz. *Signal Detection Theory*. McGraw-Hill, New York, 1966. Chapter 8.
9. Nolte, L. W. "An Adaptive Realization of the Optimum Receiver for a Sporadically Recurrent Waveform in Noise." *IEEE Trans. on Information Theory*, IT-13 (April 1967).
10. Nolte, L. W. "An Adaptive Realization of the Optimum Receiver for a Synchronous Recurrent Waveform in Noise." *IEEE Trans. on Information Theory*, IT-12 (January 1966), 78–80.
11. Rushforth, C. K. "Adaptive Communication with Sounding Signals In Random Channels." *IEEE International Convention Record,* Part 4 (March 1963), 102–106.
12. Wintz, P. A. "Optimum Adaptive Reception for Binary Sequences." *IEEE Trans. on Aerospace and Electronic Systems,* AES-6 (May 1970).

Appendixes

APPENDIX A (Chapter II)

Derivation of Fisher Discriminant Function

Let $p_i = p(x/\omega_i)$. The mean and variance of the discriminant function $U(x)$ are

$$\overline{U}_i = \int U p_i dx \quad \text{and} \quad \sigma_i^2 \, (U) = \int (U - \overline{U}_i) \, p_i dx \tag{A.1}$$

respectively. Let $U_0(x)$ be the optimal discriminant function in the Fisher sense. The method of calculus of variations may be used to find U_0. It is noted that any arbitrary $U(x)$ can be expressed as

$$U = U_0 + \alpha r(x) \tag{A.2}$$

where α is some scalar constant and $r(x)$ is a function chosen to effect the equality. Equation (A.2) is substituted into equation (A.1) and the results are substituted into equation (2.18). The resulting expression for L can be differentiated with respect to α, evaluated at $\alpha = 0$, and equated to zero, i.e.,

$$\left. \frac{\partial L}{\partial \alpha} \right|_{\alpha=0} = 0 \tag{A.3}$$

We then have the following constraints on U_0:

$$\int [(\sigma_1^2 + \sigma_2^2)(p_1 - P_2) - (\overline{U}_1 - \overline{U}_2)(U_0 p_1 - \overline{U}_1 p_1 + U_0 p_2 - \overline{U}_2 p_2)] \cdot r(x) \, dx = 0 \tag{A.4}$$

where $\overline{U}_i$ and σ_i^2 are the mean and variance of $U_0(x)$. Since $r(x)$ is a completely arbitrary function (since U is arbitrary), the coefficient of $r(x)$ in the integrand of equation (A.4) must be zero for all x. This implies that $U_0(x)$ satisfies

$$U_0(x) = \frac{\left(\dfrac{\sigma_1^2 + \sigma_2^2}{\overline{U}_1 - \overline{U}_2}\right)(p_1 - p_2) + \overline{U}_1 p_1 + \overline{U}_2 p_2}{p_1 + p_2} \tag{A.5}$$

which can be written as equation (2.19) except for a proportionality constant. In pattern classification we set $U_0(x) = 0$. So the proportionality constant does not change the optimality of $U_0(x)$.

APPENDIX B (Chapter V)

Convergence of the Supervised Estimation Process

The supervised estimation process requires the computation of $p(\theta/x_1, x_2, \ldots, x_n)$. The conditions that $p(\theta/x_1, x_2, \ldots, x_n)$ will approach the Dirac delta function at the true parameter θ_0 can be summarized as follows:[23]

1. The likelihood function approaches zero as the parameter value approaches infinity, i.e.,

$$p(x_1, x_2, \ldots, x_n/\theta) \to 0 \quad \text{as } |\,\theta\,| \to \infty$$

2. $p(x_1, x_2, \ldots, x_n/\theta)$ is continuous in θ.
3. The a priori distribution is positive for all parameter values, i.e., $p(\theta) > 0$ for every open interval.
4. The true parameter θ_0 is unique.
5. The sequence of the learning samples has the ergodic stationary distribution.
6. The expectation of the logarithm of the likelihood function with respect to the true parameter, $E_{\theta_0} \log p(x_1, x_2, \ldots, x_n/\theta)$, is continuous in θ.

It is noted that the independence of the sequence of learning samples is not required. For an example that $p(\theta/x_1, x_2, \ldots, x_n)$ does not converge when a condition stated above is not satisfied, see Berk.[24]

APPENDIX C (Chapter V)

Identifiability of Finite Mixtures

Let $F(x/\omega_i)$ be the cumulative distribution function (cdf) of $p(x/\omega_i)$. Equation (5.30) can be written as

$$H(x) = \int F(x, \omega)\, dG(\omega)$$

where the cdf G takes on values at m distinct points. Let x be the d-dimensional vector measurement. The d-dimensional cdf $H(x)$ is the image of the mapping of the m-dimensional cdf G. The distribution H is called the mixture and G the mixing distribution. H is called a finite mixture if its mixing distribution is discrete and m is finite. Let F and H be the families of distributions $F(x, \omega)$ and $H(x)$ respectively. Then H is said to be identifiable if F is a one-to-one mapping of G onto H.

The identifiability of finite mixtures has been examined by Teicher,[25] and by Yakowitz and Spragins.[26] The results of the latter are much simpler. They are stated without proof as follows.

A necessary and sufficient condition that the class H of all finite mixtures of the family F be identifiable is that F be a linearly independent set over the field of real numbers. The finite mixtures of F are identifiable if F is any one of the following: (1) the family of n products of exponential distributions, (2) the multivariate Gaussian family, (3) the union of the last two families, (4) the family of one-dimensional Cauchy distributions, or (5) the nondegenerate members of the family of one-dimensional negative binomial distributions. Also, the translation-parameter family generated by any one-dimensional cdf yields identifiable finite mixtures.

APPENDIX D (Chapter VIII)

Similarity Matrix Method

The similarity matrix method is an on-line clustering algorithm which is provided in the OLPARS system as an aid in detecting and identifying hyperellipsoidal and hyperspherical structure in subsets of a high-dimensional data set. The fundamental information regarding the clustering is obtained by computing a matrix whose ijth element is the similarity measure S_{ij} (equation 8.6) between the ith and jth input vectors. Let S be the similarity matrix with elements S_{ij}. Define a generalized similarity matrix as

$$S^* = S + (\alpha S)^2 + (\alpha S)^3 + \cdots + (\alpha S)^{N_p} \tag{D.1}$$

where $0 < \alpha < 1$ and N_p is a positive integer. The matrix S^* takes into account N_p order similarities. A typical element in the second-order matrix, S^2, for example, is

$$S_{ij}^{(2)} = \sum_{\text{all } k} S_{ik} S_{kj} \tag{D.2}$$

The element S_{ij}^* in the matrix S^* is obtained by adding N_p terms like equation (D.2). The matrix S^* is thresholded at a value (or several values of) θ supplied by the user. That is,

$$S_{ij}^* \text{ (threshold)} = \begin{cases} 1 \text{ if } S_{ij}^* \geqslant \theta \\ 0 \text{ otherwise} \end{cases} \tag{D.3}$$

Next, the sum of the number of ones in each row is computed and the row with the maximum count is identified. The vector corresponding to this row has the property that it is similar (i.e., similarity greater than θ) to the largest number of other vectors. This vector is thus identified as a cluster center and all the vectors similar to it (i.e., with a similar number of ones in the row) are elements of this cluster. These vectors are then removed from the input vector list and the corresponding rows and columns of the S^* matrix are deleted. The process then continues on the reduced S^* matrix until an identified cluster has less than the preset number of elements. At this point, the cluster configuration, i.e., the set of clusters and their respective membership, has been obtained. The cluster configuration is evaluated by the following scoring algorithm:

$$\text{Score} = \frac{1}{N_c} \sum_{k=1}^{N_c} \left[\frac{W_k}{1 + \sum_{j \neq k}^{N_c} B_{jk}} \right] \tag{D.4}$$

where

N_c = number of clusters
W_k = average within cluster similarity for cluster k
B_{jk} = average between cluster similarity between clusters j and k
M_k = number of vectors contained in cluster k

$$W_k = \frac{2}{M_k(M_k - 1)} \sum_{i}^{M_k} \sum_{\substack{j \\ i<j}}^{M_k} S_{ij}$$

$$B_{jk} = \frac{1}{M_j M_k} \sum_{p}^{M_j} \sum_{p}^{M_k} S_{pq}$$

If more than one threshold value was selected, the above clustering procedure is followed for each threshold setting. Upon completion of this task a display is presented to the user indicating the scores obtained for each cluster configuration to be stored within the OLPARS system after assigning names to each cluster.

APPENDIX E (Chapter VIII)

List of Iris Data Set

Iris setosa				*Iris versicolor*				*Iris virginica*			
Sepal length	*Sepal width*	*Petal length*	*Petal width*	*Sepal length*	*Sepal width*	*Petal length*	*Petal width*	*Sepal length*	*Sepal width*	*Petal length*	*Petal width*
5.1	3.5	1.4	0.2	7.0	3.2	4.7	1.4	6.3	3.3	6.0	2.5
4.9	3.0	1.4	0.2	6.4	3.2	4.5	1.5	5.8	2.7	5.1	1.9
4.7	3.2	1.3	0.2	6.9	3.1	4.9	1.5	7.1	3.0	5.9	2.1
4.6	3.1	1.5	0.2	5.5	2.3	4.0	1.3	6.3	2.9	5.6	1.8

(*continued next page*)

Iris setosa				*Iris versicolor*				*Iris virginica*			
Sepal length	*Sepal width*	*Petal length*	*Petal width*	*Sepal length*	*Sepal width*	*Petal length*	*Petal width*	*Sepal length*	*Sepal width*	*Petal length*	*Petal width*
5.0	3.6	1.4	0.2	6.5	2.8	4.6	1.5	6.5	3.0	5.8	2.2
5.4	3.9	1.7	0.4	5.7	2.8	4.5	1.3	7.6	3.0	6.6	2.1
4.6	3.4	1.4	0.3	6.3	3.3	4.7	1.6	4.9	2.5	4.5	1.7
5.0	3.4	1.5	0.2	4.9	2.4	3.3	1.0	7.3	2.9	6.3	1.8
4.4	2.9	1.4	0.2	6.6	2.9	4.6	1.3	6.7	2.5	5.8	1.8
4.9	3.1	1.5	0.1	5.2	2.7	3.9	1.4	7.2	3.6	6.1	2.5
5.4	3.7	1.5	0.2	5.0	2.0	3.5	1.0	6.5	3.2	5.1	2.0
4.8	3.4	1.6	0.2	5.9	3.0	4.2	1.5	6.4	2.7	5.3	1.9
4.8	3.0	1.4	0.1	6.0	2.2	4.0	1.0	6.8	3.0	5.5	2.1
4.3	3.0	1.1	0.1	6.1	2.9	4.7	1.4	5.7	2.5	5.0	2.0
5.8	4.0	1.2	0.2	5.6	2.9	3.6	1.3	5.8	2.8	5.1	2.4
5.7	4.4	1.5	0.4	6.7	3.1	4.4	1.4	6.4	3.2	5.3	2.3
5.4	3.9	1.3	0.4	5.6	3.0	4.5	1.5	6.5	3.0	5.5	1.8
5.1	3.5	1.4	0.3	5.8	2.7	4.1	1.0	7.7	3.8	6.7	2.2
5.7	3.8	1.7	0.3	6.2	2.2	4.5	1.5	7.7	2.6	6.9	2.3
5.1	3.8	1.5	0.3	5.6	2.5	3.9	1.1	6.0	2.2	5.0	1.5
5.4	3.4	1.7	0.2	5.9	3.2	4.8	1.8	6.9	3.2	5.7	2.3
5.1	3.7	1.5	0.4	6.1	2.8	4.0	1.3	5.6	2.8	4.9	2.0
4.6	3.6	1.0	0.2	6.3	2.5	4.9	1.5	7.7	2.8	6.7	2.0
5.1	3.3	1.7	0.5	6.1	2.8	4.7	1.2	6.3	2.7	4.9	1.8
4.8	3.4	1.9	0.2	6.4	2.9	4.3	1.3	6.7	3.3	5.7	2.1
5.0	3.0	1.6	0.2	6.6	3.0	4.4	1.4	7.2	3.2	6.0	1.8
5.0	3.4	1.6	0.4	6.8	2.8	4.8	1.4	6.2	2.8	4.8	1.8
5.2	3.5	1.5	0.2	6.7	3.0	5.0	1.7	6.1	3.0	4.9	1.8
5.2	3.4	1.4	0.2	6.0	2.9	4.5	1.5	6.4	2.8	5.6	2.1
4.7	3.2	1.6	0.2	5.7	2.6	3.5	1.0	7.2	3.0	5.8	1.6
4.8	3.1	1.6	0.2	5.5	2.4	3.8	1.1	7.4	2.8	6.1	1.9
5.4	3.4	1.5	0.4	5.5	2.4	3.7	1.0	7.9	3.8	6.4	2.0
5.2	4.1	1.5	0.1	5.8	2.7	3.9	1.2	6.4	2.8	5.6	2.2
5.5	4.2	1.4	0.2	6.0	2.7	5.1	1.6	6.3	2.8	5.1	1.5
4.9	3.1	1.5	0.2	5.4	3.0	4.5	1.5	6.1	2.6	5.6	1.4
5.0	3.2	1.2	0.2	6.0	3.4	4.5	1.6	7.7	3.0	6.1	2.3
5.5	3.5	1.3	0.2	6.7	3.1	4.7	1.5	6.3	3.4	5.6	2.4
4.9	3.6	1.4	0.1	6.3	2.3	4.4	1.3	6.4	3.1	5.5	1.8
4.4	3.0	1.3	0.2	5.6	3.0	4.1	1.3	6.0	3.0	4.8	1.8
5.1	3.4	1.5	0.2	5.5	2.5	4.0	1.3	6.9	3.1	5.4	2.1
5.0	3.5	1.3	0.3	5.5	2.6	4.4	1.2	6.7	3.1	5.6	2.4
4.5	2.3	1.3	0.3	6.1	3.0	4.6	1.4	6.9	3.1	5.1	2.3
4.4	3.2	1.3	0.2	5.8	2.6	4.0	1.2	5.8	2.7	5.1	1.9
5.0	3.5	1.6	0.6	5.0	2.3	3.3	1.0	6.8	3.2	5.9	2.3
5.1	3.8	1.9	0.4	5.6	2.7	4.2	1.3	6.7	3.3	5.7	2.5
4.8	3.0	1.4	0.3	5.7	3.0	4.2	1.2	6.7	3.0	5.2	2.3
5.1	3.8	1.6	0.2	5.7	2.9	4.2	1.3	6.3	2.5	5.0	1.9
4.6	3.2	1.4	0.2	6.2	2.9	4.3	1.3	6.5	3.0	5.2	2.0
5.3	3.7	1.5	0.2	5.1	2.5	3.0	1.1	6.2	3.4	5.4	2.3
5.0	3.3	1.4	0.2	5.7	2.8	4.1	1.3	5.9	3.0	5.1	1.8

SOURCE: M. G. Kendall and A. Stuart. *Advanced Theory of Statistics*, vol. 3. Hafner, New York, 1966. P. 318.

Index